TOM HORN

Last of the Bad Men

Jay Monaghan

Introduction to the Bison Books Edition
by Larry D. Ball

University of Nebraska Press
Lincoln and London

☺ The paper in this book meets the minimum requirements of American
National Standard for Information Sciences—Permanence of Paper for
Printed Library Materials, ANSI Z39.48-1984.

First Bison Books printing: 1997
Most recent printing indicated by the last digit below:
10 9   8   7   6   5   4   3   2   1

Library of Congress Cataloging-in-Publication Data
Monaghan, Jay, 1891–
[Last of the bad men]
Tom Horn: last of the bad men / Jay Monaghan; introduction to the Bison
Books edition by Larry D. Ball.
p.   cm.
Originally published: Last of the bad men. Indianapolis: Bobbs-Merrill, 1946.
Includes bibliographical references (p.   ).
ISBN 0-8032-8234-6 (pbk.: alk. paper)
1. Horn, Tom, 1860–1886.   2. Apache Indians—Wars, 1883–1886.
3. Frontier and pioneer life—West (U.S.)   4. Scouts and scouting—West
(U.S.)   5. West (U.S.)—Biography.   I. Title.
E83.88.H67H34   1997
973.8'4'092-dc21
97-1508   CIP

Reprinted from the original 1946 edition by the Bobbs-Merrill Company,
Indianapolis. This Bison Books edition follows the original in beginning the
preface on page 13; no material has been omitted.

To

Lloyd Lewis, *ranchman.*

In many ways this book is yours as much
as mine. You unearthed some of the Tom
Horn legends; tool-dressed others. Only
you and I know how close this story is to
the white ashes of our own dead campfires.

INTRODUCTION

Larry D. Ball

Few frontier personalities have aroused such interest as Thomas H. Horn, the former army scout who died on the gallows in Cheyenne, Wyoming, in 1903 for the murder of a young boy. Horn packed many experiences into his short life. In Arizona, he served as a scout in the Apache wars and participated in the bloody vendetta known as the Pleasant Valley War. As a Pinkerton operative, he pursued train robbers in Colorado. On the northern ranges, he served the great cattle interests as detective and hired assassin. This talented frontiersman also found time to become a pioneer rodeo star and to participate in the Spanish-American War. Horn abetted the growth of his own legend by producing a selective and boastful autobiography, *The Life of Tom Horn, Government Scout and Interpreter,* just before he was executed. However, this book only initiated a lengthy list of writings about this mysterious and lethal frontiersman.[1]

Tom Horn was born on a farm near Memphis, Scotland County, Missouri, on 21 November 1860. At fourteen, young Tom, who was big for his age and would eventually exceed six feet in height, sought his fortune in the West. He worked at various jobs—as a railroad laborer, teamster, livery man, and cowboy. While prospecting around Leadville, Colorado, in 1879, he reportedly signed on as a gunhand for the Denver, Rio Grande, and Western Railroad in its struggle with the Atchison, Topeka, and Santa Fe for control of the Royal Gorge of the Arkansas River.[2]

While employed by a stagecoach line in Sante Fe, New Mexico, Horn had occasion to drive a herd of company livestock to Prescott, Arizona. This remote frontier territory became his home, after a fashion. He resided there longer than in any other place. Horn dabbled in mining and claimed to have been a member of Ed Schieffelin's party that discovered and named the mining camp of Tombstone. At some point he met Al Sieber, a noted army scout, who introduced the young rover to Apache life at the San Carlos and other reservations in southeastern Arizona. Horn probably took a native wife and learned some Apache and Spanish.[3]

In his autobiography, Horn not only accords himself the position of army scout and interpreter but says that he was in the thick of the fighting in several Apache campaigns. Although he was present in some engagements, Horn's position was much more modest: army packer. The

Quartermaster General's records reveal that he served in this capacity in October 1882 and later superintended a packtrain from 13 October 1885 to 30 September 1886. Only during the last chase after Geronimo in Sonora, in 1885–86, did Horn actually reach the coveted position of chief of scouts. While serving in this capacity he was wounded—and his commanding officer, Captain Emmet Crawford, was killed—when the bluecoats blundered into a Mexican column on 10 January 1886. The following August, Horn joined Lieutenant Charles B. Gatewood's small party, which brazenly rode into Geronimo's camp and informed him that he must surrender. The tired old warrior gave up to General Nelson Miles the following September.[4]

Horn remained in southeastern Arizona after the termination of the Apache campaigns, where he continued to prospect and work for various ranches. As a cowhand for the Chiricahua Cattle Company, in Chochise County, he reportedly killed a Mexican in a fight over a woman in 1887. He participated in the bloody feud known as the Pleasant Valley (or Tonto Basin) War in 1887–88, although Horn's recollections are all too brief and misleading about this episode. Horace E. Dunlap, a Graham County ranchman and employer of Tom Horn, recalled that Horn entered Pleasant Valley not as a partisan but as a sort of bodyguard for John Rhodes. Rhodes was foreman of a ranch in Pleasant Valley, apparently owned by Robert Bowen, a Tempe hotel man. The owner desired to keep out of the fracas. Horn's task was to assist Rhodes in keeping "an armed neutrality." If so, this nonpartisan posture did not last.[5]

By the second year of the vendetta, 1888, Rhodes and Horn were clearly identified with one side in the feud, the Tewksburys. Rhodes married the widow of John Tewksbury, who was a victim of the "war," while Horn formed a close friendship with Edward Tewksbury. In August, Horn and Rhodes joined a party led by cattleman Glenn Reynolds in lynching three suspected rustlers. When Reynolds was elected sheriff of Gila County the following November, he appointed Horn as a deputy.[6]

As a deputy sheriff's duties were often part-time, Horn found a sideline on the emerging Arizona rodeo circuit. At the 1889 Fourth of July celebrations in Globe, he won the steer-tying contest handily. The *Arizona Silver Belt* was moved to characterize Horn as "the boss cattle tyer and knight of the lariat." The following fall, the gifted rider repeated this feat at the territorial fair in Phoenix. Unfortunately, such victories brought out one of the champion cowhand's greatest failings—boastfulness. Horn could not contain an exalted notion of himself. While visiting Tucson in March 1890, he issued a challenge to all comers. He "says he will wager $500 against any cowboy in Arizona, New Mexico, or Texas, that he can throw and tie a steer in less time than any one can trot into the ring," said Tucson's *Arizona Daily Star.* "Can't some of the cowmen find a man to put up against Tom Horn . . . in a cowboy tournament," moaned the *Star.*[7]

Whatever his talents with the lariat, Horn's abilities as a manhunter were much in demand. In 1890 he joined the Pinkerton National Detective Agency. Unfortunately, the novice detective embarrassed his employers on his first important case, when he was charged with robbery in Reno, Nevada. Although Horn was eventually tried and released, and demonstrated some aptitude as a sleuth, he soon left the agency. "I never did like the work," he admitted.[8]

The former Pinkerton operative was soon employed as a livestock detective for wealthy Wyoming cattlemen. The large ranchers were convinced that small cattlemen and homesteaders were wielding "the long rope" against the barons' herds. These beef lords were not above hiring such men as Tom Horn to run off or even assassinate suspected thieves. As early as spring 1892, Horn may have been at work in Johnson County, Wyoming. Although there is no evidence that he participated in the infamous "Cattleman's Invasion" of Johnson County in April 1892, Horn served as a deputy U.S. marshal in the aftermath of the incident. Later, he was suspected in the assassination of two alleged rustlers. In other instances, however, Horn merely arrested and turned over his prisoners to local authorities.[9]

The sinister nature of Horn's work, as well as the malevolent reputation that soon arose around him, ensured that he could not remain in Wyoming for long at a time. By fall 1896 he was back in Graham County, Arizona, as manager of the E. A. Jones ranch in Aravaipa Canyon. Horn's interest in mining continued as well. He informed a Globe newspaper that he had a "promising" copper claim near the San Carlos Apache Reservation. Lawmen still sought his manhunting abilities. In November 1896, U.S. Marshal William Kidder Meade asked him to serve as a posseman in the chase after the William "Black Jack" Christian band. In his reply, the veteran manhunter came very close, perhaps unconsciously, to revealing how calloused he had become toward taking human life. Horn scoffed at the typical amateurish possemen who often served the federal lawman but promised "to get them [outlaws] by going alone." However, he wanted to know "*if there is anything in it for me.*" He added, "If I undertake the job, *no cure no pay* is my mottoe [sic]. So if i dont [sic] get them it costs no one a cent." Since Horn was unable to take the job immediately, Meade continued the manhunt without him.[10]

In April 1898, Horn returned to government service as an army packer in the war against Spain. War Department records indicate that he signed up at Tampa, Florida, on 23 April 1898, in time to participate in the landing near Santiago, Cuba. When he learned that landing craft were not available for his horses and mules, Horn exhibited his practical bent. He simply pushed the mules into the sea and pointed them toward the beach. Most of them succeeded in swimming to shore; a few floated out to sea. Although Colonel Theodore Roosevelt and other officers criticized the packers for inefficiency and lack of spirit, there is no evidence that Horn was a slacker. He received a promotion to pack master on 1 August but soon fell ill with fever. The army discharged him on 6 September.[11]

Horn traveled to Wyoming, where he served as a part-time lawman and detective. When highwaymen held up a Union Pacific passenger train at Wilcox, Wyoming, in June 1899, the railroad company hired Horn as a detective to lead a party in the chase. When the brigands killed a pursuing sheriff, lawmen initiated a spirited chase. The following January, the *Cheyenne Daily Sun-Leader* reported that Horn and one Ed Taxbury—presumably Ed Tewksbury, his Arizona friend—tracked two suspects into the wilds near Jackson Hole, Wyoming, and killed them. The detectives buried their victims on the spot.[12]

A few days later, Horn sought out a reporter in order to correct errors in the initial news report. Although he objected to premature newspaper coverage of confidential detective work—in fact, he characterized journalists as "pretty tough customers" on that score—Horn went on to say,

> Yes, it is true that Ed. Taxbury and myself were compelled to kill two men a few weeks since. They were notorious horse and cattle thieves, and criminal raiders named Monte and Blair. They were not the Wilcox trainer robbers. They [the train robbers] are in British Columbia and I am going up into that country after them. We know who they are and the Union Pacific will pursue them to the end.

Whether Horn journeyed to Canada is not known. The *Cheyenne Daily Sun-Leader* later suggested that Horn and Tewksbury's victims, Monte and Blair, may have been innocent. The newswriter expressed concern at Horn's lack of regret over the matter.[13]

In the summer of 1900, Horn—using the alias Tom Hicks—obtained work in the Brown's Hole region of northwestern Colorado, where he was soon suspected of murdering two alleged rustlers, Isom Dart and Matt Rash. In an incredibly brazen exhibition, the stock detective later appeared in Cheyenne, where he gave a journalist a story about the killings—leaving his instrumentality out, of course—and averred that stock thievery had ended in northwestern Colorado. The *Cheyenne Daily Sun-Leader* remarked that the murderers "are said to be detectives imported by cattlemen" and that lawmen knew the identity of the assassins. "Only fear of vengeance from the detectives and the Wyoming [livestock] corporations which employ them," continued the news story, "prevents their names from being openly published."[14]

The gall that Horn demonstrated in reporting his own brutal deeds was a part of his stock in trade. His ego knew no bounds, and he publicly boasted about his prowess as a range detective and his proficiency with a rifle. His friends later asserted that Horn did not commit every murder attributed to him but deliberately took credit for the work of other assassins. All of this was apparently calculated to intimidate, terrorize, and discourage the potential livestock thief and thus prevent the necessity of employing more lethal measures. The mere rumor that this mysterious and menacing horseman was in the vicinity would reduce thievery. "Killing men is my specialty," he reportedly remarked, "I look at it as a business proposition." With his usual bravado, Horn concluded, "I think I have a corner on the market."[15]

By the turn of the century, the inhabitants of the northern plains were less tolerant of the highhanded methods of the great cattle interests. The days of the Tom Horns—the instruments of the beef barons—were numbered. On 18 July 1901, fourteen-year-old Willie Nickell, son of homesteader Kels Nickell, was mysteriously killed some forty miles northwest of Cheyenne. Since this regrettable incident, the presumption has been that the assassin mistook the boy for his father, whom the cattlemen desired eliminated. Joseph LeFors, a longtime deputy U.S. marshal and stock detective who was very familiar with conditions in Wyoming, assembled evidence that pointed toward Tom Horn as the murderer.[16]

LeFors devised a plan to entrap the stock detective. Pretending to arrange a similar job for Horn with Montana stockmen, the deputy marshal encouraged Horn—deep in his cups and very talkative—to make incriminating statements about himself. The unwary gunman did not know that a concealed stenographer was writing down his remarks. LeFors presented the transcript of this conversation as a "confession" to the district court in Cheyenne. Although this entire episode remains wrapped in controversy, Horn was convicted of the Nickell murder and hanged on 20 November 1903. John C. Coble, an influential cattleman and former employer of the condemned man, stood by the detective to the end. Although other barons may have contributed money toward Horn's attorney fees, they were content to sacrifice their "hit man" to an angry public. Charles Horn, older brother of Tom, buried his brother in nearby Boulder, Colorado. In a rather bizarre development, writer Chip Carlson recently arranged for an informal "retrial" of the Tom Horn case. The defendant was found not guilty.[17]

In spite of the sizeable corpus of written material about Tom Horn, this mysterious figure lacks a broadly researched and up-to-date biography. Most book-length treatments concentrate on his Wyoming years, leaving the preceding ones for incidental attention. Only one biography still stands for breadth of coverage and good storytelling—Jay Monaghan's *Last of the Bad Men: The Legend of Tom Horn*, retitled *Tom Horn: Last of the Bad Men* for this Bison Books edition. Monaghan performed considerable research and possessed a gifted pen. Furthermore, he rode the very ranges that Horn had ridden and interviewed persons who had know him. Reviewers were immediately taken with Monaghan's work. "As a tale of high adventure the career of Tom Horn exceeds the imagination of Zane Grey," said Richard W. Hantke of Lake Forest College. However, this reviewer disagreed with Monaghan's argument that Horn "was completely the product of his environment." Instead, Hantke asserted that the gunman could have just as easily have "sought an environment congenial to his character." A *Time* writer praised the author for "an excellent job of retelling the story" and even suggested that "*Last of the Bad Men* ought to be the last word."[18]

James Jay Monaghan was born in West Chester, Pennsylvania, in 1891. The son of an attorney, he attended school in Switzerland and graduated from Swarthmore College in 1913. He earned a master's degree from the University of Pennsylvania in 1918 and received a Litt.D. from Monmouth College (Illinois) in 1947. While still an undergraduate, Monaghan sought summer adventures in the West. Beginning in 1907, and continuing in subsequent summers, he served as a teamster and cowhand in Colorado and Wyoming, where he became conversant with the Tom Horn story. When revolution erupted in Mexico in 1911, Monaghan took time out from college to join the Madero partisans. He narrowly avoided death in Juarez. He recalled his early adventures in an autobiographical fragment, *Scholar, Cowboy, Mexican Spy*, which Ray Allen Billington praised as no "bland rehash of historical theories" but the recounting of "hair-raising adventures." After graduation, Monaghan devoted two decades to ranching in the region where he had spent his college summers.[19]

In middle age Monaghan began recording history. He served the Colorado Historical Society as a field researcher in 1935 and moved on to

Chicago, where he supervised a Works Progress Administration project to preserve foreign-language newspapers. He soon obtained employment at the Illinois State Historical Library and eventually became state historian. Then Monaghan relocated to Santa Barbara, California, where he became special consultant to the Wyles Collection of Lincolniana and Western Americana in 1952. All the while he produced numerous works on a variety of subjects, from Abraham Lincoln and the Civil War to George Armstrong Custer. He was the recipient of many awards and honors. Monaghan died in Santa Barbara, California, in 1980.[20]

Monaghan detected a common thread throughout the life of Tom Horn. The gunman devoted his energies to the defense of the property rights of the well-to-do. Horn was always skeptical of "men who claimed that the big [cattle] outfits were cheating the 'little fellers.'" Elsewhere, the author observes that "all the success in his [Horn's] life had come from serving the rich and powerful. Life had made him an instinctive vassal of the vested interests." When Horn encountered wealthy Colorado and Wyoming ranchers who desired "a trailer and killer," the former scout was their man.[21] When one takes into consideration Horn's experiences killing Indians without fear of punishment, his propensity to drink heavily, and his inclination to boast, the ingredients were present for a tragic ending to his life.

Tom Horn: Last of the Bad Men represents the pioneer effort to present a complete biography of Horn. It thus has its flaws. Additional research needs to be done, especially in regard to Horn's Arizona years. Furthermore, Monaghan sometimes let slip into his writing the prejudices of his time. An occasional racial slur mars the work when he refers to "Japs" and "Chinks." Isom Dart, a black victim of Horn's rifle, is described as having a face that "flashed like a black diamond." When Dart played the mouth harp, Monaghan wrote, his "jungle blood throbbed with the music." The author toys with numerology when he notes that numerous thirteens occurred in Horn's case.[22] Aside from these remarks, this book remains the most balanced and complete biography of Tom Horn. The University of Nebraska Press is to be congratulated for making it available to readers in an inexpensive paperback edition.

NOTES

1. Tom Horn, *Life of Tom Horn, Government Scout and Interpreter, Written by Himself, Together with His Letters and Statements by His Friends: A Vindication* (Denver: Louthan Book Company, 1904) and various reprints. Unless otherwise in-

dicated, references are to the 1964 University of Oklahoma Press edition with an introduction by Dean Krakel. The literature concerning Tom Horn is voluminous, but much is repetitive. See Dean Krakel, *The Saga of Tom Horn: The Story of a Cattlemen's War, with Personal Narratives, Newspaper Accounts and Official Documents and Testimonies*, Expurgated Ed. (Laramie WY: Powder River, 1954); and Doyce B. Nunis Jr., *The Life of Tom Horn Revisited* (San Marino CA: The Westerners, Los Angeles Corral, 1992), a revision and enlargement of the author's introduction to the 1987 Lakeside Classic edition of *The Life of Tom Horn*. Two recent works by Chip Carlson present new material about Horn's Wyoming years: *Tom Horn: "Killing Men Is My Specialty": The Definitive History of the Notorious Wyoming Stock Detective* (Cheyenne WY: Beartooth Corral, 1991); *Joe LeFors: "I Slickered Tom Horn." The History of the Texas Cowboy Turned Montana-Wyoming Lawman, A Sequel* (Cheyenne WY: Beartooth Corral, 1995). See also Lauran Paine, *Tom Horn: Man of the West* (London: John Long, 1962).

2. Horn, *Life of Tom Horn*, 3–10; U.S. Bureau of the Census, Population Schedules, Ninth Census of the United States, 1870, Missouri, National Archives, Washington DC, microcopy 593, roll 805, for Horn family; Jay Monaghan, *Tom Horn: Last of the Bad Men* (Lincoln: University of Nebraska Press, 1997), 29–50.

3. Horn, *Life of Tom Horn*, 10–16, 25–28.

4. Horn, *Life of Tom Horn*, 22–25, 28–212. For Horn's employment record, see W. R. Gibson, Colonel, Quartermaster Corps, to Lorenzo D. Walters, 24 June 1929, Arizona Historical Society, Tucson. Al Sieber attested to Horn's employment as a packer; see Statement of Al Sieber, 7 April 1904, in Horn, *Life of Tom Horn*, 269–71; Dan L. Thrapp, ed. and comp., *Encyclopedia of Frontier Biography*, 3 vols. (Glendale CA: Arthur H. Clark, 1988) s.v. Thomas Horn. See also Dan L. Thrapp, *Al Sieber: Chief of Scouts* (Norman: University of Oklahoma Press, 1964) for more discussion; Horace E. Dunlap, "Tom Horn, Chief of Scouts," *Arizona Historical Review* 2 (April 1929): 73–85.

5. See Monaghan, *Tom Horn*, 110–11. See also Horn, *Life of Tom Horn*, 213. Phillip G. Nickell, "Tom Horn in Arizona or—Who Killed Old Man Blevins?" *Quarterly of the National Association and Center for Outlaw and Lawman History* 14 (1990): 15–22; provides some assessment of Horn's Arizona career. For recent research, see Don Dedera, *A Little War of Our Own: The Pleasant Valley War Revisited* (Flagstaff AZ: Northland Press, 1988). Earle R. Forrest, *Arizona's Dark and Bloody Ground*, rev. and enl. ed. (Caldwell ID: Caxton, 1959) is the pioneer work, with chap. 14 devoted to Tom Horn's role.

6. Monaghan, *Tom Horn*, 111–12; see Clara T. Woody and Milton L. Schwartz, *Globe, Arizona* (Tucson: Arizona Historical Society, 1977), 168–73, for Horn's part in the lynching.

7. *Arizona Silver Belt* (Globe), 6, 13 July 1889. See Harriett Farnsworth, "Cowboys of Old Yavapai," *Frontier Times* 41 (June–July 1967): 22–24, for background on the rodeo in Arizona. See also *Arizona Silver Belt*, 15 March 1890; *Arizona Daily Star*, 11 March 1890 (Horn is erroneously called Howe); *Arizona Daily Citizen*, 12 March 1890; and Monaghan, *Tom Horn*, 112.

8. For Horn's Pinkerton experiences, see Wilson Rockwell, *Memoirs of a Law-*

man [Cyrus Shores] (Denver: Sage Books, 1962), 258–323; Kenneth Jessen, "Tom Horn—He Was a Pinkerton," *Journal of the Western Outlaw-Lawman History Association* 3 (winter 1993): 19–21, 31; see also *Arizona Silver Belt*, 17 October 1891.

9. Helena Huntington Smith, *The War on Powder River* (New York: McGraw-Hill, 1966), is the standard work. Robert K. DeArment, *Alias Frank Canton* (Norman: University of Oklahoma Press, 1996), 141–44, finds evidence of Horn's presence in Wyoming at this time. See Carlson, *Tom Horn*, 29–39, for suspected murders and 20–28, for his arrest of suspected rustlers.

10. Larry D. Ball, ed., " 'No Cure, No Pay,' A Tom Horn Letter," *Journal of Arizona History* 8 (autumn 1967): 200–202; *Arizona Silver Belt*, 8 July 1897.

11. Gibson to Walters, 24 June 1929, Arizona Historical Society; see also Monaghan, *Tom Horn*, 161–68.

12. See Carlson, *Joe LeFors*, 145–62, for the Wilcox robbery and Tom Horn's role in the pursuit and his report. Charles Kelly, *The Outlaw Trail: A History of Butch Cassidy and His Wild Bunch* (New York: Devin-Adair, 1959), 239–48, does not mention Horn in the manhunt. See also *Cheyenne Daily Sun-Leader*, 30 January 1900.

13. *Cheyenne Daily Sun-Leader*, 29 January, 2 February 1900.

14. Carlson, *Tom Horn*, 52–58. Rash was killed on 8 July and Dart on 3 October 1900. See *Rocky Mountain News* (Denver), 19 November 1900, quoting a Cheyenne dispatch. See also Wilson Rockwell, *Sunset Slope: True Epics of Western Colorado* (Denver: Big Mountain Press, 1956), 207–16.

15. See Krakel, *Saga of Tom Horn*, 54, for the Horn quote.

16. Carlson, *Tom Horn*, 66–114; William Kittredge and Steven M. Krauzer, "Marshal Joe LeFors vs. Killer Tom Horn," *American West* 22 (November–December 1985): 36–45.

17. Krakel, *Saga of Tom Horn*, is devoted to the case, with documents. See also Krakel, "Was Tom Horn Two Men?" *True West* 17 (January–February 1970): 12–17, 52–56.

18. For reviews, see *Mississippi Valley Historical Review* 33 (June 1996): 356–57 and *Time* 47 (24 June 1946): 102, 104; see also Thrapp, *Encyclopedia of Frontier Biography*, s.v. James Jay Monaghan.

19. *Contemporary Authors*, vols. 41–44, first rev., s.v. James Jay Monaghan IV; *Who's Who in America*, 40th ed., 1978–1979, 2: 2285; Monaghan, *Schoolboy, Cowboy, Mexican Spy* (Berkeley: University of California Press, 1977), Billington's observation, ix.

20. *Contemporary Authors*, s.v. Monaghan; Thrapp, *Encyclopedia of Frontier Biography*, s.v. Monaghan.

21. Monaghan, *Tom Horn*, 39, 146, 136.

22. Monaghan, *Tom Horn*, 193, 171, 227.

CONTENTS

LIST OF ILLUSTRATIONS

TOM HORN
Last of the Bad Men

PREFACE

THE last great folk tale of the last American frontier is the story of Tom Horn, a legend that has been cherished in the Northwest for almost half a century.

Nowhere in that vast region of mountains and plains has the story been preserved with more grim realism than in that isolated corner where Utah and Wyoming join Colorado. Here the country is a rolling plateau cut and crosscut by many dizzy chasms. Automobile roads cannot penetrate the primeval wastelands, radios are unknown, and the art of storytelling has been preserved. This country is an oasis of western "wilderness"—an oasis with such compelling chaotic beauty that men who have felt its spell leave it with regret—an echo of the frontier that answers some deep nostalgia inside Americans, homesickness for the gone days when Americans were pioneers in the sun and could leave a life of haggling monotony to the richer and lesser folk behind.

The legend of Tom Horn is a perfect folk tale for such a land, stark, realistic, unweakened by sentimentality. Frontiersmen of northwestern Colorado are not ones to waste time decorating a killer's memory with soft feminine romance as the outlanders of the Southwest have adorned their great legend of Billy the Kid. Lush Spanish lies have added love affairs and poetic virtues to the folk tale of William Bonney, who was the foremost assassin in the range wars of the Southwest. Tom Horn, chief killer of the northern range, has been allowed to develop in the world of legend without such obvious efflorescence. The folk tales told of him are probably far nearer the truth than those told of Billy the Kid.

The men who tell Horn's story have been rigorously independent of spirit; untouched by servility or romanticism. They have never twisted Tom Horn into the Robin Hood mold. The warmer-blooded, more chivalrous South has made its killers, Jesse James and Billy the Kid, into glamorous creatures who robbed the rich to feed the poor—

13

a mythical pattern into which the outlaws were crammed despite their obvious unfitness for the place.

Already a legend before he was dead—a favorite subject for campfire lies—Tom Horn's herculean achievements have been placed by folk fancy in countries that he never saw. His feats with saddle and gun have been told on ranges that he never visited. In collecting data on such an individual, the writer has found many conflicting stories, though only a few are recorded here. Scientific historical analysis of facts has been impossible. Much of this narrative is based on word-of-mouth testimony. All of it is valuable as a record of cowboy legend, but strangely enough the story adheres to the true outlines of Tom Horn's life. His boyhood in Missouri is least affected by conflicting accounts. This part of the history has been taken partly from Horn's autobiography. His sisters Hannah and Nancy and his brother Charles all contributed freely of their time to reconstruct Tom's early environment. Hartmann Horn, Tom's cousin, and J. M. Davidson, county superintendent of schools in Scotland County, Missouri, have also helped with this early period.

Tom's experiences on the Chisholm Trail, his livery-barn employment in Burrton, Kansas, his sojourn in Leadville and subsequent trip along the Santa Fe Trail to Arizona are contrary to his autobiography. They were first told the writer by Tom's brother, Charles Horn, and by Fay Gorham. The story appeared to be a sample of the vitality of the Tom Horn legend until a search of the records at Newton, Kansas, by Register of Deeds N. D. Kelligan, disclosed that the Horns did own land in Burrton.

Plenty of documents bear evidence of Tom Horn's activities in the Geronimo wars in Arizona, yet some military writers vehemently protest against his importance in the last struggle for the red man's continent. Britton Davis in his *Truth About Geronimo* says that no such man as Horn was in the employ of the government between 1882 and 1885. Davis was a lieutenant in the Army at the time, and helped chase Geronimo. To contradict Davis' disparaging remarks about Tom Horn is a statement by Al Sieber, dean of Arizona's Apache scouts, who says that Horn went to work for him in the government service in 1882 and was with him on numerous scouting expeditions for the next three years, including the two notable trips into Mexico in 1883 and 1885. In addition, General Nelson A. Miles commended Horn's services as chief of scouts in the Geronimo campaign, Marion P. Maus, later a general, cited Horn for gallantry, and General Leonard Wood, when a lieutenant, described in his diary hairbreadth escapes with Horn.

Colonel C. C. Smith, USA, retired, whose father was a post quartermaster during the Geronimo wars in Arizona, and who has himself done some interesting research in the period, stated that Tom Horn was an impostor, "a liar," that the credit for capturing Geronimo belonged to the military men, not to a mere civilian employee like Tom Horn who should be classed as a common workman, a man of no authority and influence, a mere laborer. Truly there is little evidence to show that Horn brought in Geronimo, but the fact that he was chief of scouts under both General Crook and General Miles cannot be denied in face of the citations of his superiors. His name as chief of scouts appeared also in the New York and San Francisco newspapers as early as 1886, and William F. Cody, the showman, offered to take Horn to Europe as a drawing card for his Wild West Show.

In this book Tom is described at both the Cibicu Creek and Chevelon Canyon fights in 1881 and 1882. Tom claimed that he took part in both. His word is the only evidence. I have noted three detailed accounts of the fight at Cibicu Creek: one by Colonel C. C. Smith from the notes of Lieutenant Thomas Cruse, who was present; a second from William A. Reigan, schoolteacher on the reservation, who heard the story from the Indians themselves; and a third from Tom Horn. No two of these accounts agree, due partly to the fact that the United States troops were in two detachments fighting contemporaneously. The version given in this book was told by Tom himself many times and finally written in his autobiography.

Regardless of Tom's importance in the Southwest, he was not destined to be immortalized in cowboy legends for his services in the Apache wars. His fame rests on his skill as a marksman while acting as United States marshal and livestock detective in Utah, Colorado and Wyoming. The same partisanship noted in Arizona appears again in the stories told about Tom Horn on the northern plains. Charles Coe, who succeeded Tom Horn as stock detective in Wyoming, stated as recently as 1930 that Tom Horn was innocent of the murders of which he was accused. An executive of the largest bank in Denver told the writer in 1936, "I was raised on a ranch in Wyoming. Tom Horn was quite a myth with our family. Father always said that if it had not been for Tom Horn every cowman in the state would have gone bankrupt. Tom Horn helped more boys to get a college education than Phillips Brooks or Horace Mann ever did. I'm sure that Father never saw Tom Horn but he contributed money to keep him from hanging."

Settlers who survived the range war with the cattle barons remember Tom Horn as an assassin, a fiend who hid outside cabins and ambushed children. As recently as 1940, mothers still frightened their youngsters with the mention of his name. For years after Tom Horn died, whenever a man was found mysteriously murdered on the plains, people said, "Somebody Tom-Horned that fellow."

His reputation probably added a new word to the English language—the verb "to drygulch," so frequent in western fiction. Occasionally a settler in Wyoming and Colorado has been drygulched without serious consequences. The writer remembers a small cattleman who attempted to frighten away a neighbor and thus get more grass for himself. First the cattleman lighted a little fire in a dry gulch. Next he scattered some Bologna sausage rinds and crusts of rye bread around it. As we rode away he said, "When Jackie finds them crumbs, he'll sure figger a Tom Horn is layin' for him and I'll bet he flies his kite."

As soon as the real Tom Horn was dead, things associated with him became immediately revered. It is not unusual for a ranchman showing a stranger his buildings to say, "See that ring spiked to the bunkhouse logs? Tom Horn used that to braid his ropes."

An example of Horn's skilled braiding is exhibited in a glass case in the Colorado State Museum in Denver.

Immediately after his burial, a guard was kept at his grave to prevent disinterment by ghouls, and showmen made handsome offers to his relatives for permission to exhibit the body, just as other men, twenty-one years before, had bid for the body of Jesse James, and still others, thirty-eight years earlier, had bid for the body of Lincoln's assassin, John Wilkes Booth.

Tom Horn was universally praised when the United States hired him to kill red men—to exterminate one civilization to make room for another. His obloquy arose when he used his talents to exterminate one class of white men to make room for another class, called "substantial property owners." It is easy enough to understand how a man of Tom Horn's mentality might turn from the first kind of assassination to the second kind; how he might become famous as a killer for a great group of people like the United States and infamous as a killer for a smaller group of capitalists. It is easy—much too easy—to comprehend the tragedy of his slow submergence into the depths, his heart hardening with the passage of the years, until he could finally describe himself with a smile of pride as "an exterminatin' son-of-a-bitch."

1

IN THE LIGHT OF BURNING BARNS

"Tom Horn! You bring me a switch!" The tall barefoot woman stared across the weed-grown garden at a boy climbing over a rail fence with a gun in his hands and a big dog at his heels. The boy stopped, scratched his leg, looked back over the fence at the rolling upland pasture. His eyes were sharp, his nose pugged, his ears crimped forward like a weasel's.

"Come here now while I lick ye." The dog's and boy's tails drooped as they came dutifully through the Jimson weeds.

"You been off prowlin' the woods all night and huntin' and this the Lord's Day!" Tears brimmed in the woman's eyes. "Where you git yer Injun ways I wanta know!" She shook the boy as a dog shakes a woodchuck.

" 'Spare the rod and spile the child,' says Scripture," the woman repeated to herself while tears trickled into the corners of her strong mouth.

It always made her cry to whip Tom. Perhaps because she could not make him beg for mercy. She wiped her eyes on her gingham apron and the boy and dog slunk under the fence and out of sight. A moment later Mrs. Horn saw the black and white figure of a skunk waddling along the path to the chicken house.

"Tom, yooh, Tom," she called in a clear penetrating voice. "Come here and kill this varmint."

The Horns were Pennsylvania-Dutch folk—not of the communistic group which came to America from the street barricades of Germany in 1848, but of the older stock that had settled along the Delaware

19

and Susquehanna Rivers in days before the American Revolution. In the Horns lived a roving strain that had seemed to die in many other Low German families the moment they began to acquire fat barns and Pennsylvania acres. Sometime in the 1840's Tom Horn's father and mother moved westward in a Conestoga wagon to Ohio; then, after a time horizon-hunger moved them farther on into Missouri. Marriage had meant children to the Horns and many happy, dirty, little faces watched the receding East from the rear of the covered wagon. On the front seat of the sausage-shaped vehicle, Tom Horn, Sr., had sat in a dusty black coat whose lapels were hidden beneath his youthful black whiskers. He had a certain strong, slender grace that was apparent too in his children. Beside him sat his wife in calico and sunbonnet. Her wedding dress, preserved for Sundays and funerals, reposed in a trunk whose interior was gay with wallpaper lining. Mrs. Horn was also strong and slim—a well of vitality out of which were drawn, all told, eight superbly built children.

The Horns were hunting land, and with a singleness of purpose they weighed the West. They were emigrants but not poor emigrants. They had money to invest and could look for a bargain. As they crossed the dun-colored waters of the Mississippi two ways lay before them. They could roll on into Iowa and settle on rich black acres or they could drive into Missouri and purchase land with black slaves to cultivate it. Iowa had Pennsylvania and Ohio traditions. Missouri was a black border state with all that that implied.

A human pride in broad acres controlled their choice. Their money would purchase only a small farm in the valleys, but it would buy a great sweep of cheaper land. So they drove into the rough clay hills of Scotland County, Missouri, where the investment of their savings bought title to six hundred acres of land fourteen miles from Memphis, the county seat. The location was ideal for stock raising. A hundred acres of bottom land skirted Wyaconda Creek. The balance was upland pasture with grass waving like wheat. On the hill where the main road cut through the farm Tom Horn, Sr., built a two-story frame house with a one-story kitchen in an ell at the side. From the stoop in summer he could look north across his cornlands, over rows of tasseled leaves sweating in the sun, to the far border of tree-tops along Wyaconda Creek. Near by and across the main road a huge Dutch barn completed the estate.

On November 21, 1860, Mrs. Horn gave birth to her baby Tom. The Civil War was breaking with particular force upon Missouri, and the first sounds the baby's ears heard were word pictures of the guerrilla atrocities that had been common talk since 1855. In that year had begun the border warfare that was waged over "Bleeding Kansas," with Jayhawkers and Border Ruffians filling the night with whips, oaths, bullets and torches. Pillage, arson and sudden death had been daily topics of conversation in the days when slave-state Missouri sent its bands to fight the free-soil riflemen of Kansas, and when Kansas, under Jim Lane, swept back, paying raid with raid.

As a youngster, little Tom Horn heard one set of neighbors praise a certain John Brown of Osawatomie for having killed men in the name of a wrathful God. He heard another set of neighbors cheer the name of Davy Atchison whose followers had shot down free-soil farmers in the name of another God called "States' Rights." Tom heard people say that Atchison had been President of the United States. The fourth of March had come on Sunday in 1849, they explained, and old General Taylor would not take the oath of office on the Lord's Day. In consequence, Atchison, President of the Senate, became chief executive of the nation for a day.

These details were confusing to a farm boy, but Tom grew up understanding that great men were men of violence, men on horseback. Tales of murders "within a day's ride from here," and of So-and-so who was whispered as having been in the raids, were daily conversation at the Horn dinner table while baby Tom was intent upon patting applesauce with his hands or attempting to wear his porridge bowl as a hat. Tom was a toddler in his father's dooryard during those days of horror when armed gangs rode through Missouri pretending to be Union men in one neighborhood and Confederates in another. Gray-clad armies halted in farm dooryards inquiring for food and horses. So did the blue-clad armies. Men of no loyalties masqueraded under both flags to steal food and horses for themselves. Little Tom heard tales of whipped farmers dying in the red light of their burning barns. He knew of farm mothers who lived in terror, running to the door every time the children cried, for fear that the wails announced the slaughter or abduction of their husbands.

In the band of a Confederate guerrilla named Charles Quantrill, rode two Missouri boys, Frank James and Cole Younger, both destined to become outlaws. And in the Missouri banditti of "Bloody Bill" Anderson, galloped another youth, Jesse James, brother of Frank.

Tom grew up as intractable and disobedient as these freebooters. He was restless, adventurous, as though the devil of night riding had settled into his blood. His life and joy were to be in the carefree greenwood. But Tom grew up with an insatiable hatred of robbers. They were the enemies of thrifty Pennsylvania-Dutch farmers.

Tom matured early. He soon outgrew the kitchen dooryard. He met and played with Sammy Griggs, a neighbor boy his own age. The Griggses were poor folks—and poverty was sharp in Civil War Missouri. The cheapest cloth, flour sacking, had rare value. Many little urchins wore as their sole summer garment flour sacks with holes cut for head and arms. Mrs. Horn, wife of a large landowner in Scotland County, did not stoop to this economy for her children, but she did save such cloth and use it secretly for her own and her daughters' lingerie. With all their wealth in land and livestock, families like the Horns seldom saw as much as five dollars in cash in a year. Barter and trade were the custom of the country. Prosperous farmers wrote orders on their deposits of grist at the mill and these orders passed for currency in the countryside as far as the endorsers were acquainted. Tom felt superior to Sammy Griggs from the beginning.

The boys' first games were "John Brown" or "Quantrill" or, when they were particularly daring, "Bloody Bill Anderson." Sometimes the boys played "Railroad," sometimes "Indian," shouting, "I'm Custer and you're Black Kettle!" Then they played "Emigrants Going to Kansas" in covered wagons.

Year in, year out, a Gargantuan parade of covered wagons had passed through the Horn farm. Caught in its spell, Tom's brothers Charles and Martin joined the cavalcade. His sisters Hannah, Maude and Alice married in time and moved farther west. Nancy, the oldest, married too but she remained by the home fire. Her years as child-mother for Tom, and later Austin, had made her identify herself more with her parents than with her brothers and sisters.

Years later, Charles remembered that Tom, as a youngster, had a sense of humor. In fun his brothers named the domestic animals after the neighbors. Tom always laughed over the idea of the preacher and the doctor, in the form of two steers, fighting in the pasture. He chuckled when he heard his brother curse the local merchant, who as a mule plowed the corn. His eyes sparkled when the neighborhood old maid, in the person of a young brood sow, was turned into the pen where the Sunday-school superintendent champed his "tushes." Best of all was butchering time when Tom's dad knocked the town banker on the head.

Mr. Horn put his growing boys into the field as soon as they could wield a hoe. Tom complained. He said the Old Man's exactions hurried all the boys toward escape with the covered wagons. Perhaps so. It was no easy task to feed ten eager mouths on farm produce alone. Country women had no facilities for canning summer fruit for winter consumption. Corn and corn alone was the staple crop. Everyone tired of the monotonous food. Every spring Mrs. Horn watched the garden for the first "greens" to cook for her children and thus "thin their blood" from a winter diet of corn and salt pork. She told over and over how she had brought wheat flour from Ohio and had distributed it among the neighbors as a Christmas treat during their first winter in Missouri.

Young Tom groaned at a life of breaking land, planting corn, cultivating corn, cutting corn and husking corn. The work was especially hard on days when his father drove away to attend sales and races. Tom Horn, Sr., was a trader, a speculator, a pusher. He liked to buy and sell. His boys, working unwillingly in the field, listened for the sound of hoofs on the Wyaconda bridge. They knew the

Old Man might come back with a new wagon, a load of hogs, or a saddle horse and drove of steers for the meadow. The sound of hoofs always urged the boys to desperate work, for the father tolerated no shirking. He lashed his boys as he did his horses when they loafed on the job. His bellowing temper and free-swinging whip inspired them always with thoughts of the covered wagons rumbling endlessly to freedom, Westward Ho!

One day Charles, Tom's oldest brother, came back from the West for a visit. Full of success, as is usual with sons who have come from a long way off, Charles gave proof to the hope that Tom had seen shining in the eyes of all emigrants who had rolled past the farm since he could remember. The procession of wagons had been like a river, a trickling stream during the Civil War, swelling in the spring of 1864 with a flood of northern draft evaders. A year later many Missouri slaveholders in battered campaign hats rumbled past, spitting the gall of defeat from their mouths. Tom noticed that the wagons he saw after the year 1865 were not like the old wagon his parents had brought from Ohio. That ancient Conestoga had looked something like a boat—the influence of fresh-water craft used by emigrants on the Ohio River. The new wagons were "prairie schooners."

Tom determined to go west someday. Fate seemed against him in Missouri. Even the schoolhouse, he said, was a mile from home and thus hard to reach. Other children walked to it eagerly from greater distances. From miles away came youngsters, three and four riding bareback on a single mule, their bare feet kicking like a centipede's. In winter, children arrived with tears frozen on their cheeks and fried pork frozen in their dinner pails.

Tom hated these walks to school, hated them doubly since they obliged him to trudge behind his sisters. He hated girls. Years later people would say—erroneously perhaps—that Tom never did like girls, nor love them; that he loved nothing in life except a few men as stoic as himself—those, and the odd thing called life itself.

He wanted to wander off alone. Tracks and trailing were his passion and instinct. The first snow of winter made tracking plainer.

Then, as Nancy led the way to school, Tom lagged behind looking at things so long that he must run now and then to catch up. A blue jay flirted by and Tom lagged again. Then he saw where a wildcat had crossed the road. Wildcats were none too plentiful. He might never have another chance to chase one. It wouldn't hurt if he followed it just a little way. Tom tracked the cat all day.

After these boyhood pursuits he was usually thrashed soundly by his father and he got no sympathy from his mother or the girls. He did not like it when they compared him unfavorably with his cousin, Bennie Markley, who had come to live in the household. Tom loathed Bennie. The boy disliked hunting, never scuffed his red-topped boots nor wore out the seat of his "britches" sliding. Always his hair was combed and his hands clean. He enjoyed going to school with the girls and answering the teacher's questions.

On hot nights Tom was often too tired to hunt. He would lie down after supper among the currant bushes in the yard. Fireflies silently bombarded the night over his head. Tom called furtively to his dog, Shedrick. He patted his head and told him of big hunts to come. Tom could see the yellow oblong of a lighted window and through it hear Bennie discussing the next Sunday-school lesson with the girls. It was hot and prisonlike inside, cool and free among the currant bushes.

Mrs. Horn wished one of her boys would emulate, as Bennie did, the esteemed General Francis Marion Drake who with other Christian soldiers was planning a university in Iowa. Tom was sure that if Bennie became a full-fledged professor he would still be a failure.

Fall came and the nights were cooler. Tom watched the corn ripening out of the milk. Tired as he was at night, he took Shedrick into the soft September gloom beneath giant trees where the corn rows marched down to "Wy'condy Crick." He knew that raccoons would be in the field and he waited for the moon and the telltale rustling of raccoon paws among the corn leaves. The knowledge that he would get "a daisy" from his mother made him dread to go home, but did not break him from hunting. Often the boy slunk into the barn to sleep in the hay rather than face a beating in the big house.

In the morning, hunger brought him to the kitchen ell. Here, in no uncertain terms, he was told that this was the Lord's Day and "How do you expect to go to church without your Saturday-night bath?" Bennie and the girls looked virtuous and shiny in their fresh clothes.

Tom's freckles would not wash off. Nancy hurt his ears and nose scrubbing him. His cleanliness gave him intolerable discomfort. The most terrible thing of all happened one Sunday when the self-conscious children had marched out to the Conestoga, now transformed to a farm wagon, filled with chairs waiting to take the family churchward. Old Shedrick, pungent with last night's skunk hunt, jumped up in friendly embrace and muddied Bennie's Sunday roundabout. With outraged rectitude Bennie gave Shedrick a blow with a hoop pole. Tom, irritable in his clean clothes, tackled Bennie with ardor and whipped him in front of all the girls. His mother, wielding an umbrella, rescued Bennie. Mr. Horn, for once in his life, made no move to chastise Tom. Tom guessed that Bennie was too good for his pa.

The Sunday look had left Tom's clothes. His mother boxed his ears and told him to stay at home so she could whip him when she got back. Then the family drove virtuously away.

As soon as the wagon was out of sight, Tom made barefoot tracks up the road to the nearest neighbor's, his mind busy with an ambition that was lifelong—to get out of sight and to do as he pleased.

His gangling young legs carried him quickly to the farm where Sammy Griggs lived. The two boys started off across the fields and into the woods with a suitable Sunday adventure clear in mind.

Two boys in the early summer. Their families safe at the little white Christian church. Their dogs curled in sleep on the leaf mold. Their own bodies resting by a rifled fox den. A canopy of grapevines over their heads. Two boys digging strong, brown toes into the cool earth, talking about girls and wondering if this and that were so about them. Wondering how it would feel to kill a man. Once at a sale Tom's pa had showed him the man who killed Jabe Tooth.

"It would be as easy to do as killin' them fox pups; but would it ha'nt you? Pa says it's all right to kill a horse thief."

An adventure with Sammy in the springtime of 1875 was one of the three reasons for Tom's departure from home. Having treed a raccoon, the boys built a fire at the foot of the trunk. They could not see the 'coon but the dogs were sure that the prey was up there somewhere among the new leaves. Sammy climbed the tree and began to shake it. The dogs jumped up and down; so did Tom. Something fell. It struck the ground and the dogs swarmed upon it. Out of the smother came Sammy's plaintive voice. The boy was bruised inside and out, bitten on neck, ear and arm. The dogs were mortified—especially Sammy's dog Sandy. There had been rivalry as to which dog was smarter. Tom thought this settled it, for Shedrick, he said, could tell a boy from a 'coon.

A coolness sprang up between Tom and Sammy. They hunted separately henceforth. Tom was indeed lonely now. He had one consolation: he had never been able to whip Sammy Griggs although he had tried a hundred times. Now he could walk about alone and whip Sammy over and over in his imagination. He might be a lonesome boy, but he was victorious.

The second incident that prepared Tom for departure happened one day while he sat on the fence by the dirt road watching covered wagons roll by. Two emigrant boys, on a horse, halted to talk to him. Tom was afraid they felt themselves better than he, just because they were following a caravan into the West. Tom noticed that one of the young riders was no larger than himself. The rider was looking at Tom critically. Tom came to the point with a slurring remark about the shotgun the riders carried. A shotgun was a buttonhole bouquet to the rifle-loving frontier.

Down off the mare slid the emigrant boys. The elder of the two grappled with Tom who speedily got the better of the scrimmage. Tom swung on top and struck downward with hot fists into a hot face. The smaller emigrant boy rushed to his brother's rescue and kicked Tom in the jaw. Arms and legs, six of each, were flying in the dust. Shedrick mistook the affair for a dogfight and leaped into the cloud. The fight stopped. The boys scrambled for the fence. The smaller emigrant boy went up the mare's leg like a tomcat up a post.

The larger emigrant boy snatched up the shotgun and did what Tom, to his dying day, thought was the most horrible thing his eyes had ever seen. The boy shot old Shed; then he jumped like a bullfrog onto the horse and galloped away with his brother down the clay road.

Tom had lost first Sammy Griggs and now old Shed. The third catastrophe was close at hand.

Feeling the dawning strength of manhood—that year he was fourteen—Tom began to eye his father critically. He noted the man's weaknesses; he questioned his strength. The time had come for the young male to test his strength with the old—the abysmal instinct of brutes. Just before haying Tom told his father that he was leaving home. This would leave the Old Man shorthanded. The two males quarreled. Mr. Horn struck at Tom with a strip of harness and Tom, for the first time in his life, struck back. His father beat him mercilessly, tossed him into the haymow and said, "Now, if you're going to leave home, go! And just remember that the last time the Old Man whipped you, he gave you a good one. Go!" he said, "but ask yer ma to pack you a lunch because you'll be back by suppertime and if you have a lunch you won't miss your dinner."

All night Tom lay prostrate in the hay and in the morning his mother and sisters carried his bruised body to a bed. For a week he could not walk, but when his feet could carry him he said good-by, and his mother watched him take the Kansas City road, go down the swale south of the house, climb the hill beyond, to the top. For a moment he seemed to stand, a tiny figure against the horizon—then disappeared.

He was going far away. No career of cheap local banditry for him. Other boys of Missouri were robbing and "shooting up" small towns. Jesse James, now twenty-seven years old, was making people hold their breath at the mention of his name. The Younger boys were riding and robbing. Such wild fellows, homeless outlaws, plundered the rich. Tom thought he might like rich people; he knew he hated poor ones.

Tom Horn set his face toward the stark and bloody plains.

2

A YOUNG MAN OFF ON HIS TRAVELS

Tom tramped down the road toward Kansas City, the great railway town, and the gateway to the pioneer West. This, the greatest city in the world to Tom, was some seventy-five miles from his home. On the second day of his walk he was passing strange farms. At night he slipped along the roadway fences, occasionally hearing a distant dog bark. In the morning freshness he walked boldly in the middle of the road and noticed the smoke of newly built fires start from farm chimneys. The smell of hot cakes and sausage brought him to farm doors. People in Missouri in 1875 generally fed a lonely boy wandering far from home. At noon he would sleep in some wood lot under elms hung with grapevines. Once a child-hungry farm woman with a song in her heart dressed him in the clothes of her own departed son while she washed his travel-stained belongings. Then she watched him as his mother had, going down the road to Kansas City. Women were often like that with Tom Horn.

Sometimes the boy got "lifts" on a farm wagon. Once he fell in with a tramp dressed in a mussed Army uniform. They sized up each other's wealth as traveling acquaintances do. The man and the boy roasted sweet potatoes and corn under a gigantic buttonwood. From the tramp Tom heard the wonders of Kansas City; how country boys were "fleeced" in the metropolis, how "they" would knock him on the head for a three-cent piece.

Young and adventurous, Tom forgot these warnings in the maelstrom of Kansas City—an eager, excited board town where men had disregarded the panic of '73 and were making money building railroads. Tom learned the meaning of a new word, "hobo." He heard that Kansas City was the hobo center of the world, not even second to Chicago. Hobo did not mean a professional tramp. Hobos were migratory, unskilled laborers who built the transcontinental railways. Only six years before, the first railroad—the Union Pacific—had reached California. People everywhere talked about the old overland stage and the pony express. Now three railroads were racing to the western ocean to compete with the Union Pacific. They were financed by land grants, and the quicker they were built the more land the companies acquired. Hobos were hired by thousands and tens of thousands to rush the work.

In front of open doorways Tom saw chalk figures on blackboards announcing big wages. He registered for work on the Santa Fe out on the plains. The workmen were herded like livestock down the muddy street to the crowded railway station. Tom saw wood-burning locomotives named after western scouts. "Kit Carson" was driven by an engineer with dignified muttonchop side whiskers, protected from the flying sparks by what appeared to be a lady's brassière. The quaint "en-jine"—as Tom called it—trundled diminutive day coaches along the tracks of the Santa Fe. A conductor passed the laborers onto the train. His blue coat and brass buttons reminded Tom of the uniforms on soldiers who came back from the Civil War.

Motley crowds occupied the day coach leaving Kansas City. Bearded "roughs" with long tickets in their hatbands piled carpet-bags and canvas sacks in the aisles. The men spat tobacco juice on the floor, and Tom could spit with the best of them. His fellow passengers were professional buffalo hunters, homeseekers and pioneer businessmen. The long barrels of Sharps and Ballard rifles rose above the wooden-slat seats. Somebody sighted a pale cavalcade of racing antelope. The bearded men grabbed their rifles, crowded to the windows, fired indiscriminately at the landscape. The white puffs from the black-powder cartridges screened the toddling train. Then the men leaned their rifles against the seats, produced bottles and passed them from hand to lip. They laughed at the way the antelope ran and said, "We shore bombarded them some."

Tom and his companions "uncarred" at Newton, Kansas. They

The Horn barn in 1941. The outside sheeting is new. The rafters, rooftree, floors and stalls were built by Tom Horn, Sr.

Wyaconda Creek on the Horn farm south of Granger, Missouri. Here Tom learned the rudiments of tracking and trailing.

Tom Blevins, storyteller, one of the men who cherish the legends of Tom Horn. Photo taken on Royle brothers' ranch, scene of the writing of the *Squaw Man*.

Cowboys on Horse Creek, Wyoming.

were assigned to a laborers' camp, where dust blew into their food and bedding. Tom found that resetting rails and replacing ties was not so romantic as he and Sammy Griggs had imagined. Custer had conquered Black Kettle once and for all time, and the wild Indians around Newton had vanished. The West which Tom had dreamed about lay like the ocean over there where the sun went down. Wooden trestles crossed creeks lined with currant bushes and choke-cherries. Buffalo bones were piled at the sidings waiting to be shipped east for the phosphate they contained. Tom had thought the work at home too hard, but this was harder. The regular hours irked his roving spirit, but he was not going back until he got what he sought in the West. It was not here on the section. It was over that horizon that ringed the little crew of human ants working on the shining rails. Out there were the greatest ranges of the world. Men with experience were killing buffalo by thousands to feed such workers as he. That was the work for which he and hundreds of other poor boys had come west, and failed to find. Rich boys, as well as poor boys, had come west for big game hunting. British lords, American millionaires and Army officers had been going over that horizon for years to kill buffalo and deer and elk and bear. Tom Horn determined that he, too, should go on a great expedition.

One day as the hobos sat on their haunches along a cut bank after dinner a grizzled veteran started to talk with a gone sound like the wind. Twenty years ago he had accompanied Sir St. George Gore on a hunting trip with two hundred guides, retainers, teamsters and packers. Tom edged nearer. The sportsmen had penetrated the Rocky Mountains and encountered a large party of Sioux Indians. They had been forced to abandon all their prized trophies. The knight asked for permission to enlist a private army to retaliate, for he was willing to stake his entire fortune rather than let a group of barbarians affront *him*. "A haw-hawing Britisher he were. Used to cuss when we didn' call him Sir Jarge. Thought he was the Lord, I guess. I called him Count because he was no account. Hee hee." The old man nudged the worker next him. "Get it? . . . Well, he's gone now," the storyteller continued, "but the Sioux Injuns is still over thar and big doin's is ahead. Seen plenty sojers goin' by on the cars last spring."

From other workers Tom learned of other great sportsmen who had passed over the horizon. Six years before, Sir John Watts Garland had built a "shooting box" out there. He also had lavish "boxes" in Africa and India. The bison and grizzly of America interested him as much as the tiger, the rhino and the elephant. The Earl of Dunraven had gone west the same year. He had a letter to General Sheridan and was given a military escort. Estes Park in Colorado was his private game preserve.

In 1871 a large party of wealthy New Yorkers had gone hunting with a great number of saddle horses and wagons. In their train were three wagons packed with ice for their wine. This was just the kind of expedition to suit a young man later to be known as Buffalo Bill, who accompanied it as scout and guide. A tall, slim, courtly young man, he quickly learned that a buckskin shirt—sure sign of poverty in the West—could be decorated until it became a mark of elegance. He was a picturesque horseman, and wealthy young men paid him big sums purely because he pleased their eyes. He showed young aristocrats how to ride after buffalo, how to shoot elk, and he initiated them into the western custom of drinking an eye opener before breakfast. In afterlife, he stated that when they got thoroughly used to this quaint habit they pronounced it more refreshing than brushing their teeth.

Two summers before Tom Horn shoveled along the Kansas roadbed, the Grand Duke Alexis of Russia went on a special Union Pacific train as far west as Denver to shoot bison. Buffalo Bill and Generals Sheridan and Custer, in all their bravest fringe, had shown the Grand Duke how to pursue bison across the plains. His royal training made him a good horseman. After a successful run young Alexis, his blond beard covering the top of his green uniform, embraced his American companions. The bison he killed were much like the aurochs of his native Russia, and the Indian horsemen that Spotted Tail brought for his inspection were probably as much like those of his native Cossacks as the plains of Kansas and Colorado were like the steppes of Russia. The life that was to thrill and grip Tom Horn forever was but a ten-day episode in the existence of Alexis. The bearded boy was destined to become an admiral in the uniform of the Czar, see fighting off the coast of Manchuria in the Russo-Japanese War, and die in a royal bed, a mediocre nobleman.

The activities of these rich men were merely tales to Tom and he had set out to see actualities. The section hands working for a dollar a day talked about the fat wages wealthy sportsmen paid cowboys who acted as game beaters. Tom longed to hunt game with picturesque noblemen and cowboys but he was considered too young. First he had hated poor people, now he hated his own poverty that kept him from doing the things more fortunate boys were doing. His first thought was to get riches, but he would have to work for a million days at a dollar a day to become a millionaire. If he could not be rich, he could serve the rich. "To the stars by exciting ways" was the motto in Tom's mind while he shoveled dirt in Kansas. Then something appeared on the southern horizon that made the fourteen-year-old boy put down his shovel forever.

It looked like an immense snake coming across the roll of the plains. Sometimes it halted and grew as vague as a cloud shadow. Then, amoebalike, it flowed out to one side and distended until it was stretched like elastic. It separated only to flow together again.

"Here comes a herd of Texas cattle!"

The herd approached. Tom noticed animals of many colors, sharp backs and hips like many peaks. Over the herd floated a mist of rocking horns. Riders encircled the drove.

After two or three months on the trail these Texas drovers were drab, unwashed fellows. Hair hung over their shirt collars and blew in front of their eyes. Their flat-crowned hats had brims as straight as the sky line. The peaked crown and curled brim of the cowboy hat did not become fashionable until riders' eyes got accustomed to the peaks and rolling valleys of the Rocky Mountains. A few of the riders wore leather over their legs. Ragged ruffians they were, with reckless eyes. Here a cotton sleeve was torn, showing bulging biceps. There an elbow was "out." Toes winked from holes in low-heeled boots.

Tom forgot these defects in dress when he saw the easy grace with which the cowboys handled their little long-tailed ponies under big-skirted, double-rigged saddles. The cowboys evidently regarded the herd as their home and their business. While it was in their charge, they were as loyal and conscientious as any workman might be. The herd was even their religion.

These drovers had nothing of the self-conscious romance of cowboys a generation later; but, if not romantic, they were as picturesque as pirates to a boy like Tom Horn. Big-eyed, he stared at them and their herds.

Each drove contained more than three thousand cattle and, as fall came on, six or seven herds crossed the railroad tracks in a day. They flowed by as endlessly as the covered wagons Tom had seen in Missouri. The West might be limitless but there could never be room for all these cattle and all these farmer emigrants. Wherever these two lines of ambition converged, one must give way.

Many herds were surging north to fill Army contracts made by quartermasters among the troops who were quelling the Indians in Wyoming. Many herds were headed for the reservations of Indians already conquered; many were destined to stock the ranges the soldiers had wrested from the red men. Some herds were sold to railroad commissary men and butchered for the construction crews. The buffalo hunters protested against all this! The Texans were taking the bread out of their mouths! Other herds were loaded on the cars and shipped to packers in Kansas City and Chicago.

Wherever the herds went, their herders were paid off the moment a sale was made. At such points saloons and gambling halls flourished. A drunken cowboy, fresh from Texas, was apt to forget that the Civil War was over and indulge in a little indiscriminate shooting at the Yanks; when "broke" he might rob a "dude" for money to finance his homeward journey. One of these cowboys, Sam Bass, having lost all his money at the end of the trail northward, held up a railway train. Cowboys immortalized Sam because his experience was epic. But the Sam Bass of folk-song legend was no figure, in reality, to compare with what Tom Horn was to be.

Young Tom had been faithful to his shovel for twenty-six days, but he was now seduced by a saddle. He quit the railroad gang and walked up the dirt street of a Kansas town, a willow-shaped youth, eying the cowboys shyly as a girl watches a boy who she imagines would make a good lover. Here were the kind of men he had always wanted to know—no Bennie Markleys among them. Tom noticed that the livery barns and saloons stood on the south side of the tracks to attract incoming cowboys. He learned that "south of the tracks" meant cheap residences and brothels. He stood bashfully at the bar drinking beer, listening to the cowboys' southern drawl. He heard them tell tales of their clashes with "nesters," farmers on the plains; how they had cut barbed-wire fences, by pounding them with rocks, to let their herds go through. "The boss says next yeah we'll carry wiah-cuttahs in our holstahs."

Tom saw outraged farmers now and then follow a herd into town and fight with the despoilers of their fences. He saw the American beginning of that immemorial conflict between horseman and farmer. He saw Kansas towns hire pistol-packing marshals to preserve order. Of the dozen or more of these professional marshals "Bat" Masterson, Wyatt Earp and "Wild Bill" Hickok appear and reappear in the life of Tom Horn. Wild Bill became the most famous, not on account of any superiority with the six-gun but on account of his later appearance in a Wild West circus.

When Tom heard shooting, he elbowed his way through crowds to look at dead men lying in new overalls and shirts purchased for the long ride home to Texas. The sight of limp, pale bodies with bullet holes affected Tom no more than had the spectacle of so many fox pups in Missouri. Tom heard the cowboys bury their dead with strange lamenting songs. He saw bareheaded crowds stand awkwardly as the shovelers threw dirt into the grave, saw the cowboys wondering what next to do until the foreman solved their dilemma by saying, "Well, boys, we've done all we can f'r Zeb. Le's get back and load them caddle." The embarrassed horsemen would be laughing before they reached the stockyards. When one of these cowboy bands rode south, Tom was with them, racing with winter over the rim of the world.

The trail was easy to follow in the late fall. It was first used by a half-breed, Jesse Chisholm—who had, so far as anybody knew, never owned a cow. Jesse scouted for the whites and traded with the Wichitas, who had fled northward in 1862 when their enemies, the rich, slaveholding tribes farther south, had sided with the Confederacy and gone on the warpath. Jesse's people held no Negroes in bondage and were driven to the free soil of Kansas with their baskets, puppies and papooses in wagons or on poles which ponies dragged as elongated shafts. Jesse made several trips in a wagon and the wheel ruts he left across the primeval sod went into history as the Chisholm Trail. There was also a John Chisum, all white, who moved great cow herds between Texas and New Mexico. He was one of the liege lords of the Southwest and tradition welded John and Jesse into the same man. The great trail was named for the man who never owned cows, not for the cattle baron who seldom used it. The mighty pathway was six years old when Tom first saw it. It had grown as a result of the Union Pacific Railroad's arrival on the northern plains. Before this railroad opened an outlet to the East, cattle had increased in Texas without profit to their owners. In 1867 cattlemen, arming against the Indians whom they were sure to meet, herded their animals toward the steel rails. The plains furnished the cheapest transportation for cattle ever known. A few men could graze immense numbers of cattle from their home range to the railroad.

As Tom jogged along this trail, listening to his superiors brag and sing, boiling coffee on fires of dry grass and buffalo chips, he hardly realized that the altitude was getting lower and the soil more sandy. He was riding back into late summer. The streams became sluggish. Rags of gray moss waved gently from the trees above malarial water. He passed San Antonio, an adobe town. He entered the brittle forest of mesquite trees with monstrous prickly pears over which a horseman could not see. Great live oaks shaded whitewashed board ranch houses. Everybody spoke Spanish with an American accent. Tom, born to English and German, soon picked up the Latin tongue. The boy had a natural aptitude for language. The people Tom met had little money but plenty of food. An extra boy or two made no difference so long as he helped fix corrals and fences, and rode after the long-horned cattle in the brakes.

Cowboy life came easily to a Missouri farm boy. Tom was more interested in braiding bridle reins than digging postholes. He practiced roping pigs and dogs and calves and finally Texas longhorns. His lariat was whale line borrowed from the sailors in the blue Gulf not far away.

Texas cowboys rode a saddle with two cinches called a "rim-fire rigging." Mexicans from south of the Rio Grande rode saddles with one broad cinch called a "center-fire saddle." Tom was told that the Texas cowboys had adopted the double-rig after the Mexican War. They did not want to copy anything from the "greasers." Tom noticed that the mesquite jungles of south Texas were so dense that a cowboy could never see a cow until he was up to it. In open country down in Mexico a cowboy had time to get off and tighten his cinch before riding up to rope an animal. He suspected that the real reason for the double-rig was the thick jungles. A man did not have time to dismount and inspect his cinch before making a throw. Two cinches, when loose, held a saddle better than one. The brush riders also used a very small looping rope with one end tied fast to the saddle horn. Tom, amazingly quick and deft with his hands, became an expert roper.

In this fairyland he was happy, but happier still when with spring the herds started north. The nomadic mess wagon was the most congenial home he had yet known—no regular hours, no Sunday schools, no girls, no mother to tell him to wash his face. At his old home he had worried because there were not enough boys to whip; now he could fight bad horses every day.

Old-timers among the cowboys, thirty years later, remembered how Tom acted when "Comanche Red" bucked him into the cactus for the third time. Tom borrowed the mess cook's file and with trembling hands and aching muscles sawed for an hour on his spur rowels. When they were sharp and jagged as a tin-can top he said, "Ol' Red may throw me ag'in, but if he does, I'll peel him from his tail butt both ways while I'm quittin' him."

Long-legged, short of waist and crotched almost to the armpits, the slim boy was built for rough riding. When chasing wild cattle through the jungle he whipped his horse if there was room to move a hand, spurred if there was room to move a foot. "Tom was big f'r his age—and knowed it," said an ancient and reminiscent cowboy of Texas in 1930. "He figgered he was better mentally, physically, yes, and by God, morally, than the rest of us boys, and damned if I know whether he was or not."

Riding with the herd, Tom saw Dodge City for the first time— "the ripsnortin'est, outshootin'est cow town" in the West, and terminus of a new Texas trail that was not so badly overstocked and eaten out as the old Chisholm trail. Outside the city, sometimes miles before they reached it, cattle buyers in plug hats, dusty frock coats and trousers wrinkled at the crotch appeared on horseback to make bids for the herd. Their purpose was to buy the cattle before the owner learned the market prices. Seasoned cowboys had fun with these unctuous frauds.

"How-de-doo, young feller," the buyer would begin, addressing the cow hand in the lead. "Whose outfit is this?"

A sophisticated cowboy would reply with glib lies, making up a fictitious name for the boss.

"These is the James Cattle Company's from Red Rock," he would say with a straight face.

"Is Mr. James along?"

The cowboy would point Indian-fashion, with his lips, directing the newcomer to the "swing-man," the rider next in line, who guarded the side of the herd. The buyer jogged back to the swing-man who would point out the "drag-man" far in the rear as "Mr. James." A dealer would ride miles before realizing that he had been "jobbed." At last he would clatter off toward Dodge City in a huff.

All this made laughter and conversation among the cowboys at suppertime. If any of them had been so slow and stupid as to tell the buyer, "Why, I don't know any Mr. James! Who told you he was with this outfit?" that man was sure to be tried in the firelight by his peers and sentenced to be whipped or saddled, ridden and spurred by his whooping comrades. These "kangaroo courts" were familiar to Tom. The name had been applied to frontier tribunals in Ohio before he was born.

Tom Horn learned, too, how to watch for robbers outside Dodge City, men who would ride up and demand the right to comb the herd for "strays." In so long a journey herds were sure to mix and to contain, at the end, many cattle wearing strange brands. Naturally a foreman anxious to make as good a showing as possible would butcher these strays in lieu of his own cattle. He would use them, too, to buy off Indians or farmers demanding settlement for damage done their crops by trampling herds. Often Texans started up the trail with no money, relying upon their acquisition of strays to pay all bills. To recover their property many cattle owners hired "stray-cutters" to meet the migratory bands outside Dodge City and salvage their particular brands. Among these legitimate representatives were thieves who, representing nobody, made large hauls for themselves. Sometimes bloody battles were waged between them and the cowboys. Tom's introduction to the West was as a defender of property rights and a doubter of all men who claimed that the big outfits were cheating the "little fellers."

Tom was glad to see a railroad town after months on the trail. He was glad to see new faces. He knew all the men of his outfit so well that he was tired of them. He was no longer amused by that grease spot on the top of the boss's flat-crowned hat where his funny bald spot rubbed the felt. But after Tom had shaved the boyish down on his lips and donned new clothes in Dodge City and walked around town for a few hours, he was overjoyed to come upon his own men in the saloons. They all looked better to one another. They looked better to themselves, too, in the barroom mirrors. Tom noticed that he was as tall as the others leaning against the bar. He liked the saloons, but he did not like to see the boys go off with women whose faces were painted as red as new hatchets. Such women laughed at him and told him not to stand with his mouth open. Tom would get even with the sex for that jibe.

The growing boy heard his companions tell strange tales about these women. Relays of cowboys herded the cattle, while the off-duty crew made merry in town, and a cowboy would say, "Them girls in Dodge City overcharged us the last time we was there—soaked us twice what the railroad men was payin'. They got us drunk, took our money and then turned us out. I couldn't sleep for thinkin' of it, so I waked Whitey and we talked things over, plannin' how to get even. Then we turned out Jed and the other boys. 'Now this is what's up,' sez I. 'We're goin' back and raid that joint, dump the whole outfit out of bed, have a roughhouse.' 'Nope,' sez Jed, pullin' on his overalls, 'I got a better idee.' So we got our hosses, saddled 'em and surrounded the house. Each man shook out his rope and built a little loop like a feller does in the brush. The windows was open. Jed made a throw and snagged a bedstead without wakin' a soul. All we could hear was snorin'. The rest of the boys tied onto bureaus, chairs and washstands. Lum Slaughter's rope upset a pitcher and I could hear a girl say, 'Are you there, dearie?' Lum's chin come even with the window sill and he sez, quiet-like, 'Yes, honey, just a minute.' He was takin' a extry dalley with his rope around her bed leg as he said it.

"When everybody was ready we turned our ponies around and Whitey sings out, 'Git up!' He wasn't talkin' to his hoss. Everybody spurred f'r camp. It sounded like Indians on the war trail back there in that house, such squealin' and yowlin'. There was furniture comin' through the windows and doors and some of it makin' *new* windows in them thin board walls.

"Jed's hoss damn near run off, he was so onused to seeing night-gowns and sheets instead of a cow at the other end of the rope.

Whitey said the old lady was still in bed when he got her outside and she hung on a-screechin' as the bed rolled along on its casters until it hit a chunk and come in two. Lookin' back we could see girls runnin' around pullin' down the tails of their shirts and yellin'. The sun was just comin' up.

"Jed alwus called his hoss 'Carpenter' after that night."

Such tales were recounted by Tom's idols. It partially explains Tom's own laughing brutality toward women in later years.

In Dodge City Tom heard that the famous marshal, Wild Bill Hickok, was dead. Hickok had quit his circus to police the mining town of Deadwood, South Dakota, and, swaggering around town in the over-dressed elegance of the successful killer, had met death by a shot in the back.

Tom heard, too, that Custer, the hero of his boyhood, had been shot down with his yellow hair flying. Wild Bill and Custer had both died as unwitting victims of the gold rush! Two elegant dandies gone to defend mines and miners.

It was as Tom left Texas for the second trip up the trail that he first became implicated in murder. With some friends he had ridden out of San Antonio to be gone for half a year. They gave the keen-edged "rebel yell" that former Confederate cavalrymen had taught the Texas riders. Drunk and happy, the whooping cowboys blazed into the air with their revolvers. At the edge of town stood a freshly whitewashed outhouse, a vivid target against the live-oak trees. Each rider shot at it as he dashed by.

The next moment they were out of sight in the cactus labyrinth. Only the dust floating over the road through the mesquite showed which way they had gone.

Hours later a man gripping his belt came running into town, howling to the world, "Ma Hawthorne and little Effie is dead down in the arroyo."

LIVERY STABLES AND SPILT BEER

Tom Horn did not dare revisit Texas. His brother Charles owned a small ranch in the Flint Hills of Kansas. Tom went to see him. The lure of cowboy life had tempted Charles as well as Tom, but having none of Tom's aversion to girls he had married and was now settled down with a small bunch of cattle on the finest grassland in all Kansas. The idea of being his own boss and building up an outfit of his own appealed to Tom and he invested his savings in his brother's venture. Long afterward Charlie's eyes would snap as he recalled how quick Tom had been to note a cow track in the grass as he rode the little herd. "Tom had better eyes than most Indians."

Before long Tom realized that his investment was a mistake. The smallness of the ranch, with its sod cabin, and its grinding necessity for narrow routine, irked a cowboy who had moved cattle by the thousand. Guarding his few cows from the all-absorbing trail herds that swept by, Tom felt inferior. He was jealous of the careless buckaroos who swapped him three or four lame animals for one of his sound steers. "Tenderfeet," these limping creatures were called— a name which soon passed to human immigrants.

Tom grew weary of the round of duties: pulling cows out of quick-sands only to be charged by the ungrateful "critters" as soon as they found their feet; seeing to it that bulls were scattered properly among the brood cows instead of being allowed to congregate on the salt grounds where unfruitful duels were the rule. While he dragged logs along little ice-sealed creeks to keep his cows from choking for water, Tom looked at steers that would take four years to mature. And four years was a long time for a seventeen-year-old to wait for

payday. The poverty of his and Charlie's resources contrasted sadly
with the big businesses Tom had seen.

No doubt Tom's attitude influenced Charlie to sell the ranch.
Moreover, their father had prospered recently. He visited the boys
in 1878, purchased some land in the town of Burrton, Kansas, and
induced Charlie and Tom to lease it from him. Town life sounded
attractive to both boys. They decided to open a livery stable. Tom,
as junior partner again and "night man," found life better than before. He had a peculiar fondness for the night and horses.

There was much loafing in the ammonia-smelling corridor between the stalls and Tom allowed riders to unroll their beds in the
stable and heard them, as they cooked meals in the street, say, "I
don't care about myself so long as my horse is took care of." He kept
spurs, guns, whips and bottles in the "office." He watched men play
cards under the tongues of cutters and spring wagons. The town
fiddler practiced there with snake rattles in his violin to make the
tone clearer. Boys sat on a bench along the front of the barn looking
at the girls coming out the back doors of their homes. When the
screens slammed all eyes would turn.

"There goes Marcella Pope; she's got a mouth as big as a horse
collar." Tom's fellows had small consideration for any girl whose
face was not painted like a signboard.

In spite of his boyhood ambition to become rich by exciting ways,
Tom was unwittingly adopted by small business and its people.
Other young men who had come up the Chisholm Trail were settling down in the Kansas towns. For sixty years they lived in the
past, telling the rising generations of the greatness of their exploits.
Years later Charles Horn said, "Our life back in Kansas was too
tame for Tom. He wasn't content to cultivate a hundred and sixty
acres, drink a little whisky, pitch horseshoes of a Sunday, marry a
brood woman and raise his own baseball nine." At the time, however, there was nothing else for Tom to do and fate might have ac-
climated him. It had been two decades since the hope of gold lured
young men across the western horizon to Pike's Peak, three since
they had been lured to California. The Deadwood gold rush was

over. People said, "All the gold out West has been discovered. The days of the Old West have passed."

Then some news clicked along the telegraph wires that reawakened the boyhood ambition of eighteen-year-old Tom. A new mineral named "galena" had been discovered in the Rocky Mountains. The news did not disturb the tranquillity of Burrton, whose young men had no desire to miss the regular Friday-night dance. Tom suggested to Charles that they go prospecting for the new mineral. Charles, who was planning to buy his father's interest in the barn, gave his younger brother an intolerant answer. Tom mentioned the subject no more. A few days later as he ate breakfast in his brother's kitchen he said, "I've been away from home for four years. I reckon I'll go back and see the folks." Charles said years later, "Tom was always like that. Instead of going home he went straight for the new diggings. I didn't see him again for twenty years."

It was easy to get a lift with covered-wagon emigrants who rolled west parallel to the railroad tracks. On either side were plains, flat as the ocean, sloping imperceptibly uphill. One evening, the snow fields of the Rockies appeared like low-flying clouds. They were over seventy miles away. Among them galena had been struck at Leadville. All around, Tom heard emigrants say that miners up there were earning wages that made a cowboy's thirty dollars a month seem dirt, but, said the wagonmen, a fellow spends it as fast as he makes it in them mining camps. Better stick to the land and make a home for yourself!

But Tom, with that singleness of purpose which had brought his parents to Missouri, left the emigrant train and struck off toward Denver. That city, in 1879, was one of false fronts and board sidewalks. Going from one building to another, Tom tripped down a flight of steps, then up another—a style of urban architecture copied from Chicago and Kansas City. Tom looked up at signboards. The places of business bore eastern names, "The New York Store," "Delmonico's Restaurant," "The Tivoli."

All the talk was of mines; all roads led to Leadville. Gold had been found in California Gulch near Leadville in 1860, but had proved too expensive to mine successfully. Now, after nineteen years, the lead carbonates that had been ignored were opened and men in red undershirts became millionaires. Here was silver and lead more golden than the gold in California Gulch.

On the streets of Denver, in its saloons, on its tiny bouncing trolley cars, Tom heard nothing but "mines—mines—mines" and the fabulous wages paid for workmen, so he took the railway back through the mountains to Red Hill. Here a Concord stage waited to carry the passengers the rest of the way to Leadville.

Tom took a seat on the "front boot" where he could see things, with a driver named Fay Gorham. The passengers' baggage was piled on the roof. Suddenly the front of the stage tipped up into the air high over the horses' backs. Tom and Fay looked at each other incredulously. Then each turned and looked under the side curtains of the stage. The cause of the upheaval sat on the back seat, a veritable giant chrysanthemum of frills and ribbons. Her face was tinted and powdered like a ripe peach, framed in a Lily Langtry coiffure and a green plush bonnet trimmed with a sprig of white flowers and two stuffed birds. An extremely affable woman, she assumed feminine helplessness, obviously insincere, and the coach rocked as she puffed and fidgeted with her voluminous petticoats. Finally she extracted something from the pocket in the back of her skirt. The driver wrinkled his forehead and said to the boy beside him, "We take lots of *them* to Leadville, nowadays. Did ye notice her hide that bottle in her muff?"

The agent signaled for the stage to start. Fay cracked his long whip, the passengers' heads snapped back as the stage started and the ascent of the Rockies began. After a time the stage rolled out upon a plain as flat as Kansas, the great basin of South Park, over nine thousand feet high—the Puma Hills behind and Pike's Peak in the southern sky, the bare green slope of the Continental Divide ahead. The breeze smelled of snow.

Fay Gorham told Tom that this country had been settled before the Horns moved to Missouri, that mines had been worked here since 1840, cattle grazed here since 1866, long before men dared turn them loose on the terrace of Kansas below. Tom learned that the West had been settled backward; first California, Oregon, Washington, then Utah by the Mormons, then Montana and Colorado by miners working their way east.

The stage bowled along merrily. Antelope colored like cinnamon and amber raced across the road. Fay said that buffalo still ranged in the aspen groves around South Park. Out on the flats men were baling the wire grass that grew wild. The stage passed ox-drawn loads of bales creeping toward the Continental Divide. At last the passengers reached Mosquito Pass—end of the prairie. The road ahead dipped into a belt of lodgepole pine, and disappeared. Fay pulled the horses to a stop, strapped himself to the seat, then gathered up his reins. With his foot on the brake, over they went. The wagon ruts were worn so deep that stumps almost bumped the axles, but the driver got the coach through. The climb was gradual at first. Soon the slopes became more precipitous, the angles more acute. At last the vehicle emerged into the alpine meadows above timber line. Some of the passengers got out to walk. Fay spat thoughtfully, then whispered to the boy beside him, "If Barnum's bay-bee back there would walk, *all* the gentlemen could ride."

Overhead eagles screamed. On the rockslides under snowbanks the leaves of the bluebells appeared greener than anything in Missouri— pure emerald against the pure white and purer blue. Conies whistled from crannies in the rocks. The driver said that bighorn sheep had been scared up on the last trip. Such rare sights always came on the last trip. Above timber line prospect holes pocked the green slopes. Human woodpeckers with beards and picks had left their hopes in holes.

The driver pointed his whip at a few deserted cabins below them under a giant red-boled spruce. "I recollect onct they was buryin' a man right thar. One of the pallbearers he seen something bright in the dirt that was piled beside the grave. He tiptoed to one side, picked up some splinters and limbs and begun stakin' out a claim right then. The preacher seed what he was doing but he didn't want to make no cartoon out of the burying, so, without changing his voice, he sez, sez he, 'Ashes to ashes, dust to dust, stake one in my name too, Lafe, f'r Jesus' sake, Amen.' "

At the crest of the pass Tom saw Leadville lying at the foot of Massive Mountain, one of a half-dozen bald headlands fluted with purple shadows. Below them canyons glowed with violet light. Beyond, distant mountainsides were mottled with groves of dainty green aspens. The spectacle burst on the travelers like triumphal music.

Fay Gorham rested his panting horses. Then he tightened his lines and the steaming horses pulled the stage over the hump. The coach started down to Leadville as a man goes down the roof of a barn in the rain, so steep and water-soaked were the rocks. On distant slopes Tom watched elk nibbling wild pea vines under the aspens. Far away grizzly bears rolled rocks to get the grubs underneath. In steep ravines water cried, sweet and clear.

Somebody called, "Stop a minute, driver! The Covered Wagon in here wants to get out. She's got the stummick-ache."

Late at night the stage rolled into Leadville where many lighted doors opened out of the darkness.

Smoke-heavy saloons—"Come, kid, have a drink"—whisky glowing in a tumbler in a boy's fingers—"No chaser? Right enough! Never put water on the fire"—another drink glowing like topaz in the light—"Bread's the staff of life, but drink's life itself"—girls, pert as wrens, pulling men's beards and sitting on their laps—the prettiest girls imaginable—girls in black silk dresses, red slippers with black pompons—girls with the first silk stockings a Missouri boy had ever seen—civilization at last—civilization on a mountaintop. Tom's attitude toward women was beginning to change.

Tom Horn walked across the ecclesiastical porch of the Little Church Saloon. He entered another whose sign read, "SMILE TWICE FOR TWO BITS." Tom saw Charlie Harrington, who was said to have killed twelve men and boasted in consequence that he had a jury in hell. Tom learned that in the mountains, as well as on the plains, prominent men shot first and argued afterward, or laughed casually about shooting. There seemed to be no difference between murder and other practical jokes, and Tom always loved practical jokes. Here was Bat Masterson of Dodge City still following the profession of pistols. How proud Tom would have been had the great man recognized him!

Young Tom heard about the Wall Streeter who had come out of his hotel one day to walk down Leadville's board sidewalks in a Prince Albert, waving a cane. A miner stepped behind him, another joined and soon it seemed that all Leadville was snake-dancing behind the Prince Albert. Any man in tailored clothes was followed by mining-stock salesmen in 1879, as closely as American tourists were followed in Naples by beggars. Not all this stock was bogus. Old-timers remembered a Jewish merchant named Guggenheim trading trinkets and notions for mining stock—odd trick of memory. Meyer Guggenheim, the immigrant, had peddled shoestrings in Philadelphia but when he came to Leadville to make his first investment in mines he was already a well-to-do merchant.

Other men had really spectacular careers in the silver city. One storekeeper, H. A. W. Tabor, grubstaked two prospectors who struck it rich. He received a half-interest in the new mine, invested his new wealth stupidly in another mine which sharpers sold him for fraud, sank a shaft ten feet below the "salted" dirt and struck a mine richer than the first. The millions rolled in and the merchant who had lived all his life in a log cabin now developed a mania for opera houses—planned building them from San Francisco to New York— planned building another city on Lake Michigan to rival Chicago. But the panic of 1893 took his fortune and he died penniless.

Leadville played for big stakes. Drummers found that feminine finery of a quality demanded nowhere west of Chicago sold readily there. So eager was the population for wealth and pleasure that nobody paid any attention to a famous man named Jesse James who was busy hunting for a claim. Leadville was lawless but not without the law. When Tom Horn was there the city had a larger percentage of lawyers, in proportion to its population, than any city in the world. New buildings were going up everywhere.

And the indulgences of the stomach rivaled all other pleasures in the city, for with the miners ready to pay the price, restaurants imported costly dainties from far away. Many kinds of game and fish from the adjacent hills and streams appeared on the tables. English visitors found in the roughest of America's mining camps ptarmigan as elegant as they had ever tasted in Balmoral or Knole. Long pack trains entered Leadville with little harness bells advertising elk meat and venison butchered in the mountains.

In its heyday Leadville claimed to be the richest city in Christendom. Tom Horn heard that four railroads were racing up the mountains, each striving to be first to tap the silver city. Tom was offered a job with a construction crew—"double pay if you'll pack a gun." What did this mean? The agent explained to Tom that only three canyons were available as rights of way for the four railroads coming to Leadville. Two of them, the Denver & Rio Grande and the Atchison, Topeka & Santa Fe, had picked the valley of the Arkansas which narrowed into the Royal Gorge—a chasm through which only one track could pass and that track must be suspended above the torrent from crossbeams mortised into the canyon walls. Each railroad was hiring section hands with guns to keep the others from laying track into the gorge. Did Tom want to make some easy money? Railroad ties were being built into blockhouses.

Tom "enlisted." He found many Missouri boys in the railroad's "army." Some of them were outlaws who had come west for their health. Tom learned that the railroad was giving passes to Quantrill men in Missouri who would come to Colorado and fight for the right of way. Tom quit. Just why is not known. Protecting the railroads and other big interests was exactly the kind of work he sought in later years. Perhaps he hated the lawless Quantrill night riders who had haunted his youth.

However that may be, Tom was soon back in Leadville, and the silver city influenced the rest of his life. It was here that he learned to know galena and the miners' lingo, how to "drill a tunnel," "sink a shaft" and "shore a stope"—knowledge that would lead him by accident to his greatest work. Five years later, when Tom had wandered over half the Rocky Mountains and had struck it rich, he warned his companions not to repeat the blunders of a miner he had known at Leadville. This man had drilled a tunnel so far that he had unconsciously circled and had come out on the same mountain-side into which he had started. He bragged that he had gone "clean through" the mountain and asked a passer-by what city that was in the valley. He could not believe that it was Leadville, his home.

At the mines Tom distinguished himself neither for his industry nor his lack of it. He was merely one of thousands who came, worked, played the allotted time and passed on. He never got to see the rich men for whom he was toiling. He craved the notice of such potentates—recognition, opportunity. He heard talk of a twenty-seven-hundred-pound nugget of silver that had been found in Arizona. Soldiers were being sent to the hot deserts of this strange country; troops were entraining now to protect miners and prospectors from hostile Indians exactly as the cavalry had tried to do in the Black Hills when Tom was too small to join.

Tom was not too young now!

A SLEEPING DICTIONARY

To REACH Arizona, the land of the great silver nugget, Tom Horn turned back to the Santa Fe Trail which, stretching from Kansas City westward, turned south in Colorado to end at Santa Fe in New Mexico. In the year that Tom set forth from Leadville, gangs of railroad workmen, spinning a silver thread from the Missouri River along the trail, had reached Las Vegas, yet for the sake of economy Tom traveled with the covered wagons that still plodded along the ancient highway. It was always easy for a boy to work his way with emigrants by tending horses and helping with the cooking.

Tom felt at home on the trail, and, like it, he was going from pioneer Missouri to the decadent civilization of Old Spain. From a seat on a covered wagon Tom looked across a sea of grama grass dotted with cactus branched like elks' horns. Cedars trimmed the edges of rocky cracks in the desert.

The covered wagons rumbled through Trinidad, the last town in the trail's course through the three-year-old state of Colorado—a medley of mud huts and hotels, banks and saloons made of tin, brick and boards. Then passing into New Mexico, the wagons climbed over Raton Pass into the glorious decay of Spain. Here backwoodsmen like Tom caught their first sight of silver bridle bits, gay Chimayo blankets, pottery whose curves somehow pleased the eye. Tom saw white adobe houses with Madonna-blue window casements and cool interiors, immaculate as no cabin in Missouri.

South of Las Vegas in Lincoln County a range war was in progress, a conflict far more serious than the steady strife between cattlemen and "nesters" in Kansas. Two cattle barons were fighting for control of unappropriated public lands. One of them was John Chisum, who had *not* named the Chisholm Trail. In this war, which took twenty-eight lives, moved a boy Tom's age, William Bonney, a New York lad better known as Billy the Kid. But Tom at this stage of his career was not interested in range or railroad wars. He pushed on to Santa Fe.

Miles before the emigrants reached the ancient city they passed clusters of adobe houses, mud churches, arched adobe corral gates so high a covered wagon could drive under them. Pigs and dogs and burros slept in the drowsy shade of quaint buildings, but the main road ahead pulsed with life, for it was down that road that the twenty-seven-hundred-pound nugget of silver had been found, and started a "gold rush."

Riders in embroidered steeple hats passed on Spanish ponies whose feet twinkled spiritedly in the yellow dust. Long whips popped like pistol shots as mule and ox-drawn freight outfits hurried into town. Santa Fe was the end of the long journey. Tom pictured the cool cantinas and the dance halls. He felt gay. Little groups of women in bright shawls sat under wax-leaved pomegranate trees, smoking cigarettes and watching the emigrants as their mothers and grandmothers had done. Tom waved to some girls. They pretended not to see him. A dark man under an embroidered steeple hat, with a poll-parrot serape around his shoulders, lolled against an adobe wall. On his bare feet he wore spurs bigger than Tom had ever seen before. He gave Tom a dark look and one hand moved under his red and green serape. The emigrant driver turned to Tom with, "You want to look out for that rooster." Tom intended to look out for no man. Nineteen years old and six feet tall, Tom saw fun ahead. "Pour the bud into them slowpoke hosses!"

The emigrants camped between their wagons and an adobe wall. Tom wandered off through the crooked streets where dark men in straw hats big as washtubs vended firewood from the backs of burros. Tom eyed the donkeys. He would need animals like them to prospect for silver. He was tired of the emigrants, bored with their mannerisms, and resolved to get a job.

He strolled to the Plaza. A crowd of white and brown men were watching something. The overland stage was letting out passengers. They were dusty from their long trip and talked about "road agents."

Tom's nose took him to the stage barn. He knew horses as well as he knew liverymen. Tom got a job driving stage—a dangerous occupation. Sometimes a stage was held up twice in one trip. Two distinct gangs were fighting for the exclusive right to rob the stages. "Holdups" held up "holdups." Matters were so serious that a strong Vigilance Committee had been organized, made up of one hundred substantial citizens, who saw that the law did not get lost in ramifications of errors and appeals. Here was a new phase of frontier justice. Men with influence said who should die, and at the next "necktie party" they died. Tom Horn never forgot the success of these private executions in New Mexico. The courts took no steps to hang the hangers, who were, of course, the prominent, substantial men of the country. The courts not only took no steps to punish the lynchers, but worked in conjunction with them. One day two highwaymen were arrested. Their preliminary hearing was held in the Palace of Governors. Tom was told that the shackled men sat on the floor in one corner of a room and spat tobacco juice into the fireplace while the Territorial Commissioner sat at a table in the same room, took testimony as among friends, and instead of ordering the culprits to be tried at the next session of the territorial court delivered them in the Plaza to the hundred substantial citizens with their ropes. Such an American Reign of Terror was needed to bring order out of chaos. The big, substantial citizens of New Mexico in the eighties had unlimited power, and Tom's first job was serving them. But serving the rich did not hold him now as it did in later years. He wanted to go to Arizona where he might find his silver mine and become rich himself.

His chance was close at hand. Still serving these powerful transportation men, Tom helped take a drove of mules to an isolated stage station in the heart of the Indian country in Arizona. The soldiers who had been shipped south when Tom left Leadville were stationed here, protecting the prospectors from the Indians. Tom did not have enough money to buy an outfit and go prospecting. His next job, near Prescott, was night-herding oxen for the man who had a contract to furnish wood to the government post. A boy who had night-herded longhorns on the Chisholm Trail had no trouble night-herding work cattle in Arizona. When this job was finished Tom found congenial employment around the old tumble-down stockade a mile out of town, known as Fort Whipple. He was hired first to day-herd a shipment of cavalry horses. Thus the tall boy became known to the Army contractors who supplied the Army posts. Soon the cavalry remounts were distributed among the troops and Tom found work with Tully, Ochoa & DeLong, delivering beef at the Indian agency.

The Indians Tom saw in the Southwest were not like those he had seen in Kansas. Some of them down here lived in adobe villages like Mexicans. Tom never could be sure whether he was in a Mexican village or an Indian village until he learned to look for the kiva—a round underground council room, used by the red men. Tom found that the Navahos and Apaches lived in brush domes called "wicki-ups" and he noticed that Mexican sheepherders also built wickiups when they camped in the hills. Some of the Mexicans and Indians dressed alike except on feast days when their garbs were widely different. The Indians Tom had seen in Kansas roached their hair like a horse's mane. They wore gaudy feathers. Few of the Arizona Indians wore feathers. Most of them wore hats. Some of the poorer ones, and these included the Apaches, wore around their heads bands full of aspen leaves to keep their foreheads cool. Sometimes the top of the head was covered and sometimes it was bare. The Indians were the poorest people Tom had ever seen. They dressed in ragged coats, no trousers, and they ate anything they could find in the hills.

Tom noticed other young fellows like himself loafing around the Army posts. He saw older men, too, who had been in the country for years, knew the mountains and deserts as well as the Indians. Such fellows hired themselves as scouts and guides to the soldiers. Tom looked at the scouts with awe. He heard people mention Al

Sieber as the greatest of them all. One day Tom met Al outside the unbarked log wall of Fort Whipple. Both were unemployed. Sieber said that there was work down at the San Carlos Indian agency only a hundred miles away. Tom and Al rode off together across the Tonto Basin. For days they jogged side by side and camped out at night. The grass was good and Tom learned that it was cheaper to keep moving in Arizona than stay in town.

Tom considered Al Sieber an old man. Thirty-six was ancient to a nineteen-year-old, but in spite of the difference a strange friendship grew up between them. Both spoke German. Sieber had outgrown the theatrical love of long hair and beads so typical of professional scouts, yet at heart he was as much Indian as white man. Tom admired Al's massive torso. His own body was slim, Grecian, athletic. Al Sieber's knotty muscles had twisted all beauty from his frame. The beauty of strength had been made grotesque by an excess of strength. His gnarled muscles were warped and strictured with twenty-eight wounds, and during his acquaintance with Tom he received his twenty-ninth, and lost a leg. He was like the archetype of the barbarian gladiator, a savage from the caves of Europe among savages from the caves of the Mogollons. He could ride three days without eating, cut an enemy's throat in a personal altercation, and dally a week under a mudbank, sleeping, trading and singing. It took a rockslide to kill him, more than a generation later, while he bossed Indian laborers on a road near the Roosevelt Dam.

Sieber had gained renown by knowing mountains, horses, Mexicans and Indians from the "dust up." He and Horn prowled among the wickiups, jacals and pueblos of the brown natives. An invitation to a meal now and then cut down their cost of living. Al explained too that a fellow sometimes learned things in the wickiups that helped him get a job scouting with the soldiers. Tom wanted to be a great scout like Al. Sieber taught him the mysteries of the profession: how to distinguish different tribes by their dress and by their tracks in the dust. He pointed out the peculiar imprint of a Mexican sandal. He explained that a Pueblo Indian wore moccasins with tops like funnels. Apaches wore moccasins with tops like boots and toes that turned up with bobtails in front. A Pueblo woman made tracks wide apart; an Apache woman put down her feet close together. A Hopi runner wore no moccasins at all and he could outrun a horse in fifty miles.

One day Tom and Sieber camped at the junction of the Black and White Rivers. A company of cavalry trotted down to the stream to water the horses. Tom saw the funniest little man he had ever seen in his life, riding beside the commanding officer. The little gnome was evidently guide and scout for the soldiers. To friends in Colorado, twenty years later, Tom described Mickey Free as a little redheaded Apache with one eye, sired by an Irishman and out of a Mexican mother. Both parents had been massacred by the Indians who reared Mickey in their tribe. He could speak no word of English, but he enjoyed scouting for the white troopers—a soldier of fortune, happiest when he led a squad of blue-clad cavalry into a desperate charge through which he would fight like a devil, then escape before everybody was slaughtered. Mickey prayed to red ghost-gods but his character was Irish from his moccasins to his huge upper lip. Tom remembered him as standing only five feet five inches tall, and owning a face wrinkled like a monkey's. He seemed to be a cross between a jockey and a weasel. He was near Tom's age. Later Tom liked to tell how he and Mickey rode, hunted and played together. "He called me 'Talking Boy' because I could speak four languages," Tom used to say, remembering him.

Tom determined to lead a carefree life like Sieber and Mickey. Why not use his skill at trailing and his gift for languages and become a scout and interpreter himself? Sieber suggested that the best way to become proficient in Apache was to "go back to the blanket" and get "a sleeping dictionary." He showed Tom an opportunity to buy a half-interest in a squaw, three Indian children, four horses and five dogs, none of whom understood anything but Apache. Tom hesitated. He had never cared much for white girls. Finally he gave in and resigned himself to a slothful winter in the little group of huts, surrounded by withered corn and melon patches, called "Pedro's village." Pedro was an old Apache who had once traveled to Washington to shake hands with the President. He was now decrepit and peaceful. The wonders he told about Washington caused his people to believe him a liar. He could not hear without the aid of an ear trumpet, so he was deaf to the wild minor key of the war songs and the exotic recurrences of Apache religious music. When these blood songs wailed in the night, every other clan on the reservation might feel the pulsing urge to leave the melon patches and go raiding, fighting and burning across the waste world. Pedro and his clan remained.

Until corn-planting time Tom lived with his red partners. The saltless food did queer things to his insides. The peculiarly sweet Indian smell in the wickiup permeated Tom's own clothes and blankets. At first he liked it. Then the sweetness cloyed on him. Soon he ceased to notice it. Tom watched children five years old prattling fluently the language he wracked his memory to master. He could have learned much from playing with them, but his age and dignity prohibited such familiarity. He scuffled occasionally with householders his own age but the accepted occupation for red men in his status was to ride horseback, wear finely embroidered clothes, visit, sing religious songs and gamble by the hour.

Tom noticed that the Indians were gentle with their children and he wondered about the stories of cruelty to their enemies. He saw that they were talkative, giggling and laughing and constantly railing at one another in good humor. He noticed that the Apaches valued horses for food as much as they valued them for riding. When they really wanted to get somewhere quickly, they abandoned their horses and took to the rocks on foot.

Riding, singing, sleeping with the Indians, Tom learned that they were unhappy. A generation ago they had been conquered by the whites and put on reservations. Issues of food had been promised them. Fellow tribesmen had been appointed to act as policemen, keep order and see that no Indian left the reservation without a pass. Many of the Indian boys of Tom's age fretted in their imprisonment. Restless as caged yearling bears, they wanted to see over the hills that walled their reservation. These young savages became more curious when their tribal music thrilled them to religious ecstasy.

Constantly little groups of adventurers stole away to hunt, explore and perhaps kill some prospector who, gone crazy for the silver Tom had come to find, traveled secretively alone.

Old Indians sympathized with the eager young men. They complained that the Indian agents issued food unfit to eat, squandered the Indians' money on corrupt contracts to enrich themselves. The Indian had no recourse. He could not even talk the conqueror's language. Let the young men get satisfaction on the warpath if they could.

In the spring of 1881 Tom left Pedro's village and moved into the agency. He knew how precariously the white men ruled. In case of trouble his knowledge of the language might give him a great opportunity. In the sutler's shop Tom heard civilians curse Army administration of the Indians—no chance to make a dollar selling supplies. In the next breath the civilians wished the Army would come in force and protect them from a possible uprising. General George Crook had been in command until 1875. Then he had gone north to fight the Sioux. The Apaches had been getting worse every year since his departure.

Spring turned quickly into a scorching Arizona summer. Clerks worked in the agency buildings with all the windows open. Hot air and hot sand burned their faces in the shade. Tom loafed in the cool of the adobe stables. Indians, dressed heavily to keep out the heat, jogged into the post. Their moccasined feet stepped silently across the agency porch. They told the White Father that a prophet, Na-kay-do-klunni, was gathering converts on Cibicu Creek. He preached that all dead Indians would come to life. The old days would return. White men would not have to be respected. Many Indians, so the messengers said, had left their reservations. On Cibicu Creek Prophet 'Do-klunni was teaching them his new songs and magic dances.

The bad news spread through the agency buildings like the hot wind. Word was sent to the distant military post: "Kill the uprising while it is a pup." Two companies of soldiers assembled. Indian scouts were mustered. Tom remembered years later that he, Mickey Free and Al Sieber went along as guides and interpreters. The three civilians soon learned that the Indian scouts were in league with the renegades. The party was being led into an ambush. The guides went to Captain Edmund Hentig, the white commander. He would not listen to their arguments. White guides were proverbially suspected of not wishing to catch troublemakers. Did they not make their living in Indian warfare?

The cavalcade came to the enemy's country. They camped on Cañon Creek, prepared to march against the prophet and arrest him in the morning. Late that night a small Mexican girl crept to Tom's blankets and roused him with fingers dainty as fern tips. She whispered in his ear that an ambush was set for the morrow. A war party was waiting for them on Cibicu Creek. Then the child vanished.

This tale of the dark-skinned girl saving the life of the apple-cheeked youth of twenty-one who was destined to become the Tiger of the North is a strangely distorted Pocahontas legend. Tom's account of his experience the following day does not correspond with the military records, but as the catastrophe in no way redounded to the glory of the Army there may be some truth in the scout's version. Tom said that he relayed the girl's message to Captain Hentig. The officer sneered. Let the scouts take their fears back to safety! The expedition would go forward! And on it went, with Tom and Mickey Free riding behind the treacherous pair of Indian scouts, muttering promises to kill them at the first sign of a sellout. Furiously the captain ordered Tom and Mickey to ride at the column's rear.

Into the dread canyon of Cibicu Creek went the party, the Indian guides insisting that the bottom of the canyon be followed. Sieber countered by demanding that the soldiers traverse the side of the canyon, edging always toward higher ground. When the Indian guides chattered and pointed to the base of the big ravine, Sieber kept saying "Yes" to them and misinterpreting to the captain. From the rear Tom and Mickey noticed what Sieber was doing, and wondered if his angle of diversion would be sharp enough to miss the ambush somewhere ahead.

Mickey noticed a magpie come sailing across the canyon on black and white wings, light on a pine stub, cock first one eye then the other at something behind a piñon log and scold raucously. Tom noticed that everything was too quiet—there were no sparrows chirping in the trees, no mountain rats sitting on the brush piles under the rocks.

Crash came the expected volley! Horses plunged, falling as though they had slipped on the ice. Some sat up like dogs. Soldiers dived through the air, reached for an invisible trapeze, crawled in the dirt, swearing, calling for help.

No enemy could be seen. Captain Hentig had disappeared. Tom heard Sieber yell like an old sea captain in a hurricane, "Get up the hill! Get up the hill! If they get the top we're gone fawn skins."

Tom and Mickey panted up the hill, abandoning their horses as Apaches did in time of emergency. Brush gashed them like bull whips. On the summit they dropped on their bellies and poured a hasty fire into the red men who were swarming up the other slope. Surprised, the Indians turned and skimmed away over the rocks like the shadows of flying birds.

The valley became as silent as it had been before the attack. Now and then Tom heard Indians calling to one another as they slipped away through the piñons. A squad of puffing soldiers came to the hilltop. Down below, the rest of the troopers were helping the wounded. Captain Hentig was reported dead, a third of the soldiers disabled. The red scouts had fled.

Tom wiped the grime from the sweaty welts on his face and arms. The brush had been cruel to him. He looked down into the death-trap. Had the soldiers marched straight into it not a man would have escaped. Had he and Mickey failed to seize the hilltop not even Sieber's strategy would have saved the force.

The survivors reorganized the cavalcade. They buried Captain Hentig in the mountains he did not understand and picked their way through the dark toward Camp Apache. Next day they arrived. The telegraph was ticking. The "little brush" on Cibicu had become a signal for a general Indian war. The border was mobilizing. Let the war come. Talking Boy saw the chance of a lifetime for a man with his training.

5

GERONIMO

Tom waited expectantly at San Carlos. The Indian uprising did not materialize. The government offered him no permanent position. Tom pitched camp on the river a few miles from the agency. He could live cheaply there and be available when an interpreter was needed at the post. White men were not usually allowed on the reservation without a pass, but interpreters were an exception. Tom settled into the Indian life much as he had in Pedro's village. From conversations with his neighbors he learned that the Indians deemed themselves hopelessly outnumbered by the whites. 'Do-klunni had been killed in the Cibicu skirmish. No other prophet offered leadership. Adventurous Indians must hunt elsewhere for excitement. Tom heard them chat endlessly about a ghost line called the Mexican border, across which American soldiers dared not ride. The Indians had learned, too, that the Mexican soldiers halted at this invisible barrier. Tom listened to—and pretended not to hear—the Indians plan little war parties to leave the reservation, rob, kill, and then flee into Mexico ahead of a sheriff's posse or a squad of cavalry. In the neighboring land they would plunder haciendas, recruit horses and, when cornered by the Mexican Army, send for the United States government to come and protect its wards. On the American border sheriffs and prosecutors might be waiting to hail the red men before civil courts for murder but the renegades had the advantage. They could drive bargains with the American Army, say they would return if the troops promised them safe passage to their reservations upon which the civil authorities could not come.

Tom knew that the Army officers were quick to agree to the

Indians' terms, for it meant glory to themselves, riding back with the captives. Furthermore, the troopers could appropriate unto them-selves part of the plunder which the Indians had amassed in their raids. Nevertheless the Indians usually got home with enough booty to keep them satisfied for the remainder of the year; then they would repeat the whole performance.

Tom heard in the jargon of voices around him one name repeated over and over, "Goylothay"—a great medicine man who walked and talked with God. He had induced his clan, the Chiricahuas, to fol-low him into Mexico on several forays, as a protest against civil Indian agents. Some of these people stayed there. The Mexicans called this fighting preacher San Geronimo or Saint Jerome, on account of his ability to debate. Fifty-one years before, when he was born, his mother had named him "The Yawner"—some said "The Laugher." Either title was now highly ironic for, in adulthood, Geronimo was notorious for cruelty, quick actions and bold speech. General Nelson A. Miles, of the United States Army, once looked at Geronimo's six feet of brown magnificence, and jotted down in his memoirs, "He was one of the brightest, most resolute, determined looking men that I have ever encountered."

Tom learned from his red and white friends that a constant dribble of braves came to the reservation from across the Mexican border to woo new wives and to tell their cousins the glory of freedom. Dances were held for these wild brothers and the pulses of the music fired reservation boys to return with the renegades.

Once, in March 1882, as Tom lay at night on his blankets by the dead fire among his snoring companions, some indescribable change in the noises of the night told him that morning was close at hand. He got up, gathered his blanket around his neck and shoulders, Apache-fashion, and stepped out of the wickiup. Other men, equally silent and grave, were emerging from their hovels. The savages looked at the morning star, the paling sky. What was wrong?

A few young men started to hum an Indian chant. They tapped the earth with little feathered wands. Day dawned and a runner arrived, barefooted, naked-legged, wearing a twisted breechcloth, and tinkling amulets around his neck. He had come from the next village up the creek two miles away. The Indians crowded around him to hear his story: A party of Geronimo's warriors, said the runner, were visiting all the villages, bringing medicine from Goylothay. Warriors in Ju's village up the creek had danced all night. They were determined to break for freedom—join Geronimo in the Sierra Madres.

Tom and his red "brothers" trudged up the creek to see the untamed savages. Tom looked curiously at their hard, wild faces. He compared their strength to his own and felt satisfied.

The wild brothers remained at the wickiups quietly but their presence upset the nerves of the agency officials. White men twitched whenever a distant shot was heard. The roar of hoofs of a galloping horse set their nerves on edge. Tom was told to move into the agency. Instead he moved deeper among the Indian camps.

April came. One day an Indian policeman attempted to arrest a young Indian for a petty offense. A riot started. The constabulary, shooting wild, killed a squaw. Then the devil broke loose. Drums sounded, shouts and wails arose. Horsemen charged through the chaparral. Rifles were cocked and bows drawn to the arrowhead. In wickiups the Apaches started drinking. The alcoholic fumes floated through their brains. Tom heard the tribal death chant throb along the brushy creek bottom. He sat impassive but alert as the superstitious minds of the savages kindled to Geronimo's alluring tales of freedom in Mexico. Tom had never before seen Indians work themselves into war fury.

The song became more savage. Young men ran from wickiup to wickiup, old women brushed the hair out of their eyes and listened.

"Bad," said an old Indian squatting beside Horn. "Bad." The old man shrank into his blanket. The sun set. The shadow of evening crept up the mountainside. No sleep came during the night to the little village. At dawn the wind brought the sound of rifles—a distant volley. Tom looked inquiringly at his red friends. A few minutes later a runner burst from the brush. Ju had made his break for freedom! The chief of police, George Sterling, had ridden out and commanded him to halt. A bullet had knocked Sterling from his saddle. The runner emphasized his words with quick gestures in sign language. A squaw, he continued, had cut off Sterling's head, kicked it like a ball. Bullets and arrows shredded his headless body. Revenge for the death of a sister!

The runner said also that friendly clans, peaceable up to now, were joining the exodus. Loco's village near by was packing to move. Tom glanced stealthily at the listening circle of Indians. There would be trouble indeed now, for Loco had been tractable. He was middle-aged and had, over one eye, a cataract that made him squint like a man looking through a telescope. The deformity gave a sinister cast to his pacific appearance. Knowing that if Loco was angry the disaffection must be serious, Tom and a few friends—fifteen men in all, with dogs, women and children—fled to the broad valley of the Gila, where a natural fortification awaited behind some iron spires. In this refuge they felt safe. Soon after sunup Loco's band, strung out for a mile, came in sight. Twenty warriors rode ahead. Ju's band was somewhere behind. From the spires Tom saw seven little figures—Indian police—riding along beyond the column, watching the procession from a distance. Directly one of these seven dashed toward the column. Tom saw a little blossom of white smoke puff from the rider's gun. Instantly the horseman swerved away. Revenge for Sterling! The Indian policeman was galloping toward his companions before the sound of the report reached Tom's ears.

The tragedy did not divert the column. A few men stopped, tossed their fallen comrade across a horse's back, then continued with the multitude. The Indians streamed past the spires, driving horses and mules ahead of them, shouting in the dust. The last of them disappeared. Tom whipped his horse to the San Carlos agency. Everything was in confusion. Excited agency clerks were handing out rifles and ammunition to every Indian who promised to be friendly and fight the renegades. Tom turned away disgusted. Where was Sieber? Tom spurred his horse to Camp Thomas, the nearest mili-

Al Sieber, born in Germany in 1844, served as a sharpshooter in the Army of the Potomac during the Civil War, was wounded at Gettysburg and went west in 1866. Al Sieber was a veteran chief of scouts when Tom knew him in 1880.

Mickey Free, captured by the Apaches when a baby. His red hair always flamed where the fighting was hottest.

tary post, thirty-two miles away. Sieber and forty troopers returned with him to the scene of action. Loco, Ju and Geronimo, with many fanatic followers, had left the reservation.

Troops of cavalry, summoned by telegraph, came from several posts. Converging on the renegades, they deployed and charged in regulation waves, lost a few soldiers and accomplished nothing. It was like trying to stop a flood with handfuls of mud. Tom galloped proudly beside Sieber, attempting to form contact between the several squads. Mickey Free joined them for the chase.

The red horde crossed the newly constructed Southern Pacific railroad tracks. Tourists saw, in the frame of Pullman windows, a picture of Indians waving cheerily at the "iron horse," then looking menacingly over their shoulders at the horizon whence soldiers were coming.

To the scouts the pursuit was hopeless. The soldiers, eternally waiting for their supplies and bedding to arrive, were slower than the Indians in spite of all the driven horses, women and children that encumbered the red men's flight. Splitting into small bands, the Apaches stole fresh horses as they progressed, abandoned their worn-out steeds to the soldiers, and kept well in advance.

Days passed bootlessly. The fugitives flitted like desert "dust devils" across Arizona into southern New Mexico Territory. One afternoon Tom, Sieber and Mickey sat on a hill watching the Indians pass into Mexico, safe from pursuit. The war was over. The Indians had escaped!

The three men turned their horses toward Cloverdale with regret. Below them they saw a troop of forty cavalrymen clattering toward the border. The captain spied the scouts and called a halt. Captain Tullius Cicero Tupper asked where he could find the Indians. He was not interested in the location of the international boundary. Tom watched him curiously. The higher a man ranked, the less he seemed bound by laws. The rich men of New Mexico were not bound by the law of the territory. Here was a man not bound by the law of nations.

Captain Tupper had trained his men to do certain things if ever they got under fire. Now was a good chance to see how well they had learned their lessons. Besides, he wanted an Indian pony for his little daughter back at the Army post. Tupper lent Sieber his telescope. The scout picked out the Apaches squatting like locusts on the cow-hipped headland above the Mexican desert. Sieber said that the Indians felt safe. They would have a big dance and sing their songs. The captain listened to him. Tupper had fought in the Civil War and he liked the soldier's trade. As the sun went down he sat talking and thinking. Then when it was pitch-dark he ordered the bugle to blow "Boots and Saddles." Tom was the happiest boy in the Southwest. They were going into Mexico, to hell with the boundary line!

THIS LAWLESSNESS MUST STOP!

THE summer night was pleasant; horses' hoofs whispered in the sand. The men whispered, too, for orders had been given to strike no matches, make no unnecessary noise. The only hope of victory lay in a surprise, since the attackers would be outnumbered five to one. Stealing forward to spy the village that had risen so quickly, Tom realized that he would get revenge for Cibicu Creek. Behind him the soldiers came across the sandy ground in squads. Gnarled bushes furnished excellent cover as the morning stars paled in the sky. Now and then Tom heard the quick click of a rifle as a nervous soldier looked at it to be sure it was loaded. They neared the hostile camp.

A volley crashed in the dawn and Tom saw a trooper on a white horse rush toward the Indian camp. A soldier beside him fired—a red flash in the dying night. Tom and the sergeant of the platoon he was guiding spurred ahead. There was the *whack* of a soft lead bullet against flesh. The sergeant's saddle was empty. Tom jerked his horse to a stop, dismounted and ran back. The grizzled soldier was trying to stand up. A red spot widened on the side of his shirt. Tom lifted the wounded man on his horse and started to lead him away, but the horse jerked its head and refused. Bullets flipped the sand all around them. The horse had a broken leg. Tom shouldered the sergeant and staggered to the rear until he collapsed behind a hummock, then, when his wind returned, raced back to the spot where both men had dropped their rifles. Getting the Springfields, he rejoined the sergeant who was recovering—and swearing.

The fight was over and Tupper counted five Indians and only one blue-uniformed trooper dead. Tom, in telling about the fight, said

Tupper was in high spirits, with two hundred and sixty ponies for his little girl.

The white men fell back from the rocks into which the Indians had disappeared before broad daylight would tell the Indians that they were a mere handful. The soldiers slept through the heat of the day and awoke at sundown to see another and larger detachment of cavalry riding up. In after years Tom Horn remembered that the officer at the head of the column was one of the idols of his boyhood, Colonel George A. Forsyth, an aide to General Sheridan during the bison chase on the plains with Grand Duke Alexis. Colonel Forsyth had no more respect for the international boundary than had Tupper. The Indians had only a twelve-hour start. The colonel and the captain talked the matter over. There were enough soldiers now to do something. It was a wild country and nobody would ever know. So the column pressed on through the night. At dawn the soldiers "shaded up" under ·bushes. The scouts pushed ahead and heard a bombardment. At the news, Forsyth urged his tired troopers on again and two hours later came upon Mexican soldiers dragging into a pile dead Indians, women and children, more than a hundred of them. The Mexican regulars had seen the dust from the fleeing Indians and, ambushing them, had waited until the warriors passed, then shooting into the flank of the irregular column, had slaughtered the women and children. The swarthy Mexican colonel bowed and informed the white officers that they were his prisoners; would they breakfast with him? They might retain their side. arms! When the scanty meal was over, Forsyth asked the Mexican if he would not breakfast with *him*. Forsyth and Tupper knew that they were bad boys caught red-handed but they had had a glorious chase— and were not finished yet. Forsyth had noticed that the Mexicans were out of ammunition as well as food, so, while his guest picked his teeth, Forsyth gave orders in English, unintelligible to the Mexican, for his men to pack their things and be ready to move. Then he bowed to his guest and led his men north—while the Spanish American looked helplessly at his prisoners' escape.

Tom smiled sardonically. Brute force ruled the world. The man with the gun dictated the terms.

Tom and Sieber were ordered back to the San Carlos reservation. They took up their old life with the Indians and looked forward to employment in the next "war." Trouble came in July 1882. Massacres were reported in Green Valley. Tom heard that scouts were enlisted from Pedro's village—Tom's old "brothers." He hurried north and got a job leading them. Chief of scouts at last, at twenty-two, Tom looked with pride on his ragged troop. A veteran of two brief campaigns, he felt himself a match for any Indians.

Up Green Valley Tom led his ragamuffins on the trail of the renegades, past dead settlers and burned cabins. From his saddle he looked down on mutilated torsos—hearts hacked out with knives. He saw raw and bleeding heads whose scalps had been ripped off, then thrown back in their faces. Scalping was an atrocity the Apaches had learned from the Plains Indians, but as yet the Apaches were not sure what to do with a scalp once they had removed it.

Tom met a column of cavalry. His patron saint, Al Sieber, rode at the head beside a grim, rugged-faced officer. Captain Adna Romanza Chaffee was reputed to be the best swearer in the Army. Tom's cup of happiness brimmed with glory in the company of the two great men.

The trail led up the Mogollon escarpment. Under tall longleaf pines the Indian "sign" became fresh. At noon a shot from the trees ahead brought the troops to a standstill. Dismounting, they deployed and charged, answering the Apache's fire. Red bark sprayed like sparks. A limb fell. The grass waved with bullets. "There they go!"

One dead Indian lay in the grass. Irish troopers looked at him, grinned and ran back to their horses. Pursuit again! Within a mile they came upon a wounded Indian crawling desperately for the rocks. Tom's scouts pounced on him like cats and when Tom pawed them away, the man was dead. Lifting the limp head, Tom saw it was one of the guides who had led Hentig to his death.

His scouts were mewing like wild animals. The galloping soldiers

rocked through the tall pines, Tom in the lead, certain that the renegades were bound for a canyon ahead. If the pursuers could reach
the brink in time they might shoot the Indians in the canyon as farm
boys shoot pigs in a pen.

Chevelon Canyon cut the grass-floored forest like a saw, and the
astonished soldiers were on the edge before they knew it. Yonder,
on the opposite wall, the renegades were climbing out, scrambling
up rockslides. The red scouts and white troopers lay down along the
canyon rim. To the obbligato of Chaffee's God-damning they began
to fire. The Indians, small figures against the painted rocks, scattered like insects, some on foot, some on horseback.

Tom, from the corner of his eye, saw the prone sharpshooters,
raised on their elbows, shoot their rifles, and yelp in triumph when
a little brown man hurtled down the distant slope. Crafty old Sieber
beckoned Tom and a crack-shot sergeant near by. He pointed out
a narrow trail near the top of the canyon, through which the fugitives
must pass to escape. The three men trained their rifle sights on this
pass. Toward the spot came horses, a lunging gray in the lead,
naked figures like monkeys on their backs. The gray horse suddenly
filled three sights and Tom, Sieber and the sergeant fired in a split
second. Down came the gray horse, somersaulting like a broken-
backed rabbit. The horses behind sprawled into a tangle of thrash-
ing legs. The pass was blocked. As fugitives came to the clogged
runway to tug at the dead gray horse, the white troopers crumpled
them with bullets.

The Indians abandoned their horses, quit the trail and scrambled
over the rocks. Each brave, as he escaped over the brim, patted his
rump at the distant troopers. Damn the Apaches; Tom liked the
little cusses.

All afternoon Tom heard the battle continue on the far side of the
canyon. Another detachment of soldiers had overtaken the Indians
there. The soldiers with Tom spent the time gathering the dead and
wounded in the canyon, then called it a day. They marched back
to the post and the scouts were paid off.

Tom and Sieber sank back into a life of savage slothfulness, sleep-

ing and eating for days on end. They braided ropes, made silver ornaments, hummed Indian chants, and slept again. Tom had found the
savage life for which he was born. Immediate happiness had broken
down the old urge to prospect for a silver mine.

Indian women brought food to Tom and Sieber. They apologized
because the season was too late for that tenderest of Apache delicacies,
unborn fawn. The women crushed mesquite beans in their stone
grinders, tempered the meal with grass seed which they had knocked
with sticks into their conical baskets. The closer Tom saw into the
lives of the Apaches, the clearer it became that the government
would have to spend years subjugating so savage and thrifty a people.
They could find food on the barest desert.

Apaches were as willing to eat jack rabbit and desert rat as they
were to eat horse, cow, burro or antelope. They would roast a rat
on a fire the size of a man's hand, lying on their sides to blow the
coals under the sizzling rodent.

An Indian fire was different from a white man's fire. The red-
skin reasoned from a different premise. His fire was so small that
he could circle it with his body and thus warm his vitals. A white
man built a fire so large that he could not get near enough to it to
warm himself. If a white man, meeting an Indian in the forest, asked
him if he were lost, the Indian would reply, "Me no lost. Wickiup
lost." Cowboys mounted a horse from the left side, Indians from the
right. White men shod a tender-footed horse in front, saying that a
horse needed protection where most of his weight rested. Indians
replied that the pony could see where to put his front feet and that
his hind feet, which had to trust more to luck, needed shoes.

Tom was as interested in strange peoples' ways of living as he was
in their languages. He noticed that when all meat failed the Apache,
he could always find mesquite beans, wild cherries or nopal figs.
The high grassy swales afforded him wild potatoes. The century
plant was his staff of life. It took him three days to bake it properly
in a long pit. When it was done he had his favorite food. Distilled
century plant made his favorite drink—the aloe drug which quick-
ened his pulse for singing and dancing. The barley which General

Crook had encouraged the Apaches to raise was moonshined into beer called "tiswin."

Tom was becoming Indian-minded, like Al Sieber. At twenty-two, he believed himself, with reason, to be a great man among the savages. He looked patronizingly on common white soldiers. Red scouts seemed much superior to them. Apache warriors traveled for days without baggage or supplies. A young brave on his first four raids must carry a reed through which to suck his drinking water and a stick with which to scratch himself—traditional impedimenta—but nothing else except his clothes and weapons. For amusement a warrior might take a pack of monte cards or hidebound wands for the "stick game," but these were not necessities and they took little room. No rumbling wagon train, with tents and supplies, raised a column of dust to disclose the whereabouts of raiding Apaches.

Tom noticed too that the Army officers seemed to recognize his position of influence among the Indians. They smiled at him with distant friendliness. He heard that General Orlando B. Willcox, commander of the Department of Arizona, had cited him for gallantry in saving the wounded sergeant during Captain Tupper's battle for the Indian ponies. That summer of 1882 Tom earned the further gratitude of military men by his failure to remember anything definite about Tupper's expedition into Mexico. An international board of officers had arrived to inquire into the violation of Mexican sovereignty by the United States, and neither Tom nor Sieber could recall anything incriminating against their superiors.

After the inquiry Tom lolled around the Indian camps waiting for another job and thinking, cynically, how little difference there was between white, brown and red men, when they wanted to steal horses. On the frontier horses passed as currency and each color of man had his own peculiar way of obtaining them.

Years later Tom joked about the morning when he opened the flap of his wickiup to sniff the air and discovered his red brothers outside talking excitedly. Someone had stolen a bunch of horses. The trail was plain. Tom and a few of his red friends galloped off on a short cut to the nearest watering place. They arrived ahead of the thieves and hid in the brush. Soon the stolen horses appeared against the sky and clattered down to drink in the stream. The thieves, three Mexicans, followed, and sat grinning at one another while their mounts thrust hot noses deep into the mountain torrent.

Tom gave the word. The Indians fired. One Mexican fell dead and the remaining two slashed off through the brush, the Indians after them like hounds. Tom sat still, adding nothing but whoops to the fun. Shots and howls came from the thicket and soon a grinning Apache dragged in a dead Mexican by a rope fast to his saddle. Laughing Indians came out of the brush, lay on their stomachs to drink from the stream, and gloated over their triumph.

Suddenly they heard the ripple that could only come from the shod hoofs of cavalry horses marching down the government road. In a few minutes a troop escorting no less a dignitary than the inspector general of the district, accompanied by the commanding General Willcox and his young son Charles, came to the stream to eat their luncheon. General Willcox was surprised to see armed Indians grouped around a white boy and two dead Mexicans. Tom knew this was the general who had lately commended him for gallantry, and with a shamed face he rode to meet him.

Tom eyed the ground while the general spat out blistering words. Murder had been done! Murderers must go to the fort and wear irons. This goddam lawlessness must stop!

As the lecture continued Tom saw, from the tail of his eye, the Indians squatting among the bushes wondering what was being said. Then Tom stopped listening to the general. What was that noise in the brush—coming nearer? Willcox stopped his harangue to look. Tom peered over his shoulder. Two of the Indians were dragging a third dead Mexican up to the group. They tugged until the corpse was laid at Tom's feet like a dog dropping a quail at the feet of its master.

The general's face reddened under his white hair, and he began to bombard the sheepish boy with every expletive in a veteran soldier's vocabulary. Finally the great man rode away without remembering to put Tom under arrest. Tom, accompanied by his savages, stole back to the tribe. Again he had discovered that even the biggest of the rich men did not care if a man were killed so long as he deserved killing. The formality of the law could be preserved by reprimands; the lawbreakers could be excused if 'their crimes had the appearance of justice.

For months Tom lived amid all this primitive cruelty, hearing Indians tell how they had killed white men, hearing soldiers tell how they had slaughtered red men. When parties of renegades escaped from the reservation Tom and Sieber followed them and, if they failed to make a capture, returned to the wickiups where sooner or later the braves would quietly reappear and resume their idle life. It was convenient to make no report of a fugitive's return. Probably the Indian was one of Tom's special friends.

On the other hand, if an order was sent out to arrest one of these braves it was a scout's duty to deliver his onetime friend to the guardhouse. When imprisoned on sentence of death Apaches sometimes used buckskin for their deliverance. Jailers, knowing how often doomed Apaches sought suicide in their cells, removed from their captives all garments that might be converted into a noose. Leaving the red men naked save for their moccasins, the jailers felt satisfied that the prisoners could do themselves no harm. In the night, however, the Apaches tore their buckskin moccasins into strips, chewed the thongs until they were wet, then tied them tightly about their throats and sat waiting, waiting for the skin to tighten as it dried and thus bring blessed death.

Tom was developing into a man as calloused toward death as toward the international boundary laws. He and Sieber crossed the border line with cynical disdain, killed renegades for fun or for their women, and returned, certain that if they were caught their superiors would scold and wink, much as Tom's mother had done in Missouri. Once, indeed, a commission sitting on a particularly flagrant violation by the two scouts handed down a stern reprimand which was read to the guilty pair by an officer so ironic of nature as to add at its conclusion, "Now, let's go and get a drink."

7

MEN'S SCALPS AND BIRDS' EGGS

FOR more than two years Tom Horn hunted, wrestled, raced horses, and braided ropes around the frontier Army posts, his heart hardening with the passing of each day. Occasionally he remembered Leadville and his ambition to become rich. As he crossed and camped in the mountains he noticed the rocks and collected samples of minerals that looked like galena. He remembered where he found these specimens but he was having too good a time with his savage friends to give ore serious consideration. The government was paying him seventy-five dollars a month, the work was congenial and he was satisfied.

In the summer of 1882 Tom was told that General George Crook was coming back to Arizona to awe the Apaches into quietude with his reputation. Tom heard friends say that Crook was a man who could beat the Indians at their own game. He had spent his life fighting them—except four years when he fought rebels in the Civil War. An Ohio farm boy who never outgrew his desire to shoot rabbits in the wood lot, Crook had campaigned across California, Oregon, Washington, Idaho, Montana, the Dakotas and Wyoming, conquering the Bannocks, Paiutes, Nez Percés, Sioux and Cheyennes. Tom was curious. He talked with many men who remembered Crook when he was in the country seven years ago. These men said that Crook was invincible with the Indians because he employed the red men themselves. He invariably hired rival tribes to catch renegades and officered them with squaw men. Crook himself rode the range with his mongrel allies. Army paper work he left to aides and adjutants. His tastes were active, military and Spartan as any Apache's.

At a later date, General Charles King, who was associated with Crook for sixteen years, said that the only time he had ever seen the general dressed in the uniform of his rank was when he lay in his casket.

This doughty fighter arrived in Arizona and his first order was: "Stow away your sabers, your sashes, plumes and even your uniforms; you won't need them." Eastern recruits would not have much place in the coming campaign. Tom and Sieber knew that men with their training had come into their own. They knew also that a new "Hot Trail" Treaty between the United States and Mexico permitted soldiers from either country to follow red renegades across the border.

The Indians sensed this Hot Trail Treaty, too, and refrained from raiding. The promised campaign was postponed. Peace lay over the Apache reservation and Tom Horn and Al Sieber lost their jobs. Tom remembered the minerals he had found in the mountains. He and Sieber rode away to Tombstone, Arizona, to try their luck at mining and also their skill at barroom feats. Tombstone was a second Leadville. Tom Horn felt at home. He saw many familiar faces. Men trained to lawlessness, or its suppression, had come to Arizona to engage in the business that they understood. Here was Wyatt Earp still making his living with his dexterous pistol.

Tom staked a mine and was enjoying drunken revelry with Sieber in March 1883, when a dispatch came from Crook. War had come! Chato, one of Geronimo's renegades in Mexico, had crossed the border with a handful of young warriors. They were killing white men in the Whetstone and Dragoon Mountains. Crook had a chance to try his Hot Trail Treaty at last. He wanted Al Sieber to report at San Carlos at once. Tom determined to go with him. Surely there would be jobs for them both.

Tipsy friends in Tombstone would not let the scouts depart. "Just one more drink," they coaxed, and threatened to fight when Al and Tom tried to say good-by. Finally the two scouts whispered to the

town marshal to bring their horses to the rear of the Bird Cage
Theatre. Between the acts they stepped out "for a minute." In
their saddles they clattered from town, heads rolling on shoulders,
thick tongues licking at the cool air like steers at rock salt.

Tom could get no job with the scouts but Crook was organizing
five pack trains. The general loved his pack mules the way Napoleon
loved his artillery. Tom, tall and strong, was built for lifting a heavy
load upon a mule. He knew that he could make good and hired
himself in the train. The great Indian fighter was sure to notice him.

Crook determined to strike straight for Geronimo in Mexico—
crush the heart of the Indian trouble. He set off at once with a hundred white troopers, two hundred red trackers and his five pack
trains. He crossed the international border and climbed up on the
Sierra Madres highlands. Tom, seated on a mule behind the bobbing packs, watched Crook as the cavalcade wound through the high
grass and huge scarlet flowers under the tall Mexican pines. Crook
rode like a farmer—or rather, like his old Union commander,
Grant—slouchily dressed, a mule between his knees, a shotgun in his
lap, a General collecting birds and birds' eggs. He was as happy as a
boy, when he killed a giant ivory-billed woodpecker. Wars had been
endless with him for thirty years, but this was the first ivory-billed
woodpecker he had ever shot. His men said he reminded them of a
Jew peddler.

One day a runner met the soldiers. The great Goylothay had seen
the white men cross the border. He knew that the rumor about the
Hot Trail Treaty was a fact. The boundary that had protected him
for years would no longer protect him. He wanted to negotiate a
surrender—so the messenger said.

Crook designated a time and place. His own runners brought
word that the Indians back on the Arizona reservations threatened to
break out. He ordered Sieber to go back and curb the insurrection.
Tom Horn said later that he was given Al's place as chief of scouts.
Proud of his position, he watched Crook and Geronimo powwow in
1883. Tom noted that the red man talked endlessly while in the recesses of his cunning brain he still debated what to do. The great

medicine man evidently enjoyed ceremonious orations between himself and white officers, preferably generals. The Mexicans had understood the red man when they named him San Geronimo, the debater.

Tom attended to the simple menial tasks around camp while Crook and Geronimo killed time speaking of grievances, peace, war, the fires that flare in young men, and the sad approach of death for all men wherever they might be. When the two leaders had talked themselves out, the renegades returned to the reservation. So ended Crook's expedition against Geronimo. Tom Horn slumped back into the life of the red man—singing, gambling, playing pranks.

Once he met a curiosity: a blonde girl, burdened with many petticoats, in that casual country where a chemise was considered ample covering for a brunette beauty. The girl acted as though she were stuck-up—and didn't care. The collar on her dress was whaleboned a little higher, her pneumatic bust was pumped a little fuller, her stays were laced a little tighter, and she flirted her bustle a little more saucily than any girl that Tom had ever seen before. Schooled at Leadville and Dodge City, Tom decided to give his comrades a good laugh at the expense of the coquette. She fell eagerly into his trap, in fact set a trap of her own, for Tom. Attracted by Chief Horn's hard eye and narrow hips, she described herself as tremendously interested in his horse, his saddle and the way his corps of Apache scouts lived. Tom took her to see his men. The brown fellows, dressed in coats and no trousers, looked up as they chanted their gambling songs, but they never stopped the quivering cadences of their bodies.

Tom took the blonde to see Mickey Free, now a first sergeant and proud of his rank. Mickey sat on a roll of bedding, employing forceps to pluck stray hairs off his Hibernian lips and surveying his work in a pocket mirror. Tom patted Mickey on the shoulder and told the girl in English what a villainous cutthroat he was. Mickey, who—according to Tom's story—still refused to learn English, thought he was being introduced to the woman and lavished upon· her a broad Irish grin.

Tom and the blonde sat down. Mickey produced tobacco and

corn husks. He cut the husks into cigarette paper with deft slices from his wicked knife. Mickey rolled a smoke, then took a little block of wood from his tobacco pouch. One end of the block was coated with a dry paste of phosphorus and sulphur. He split a sliver from the block and scratched it on the sole of his bare foot until it sputtered into flame. He liked to display these matches. Most of the scouts lighted cigarettes with flint and steel. The blonde had many things to learn from Tom's scouts.

Indians who had been sleeping joined the group. Everybody squatted in the warm winter sunshine. The scouts talked and laughed but understood no English. The girl did not know Spanish or Apache. Tom Horn, understanding all tongues, was the center of conversation and translated with western freedom.

At length he grew tired of translating, took to moving about the camp and managed to secrete a gopher trap under the bedding roll against which Mickey leaned. Then he said to the blonde woman, "Mickey has hidden an embroidered tobacco pouch under that bedding—right where you see the rope go under. Steal it and we'll have some fun with Mickey."

The blonde snickered at the happy prospect of being an ally of the chief of scouts in a practical joke on Mickey. She sat down beside the redheaded Mexican, crowding him a little so that her mischief would be screened. Then with her face close to the half-breed's, chatting and smiling like a professional entertainer, she slipped her right hand under the canvas.

Tom saw her jump. A shadow passed across her face. Her eyebrows bowed into question marks. Ouch! Tom blew a cloud of contented smoke into the air. The woman was ten years his senior and no better than she should be—fair game for a youth of twenty-two. The blonde might have endured this injury but Tom added to it by calling her Mickey's girl and laughing about the lovesick couple. The blonde must have wished that Tom would get paid off and leave the country, but this time the government kept the chiefs of scouts in spite of the fact that Geronimo settled down quietly on the reservation. General Crook believed in the Indian scouts. He noticed that Geronimo's young men had not given up their wild ways. They persisted in slipping away to Mexico to steal horses. Crook ordered his Indian scouts with their white chiefs to patrol the international border. The monotony was interrupted every month or two by a skirmish. Tom liked to tell, in later years, how his scouts, a troop of cavalry and a squad of volunteer cowboys once annihilated a party of fifteen renegade Apaches. The white men had spied a suspicious column of dust far out in the desert—plainly a band of horses being driven north from Mexico.

The cowboys ached for a fight. Tom saw them cluster instinctively around Mickey Free. If any man in the Southwest could lead them into the thickest of the fray, it would be this dusky Irishman with the charmed life. The officer commanding the troopers ordered each man to tie his blue blouse behind his saddle. Tom had an idea: those blouses, if put on his own red scouts, would prevent the cowboys and troopers from killing a lot of friends in the hurly-burly. Tom asked the lieutenant for the loan. It was made. The red scouts strutted in their blue finery. Mickey Free whetted his knife on the rawhide sole of his moccasin and cocked his good eye at the ridge where the renegades were expected. Tom put his ear to the ground and caught a faint rumble. The Apaches were close at hand.

The soldiers, scouts and cowboys dropped into arroyos out of sight. Tom's twenty-five savages practiced sighting their rifles, their snakelike eyes glittering. The cowboys spurred their horses in pantomime, then looked at Mickey and grinned. The white troopers tightened their belts. A faint noise throbbed in the air—the distant crooning of voices. The trail song of the Indians had a lilt different from any cowboy ballad. Indians rode a different stirrup. The song almost died away, then swelled up in deep, exultant cadences, the shrill treble of the squaws piping thinly over all like birds high in the air.

The Indians jogged into view, their stolen horses grouped in advance. A shot rang out. Tom saw troopers spur in, with pistols poised over their shoulders. He saw Mickey Free lead the cowboys at a dead run, red pigtails flying. The renegades turned to flee, clinging like bugs to their horses' sides. Tom yelled to his twenty-five snake-eyed braves and struck the fugitives in the rear. Brush crackled, revolvers boomed, dust hid everything; lifted; horses bumped against one another, voices screamed and cursed. Tom saw a Mexican cowboy whirling his lariat in a cloud of golden dust.

Five minutes later it was all over. A dozen of the fourteen renegades lay dead on the trampled ground. One squaw was captured and one man unaccounted for. Two cowboys had been wounded. Mickey Free nursed a bad arm, slashed when he reached forward to sink his knife in a fugitive's back. A tall Texas cowboy laughed, "It's sho' lucky, Ho'n, yo' little ol' scouts woah Ahmy jumpahs. If they hadn't, I'd naturally have sho' got me some moah Injuns."

Tom knew Crook did not want his scouts to come back to the reservation with stolen Mexican ponies. He gave the rich haul of horses to the cowboys and rode along to headquarters with the victory chant of his snake-headed scouts rising and falling in time with the drumbeats of horses' hoofs.

"SNAKE-HEADS" BEHIND HIM

ALMOST a year and a half after Crook brought in Geronimo, the red leader made another break for freedom.

Tom Horn always maintained that he and Mickey Free were not on the reservation at the time. He said they were patrolling the border with a squad of scouts and a troop of soldiers when they came suddenly upon a small group of Indians butchering a stolen steer. No Indians had a right to be off the reservation, so the soldiers slipped forward silently and fired into the ravenous savages who hopped around the carcass. At the volley the Indians scattered like flapping birds—all save those who lay kicking or dead by the dead steer. The scouts chased and caught what squaws they could and Mickey treed a big one. Under threat of death she climbed down backward like a bear. She had a fat person's love of jewelry and her Falstaffian paunch was trussed with a leather belt upon which were threaded silver ornaments as large as dinner plates. Her small feet, at the end of buckskin-wrapped legs, looked like stubs. Mickey drove her before him down to a supply wagon in which all the captured squaws were moved campward. Mickey Free had lost his horse in the skirmish, so the poor fellow had to ride in the wagon with the women. The scouts tormented Mickey all the way, telling him how angry his blonde would be if she knew that he was buggy-riding with other girls. Mickey dangled his moccasins over the endgate and seemed pleased.

The captured squaws told the officer in charge, "Geronimo, him out." Frightful words: work, sweat and excitement for the Army! The officer called a halt, supplied Mickey with a fresh horse and selected a detail to pursue the renegades. He ordered Tom Horn to escort the smelly squaws to the reservation. Mickey Free had a saucy lilt in his blue Irish eye as he jogged off beside the lieutenant toward fresh adventures. He was trotting out of Tom's life forever.

When Tom reached the reservation the vast bustle of Crook's army, preparing to follow and capture Geronimo, dominated everything. This was the greatest exodus of Apaches Tom had ever seen. Natchez, hereditary chief of the Chiricahuas, and Chihuahua, the war chief, had both gone. Thousands of soldiers trotted in long lines across valleys of shadowless death. Hundreds of snake-headed Apache scouts fringed the troops, studying the sky line, and the dust, for signs of Geronimo. Troop after troop caught up with renegade bands. There were stealthy attacks and bold charges but the net result was a few captured squaws and one papoose. Geronimo slipped by devious deserts into Mexico. Then he decided to have fun with the soldiers.

He sent back a young chieftain, Josanine, with ten warriors to harry the border. Evading the troops, the renegades followed the rock ridges and desert paths, traveling on stolen horses, eating lizards, rabbits—and their horses. They fell like a sandstorm on the unprotected reservation, killing twenty-one of their own people, presumably as punishment for having helped Crook. They also butchered thirty-eight whites; then they returned to Geronimo, covering twelve hundred miles in four weeks and passing through a country where forty-three companies of infantry and forty troops of cavalry, and the gods only knew how many of their brothers, the Apache scouts, were looking for them.

This was too much for Crook. He prepared his second "final" offensive against Geronimo's mountain stronghold. This time he did not go in person but sent Captain Emmet Crawford, with Tom Horn as chief of scouts to guide a party of friendly Apaches along Josanine's trail until it led to the main camp of Geronimo. Tom, jogging ahead, looked back at the command—one hundred "snake-heads" officered by four commissioned white men: Captain Emmet Crawford, thin as whalebone, tanned but delicate in appearance, straight and stiff, with a mustache and goatee; First Lieutenant Marion P. Maus, thickset, bright-eyed and energetic as a fox terrier; William E. Shipp, dark, dashing Southern cavalier, second lieutenant of the 10th Cavalry; Samson L. Faison, sturdy, slow, young North Carolinian, second lieutenant from the 1st Infantry. Acting Assistant Surgeon T. B. Davis and Tom Horn, chief of scouts, filled the complement.

The Apache scouts had been issued Army uniforms but wore only the undershirts and tunics. They discarded the trousers, disdained shoes and clung to their boot-topped moccasins.

One hundred little brown men of hammered iron, six towering white men, with Tom Horn towering above them all—Tom with dark eyes dull in repose, his large ears crimped forward, his body barreled like a rifle—a veteran at twenty-five.

The party wound through the Dragoon Mountains. Tom was kept busy adjusting the white commanders to the prejudices of the Indians. Once a lieutenant caught an owl and, laughing, showed it to his comrades. The men stuck their fingers at the little snapping beak. The red scouts began weird croonings to themselves. They beat the earth with feathered sticks and sang songs against evil spirits. Their hum grew angry. Suddenly the officers dropped the owl and ran to the pack mules that bore the ammunition. Immediately the song stopped, the danger was passed and the little owl scuttled wrathfully under a rock. Tom explained to the West Pointers that owls were sacred to these red men, with whom he had spent half of his adult life, that the Apache name for "owl," like "bear," "snake," "lightning" and a great many other nouns, must not be spoken without prefixing *"ostin,"* which they could translate as "Mister," "Professor," "Reverend"—anything they liked.

Once a sheriff from Arizona caught up with the troop and handed Crawford a warrant for the arrest of a red scout called "Dutchy," a heathen-eyed villain, charged with murder. Crawford confided to the official that an arrest here might mean the massacre of all the officers, including the esteemed sheriff himself; so the latter jogged off on the homeward trail alone. Dutchy grinned in embarrassment and pleasure. Captain Crawford made him his personal bodyguard. Reward for crime!

Again and again Tom was impressed by the fact that when men in authority—the government—had use for a murderer they held him from the clutches of the law.

Every few days the party camped to rest. The Indians roasted the broad leaves of the century plant to get their favorite food, danced to relieve their exuberant spirits, and fired into the air. It was a skittish little army to command. The inhabitants of Mexican towns feared them, indeed seemed ready at times to wipe out these ancient Apache enemies and the six white men with them.

A crisis came at Christmas when the scouts obtained mescal near the town of Huasavas, an oasis in the desert, with an adobe church and huts surrounded by orange and lemon trees, heavy with golden spheres, and orchards of peach trees loaded with dusty, red-cheeked fruit. Late at night a slit-eyed scout full of drink, wearing his tunic inside out and his black-snake hair bound back with a red headband, came unexpectedly upon a Huasavas policeman uniformed in sandals and canary-yellow pajamas. They looked at each other in the light of the policeman's lantern, then the chattering Mexican shot down the Indian. The news reached the camp and the Apaches began their war dance. The town of Huasavas prayed and the West Pointers wondered. If the Indians were still drunk at daylight the five white officers and the Mexican population might all be obliterated. Tom Horn alone believed that he had a chance of escape, since it was unlikely that the Apaches would kill Talking Boy.

Fortunately the Indians danced the liquor well out of themselves by dawn and, childlike, forgot their wounded comrade. The white officers got them under way. Town after town they put behind them. Tom observed the frightened faces of peons in glassless windows and at roadside shrines. For a hundred and fifty years these people had crossed themselves whenever they came upon moccasin tracks with the toes turned up in front, Apache-fashion.

The scouts marched on to the Sierra Madres, the highland home of the Apaches. Wild turkeys flew up from scratching grounds into the tall pine trees, and coveys of quail, rolling through the grass like cannon balls, exploded into fragments. Tom found Josanine's tracks in the soft earth of the high mountains. With ten scouts Tom prepared to push ahead of the column into the foggy winter mountains. From the scouts' mess each of his men took five days' rations of pinole, parched corn dried in brown sugar. Mexicans and Indians loved it and the American Army had abandoned pork for pinole as the mainstay on campaigns in the Southwest. It answered admirably the craving of old troopers for liquor, which had been rationed to them during the Civil War. It kept the young troopers from developing the liquor habit—some of them at least. In addition to pinole, Tom and his scouts carried jerked meat, rattling like clinkers, in their pockets.

An inexperienced scout might have followed Josanine's trail as a hound follows a fox. Not Tom. He was too familiar with Indian woodcraft to trail Josanine boldly, let his rear guard see him coming, and make a false track that would not lead to Geronimo's camp. Tom knew that he must outwit Josanine. He believed himself a match for any Indian, mentally or physically. He was sure that Josanine would try all the wiles of Indian warfare and would be on his guard for all forms of Indian surprises. Tom would have to use some tracking trick more cunning than any taught him in Pedro's camp. Trailing had been a lifelong study with Tom. He had noticed one animal more deadly in the pursuit of its prey than even the Apache. A cougar invariably trailed a band of deer without dogging their tracks. Cougarlike, Tom set off traveling parallel to the Indians' trail—not along it. Every day he crossed the trail at right angles to be sure he had not lost it, then traveled parallel to the renegades' path on the other side. Tom soon made his scouts enthusiastic, sure that they were outwitting their cousins. They consented to travel after dark. By this routine they advanced while the fugitives slept and took their own rest while the fugitives were abroad. As each dawn paled the foggy winter sky Tom scattered his watchmen to the mountaintops where they would doze and watch for smoke or listen for a distant shot or any sign of their prey. At dusk he would assemble his little iron men and begin another thirty-mile walk.

Daily Tom sent back two runners, to hurry Crawford along. His food gave out but he kept on. One foggy morning when he knew the report of a rifle would be deadened by the damp air, he shot a buck in a deep canyon. The men gorged themselves on the dark red meat for an hour. They trotted off with dripping bundles of flesh for supper and breakfast.

Coming upon racks where squaws had dried meat, the scouts replenished their larder on refuse. Tom studied the camp site. By the moccasin tracks he estimated the enemy to be four hundred. This was more than Josanine and his warriors! Could it be that they had joined with Geronimo?

Tom drove his men ahead rapidly. The scouts sent as messengers never caught up with him again once they had delivered word to Crawford.

One midnight two of his few remaining scouts reported a red glow up the Aros River. Tom sent a runner to Crawford. He was alone now with four Apaches. At noon, edging nearer, Tom smelled mescal smoke. The renegades must feel safe to be roasting mescal. They were obviously planning to camp for at least a week. At twilight the five men scattered to the mountaintops to locate the camp. As the gray sky turned black, they saw the shadows of fires on the clouds ten miles away. Tom sent two of his men on a trot for Crawford, and hoped that he was close at hand. Tom and his two remaining veterans wormed their way toward the glowing shadows.

At last the radiance was overhead. They sat down against trees, shivered and dozed through the rainy night. They were tired and hungry. At dawn, bleak and cold, they counted fifty plumes of smoke a mile away. Soon small figures appeared, driving horses, and the garrulous, joking prattle of an Indian camp came to their ears. Tom studied the ground, then, with his men, ran at a dogtrot hunting Crawford. Three hours later they found him, dead-tired too, his men all but exhausted. Tom ate, then slept, whimpering in his sleep like a dog. The five officers exchanged their boots for moccasins so that they could march in silence.

It was the ninth day of January 1886 and Crawford knew that it was to be his big day. Late in the afternoon the little army, stimulated by the thought of battle, set out. They passed deer and a grumbling jaguar whose tiger head seemed too large for his leopard body. Tom warned the men not to shoot. A covey of quail flew up with thunderous wings. The whole troop fell flat in the grass, thinking it an Apache volley. Night came and the men's sweat-drenched clothing grew cold and stiff, rasping their flesh, lashing their drowsy spirits. Dr. Davis, the company surgeon, dropped out and was left behind. Captain Crawford's rifle dragged. Lieutenant Maus, whose receding chin belied his terrier vitality, carried on magnificently. Lieutenant Shipp, dark cavalier with Rameses whiskers, felt sorry for Crawford. It was tragic for a commander to lead his men through weeks of hardship, past dangers, all for one great moment, then to become too tired to strike when that great moment came. The lieutenants wondered if Crawford would last these few final miles.

Deep in the night they arrived before the hostile camp. Crawford had made it. Maus was the only man in the troop who did not appear fagged out. He took his quota of scouts to the far side of the Apache village in order to bottle the probable retreat of the Indians. Cavalier Shipp slipped off to place his men between the camp and the river. Tom and his reassembled scouts went down between the village and the mountains with Crawford. The plan was to surround the Indians completely. When Maus, who had the farthest to go, opened fire all were to attack. Daylight came and two burros blundered upon Tom's scouts, studied the situation for a time with ears bent forward, then with tails clamped tightly down, raced for the wickiups, serving better than watchdogs. Indians with rifles came out to see what had alarmed the burros. Shooting began, the soldiers and scouts charged in irregular lines. The wickiups shook with yelling squaws, children clutched with soft hands at the legs of warriors who brushed them aside as they fired at the advancing enemy. Above the stampede could be heard a big voice shouting commands.

Tom, running with his men, heard it and knew it for Geronimo's.

The old Roman nose himself was here, eh? Tom ran toward the sound, while his men, combining with Shipp's, poured volleys into the crowd of squaws and children.

In after years Tom was fond of telling friends in Denver that he had bounded among the rocks with poised rifle trying to discover Geronimo among the fleeing braves. He said he had wanted to kill him, but all naked Indians looked alike from behind, so the hunter was disappointed.

Maus had not had time to reach his position, and the Apaches escaped through the bottleneck.

Crawford, heartsick, was sure that Horn's men had betrayed him. There was no excuse for scaring the burros. It was treachery. What more could anyone expect, after all, when he took scouts from the same villages that had raised Geronimo's men? Back at Fort Leavenworth, General Nelson A. Miles, reading reports of the battle, blamed Tom Horn for the failure of the expedition, since it had been his men who had given the warning.

The looted camp was piled in a heap and set on fire. While it burned, the exhausted scouts slept. They had killed many of their relatives, but felt satisfied since it meant revenge for the slaughter Josanine had wreaked on the reservation. Men slept even while their ears were being torn with that most jagged of noises, the long-held wails of captive Indian women lying flat on their paunches with their screeching mouths to the ground.

Neither sleep nor contentment was on Captain Crawford's face as he lay down beside Tom Horn. He could get nobody to man outposts when sleep was so insistent. He had missed catching Geronimo. He was worn out. Besides he was quarreling through the mails with a fashionable sweetheart back east. He loved the girl but he loved more the sweet routine of monastic barracks with no Geronimo— and no girls. Sleep came to the harried captain. His next sleep after this would be the long one—and the best.

9

BLOOD ON THE ROCKS

CRAWFORD and Horn came out of their deep sleep. A sentry announced that a new enemy, Mexicans, approached. Shots banged in the morning mists. Brown men in light-colored uniforms charged the bivouac. The scouts fired at them. The enemy stopped, then retreated to the shelter of the rocks. Horn noticed wounded men crawling after their fellows. Bullets kicked up dirt around the broken bodies and they grew quiet.

A great lull now settled down. A group of Mexican officers appeared with a flag of truce. Captain Crawford beckoned to Horn and Maus. The three white men stepped out between the lines to meet the emissaries. The Americans learned that the Mexicans were, like themselves, regular army officers commanding Indian irregulars. The Mexicans commanded Tarahumare Indians, hereditary enemies of the Apaches. The Tarahumares, unlike the Apaches, had not thrown away the trousers their employers had given them. Instead they wore them around their shoulders like shawls, the legs tied together at their throats. Otherwise the two hordes were indistinguishable.

The brown and white officers, standing together making terms, had ceased to be commanders, had they only known it. Behind them rose the clicking of ejectors. Old tribal hatreds were coming to a boil. The officers all turned, yelling, "Don't fire!" Then they looked at one another, mutually suspecting treachery. In the rocks the rival tribesmen had forgotten them.

A single shot cracked in the fog. A moment's silence—like the hush before a bolt of lightning—then red flashes from scores of rifles set the mists whirling. Two of the mustached Mexican officers fell dead. The survivors, Mexican and American, caught between both fires, rushed toward their respective commands. Tom saw Captain Crawford running ahead of him. Terrier Maus scampered at his side. Suddenly Tom's head jerked back. The treetops wheeled around in the milky fog. The ground rose up and hit him in the face. Tom lay numb and listless in a tepid sea. He tasted wet earth, heard shouting and shooting far above him. He was not uncomfortable, lulled by a dull ache, and caring about nothing.

A buzzing, whirring sound was in his ears and a red-hot iron in the thick of his arm. Then he understood why he tasted wet earth. The trees and fog and wet ground came back to his paralyzed senses, and with them came the desire to live. He drew his legs up and saw that he could still run. His consciousness flashed back as suddenly as it had died. He made a great effort, got up, and ran for shelter. In the rocks, he saw Captain Crawford lying on his back— a red handkerchief over his face. His hand clutched at the handkerchief in spasms. Heathen-eyed Dutchy stood beside him on guard. Tom saw Lieutenant Maus near by. "Poor chap," Maus said, looking down at Crawford, "shot in the head." He added that all the Mexican officers had been killed before they reached their lines. Then Maus looked at Tom. Surprise came into his bright eyes. Tom felt hot waves of pain playing down his left arm. Blood was dripping from his fingers. Scouts crowded around him, cut off his sopping sleeve, and plugged the hole in his biceps where a .44 ball had gone through. Maus trotted off, swearing at the sputtering line. The ammunition was running low.

Tom was weak and trembling from the bullet shock. He sat down to rest. Soon he felt better and did a little shooting himself, handling his 45-70 octagon-barrel rifle in one hand, like a revolver, a feat of strength his friends liked to remember. The giant had a wrist like a horse's leg. For two hours the officers tried to stop the aimless firing. At last the wet hills were silent.

Across the valley Tom saw the Mexicans signal for another parley. Maus walked out between the lines. Taking a chance surely! Tom knew that the lieutenant could speak only broken Spanish and that the Mexican survivors were Indians who spoke as little Spanish as Maus himself. Tribal hatreds were apt to get out of hand again, but the Americans were out of supplies and almost out of ammunition. Perhaps the risk was necessary. A fight could not be kept up long. Tom watched with interest. What reception would Maus receive? The Tarahumare dead and wounded dotted the dripping valley. Their officers had been shot down by the Americans. Maus disappeared in the enemy lines. Tom and the Apaches waited. Before long the tiny figure of the lieutenant appeared again. He shouted that he was a prisoner. The enemy would not free him unless he surrendered the pack mules so they could move the wounded out of the mountains. "Send the mules!"

Tom turned to Lieutenant Shipp, the second in command. Shipp wore a broad hat jauntily over one eye. He shouted that the Apaches objected to sending the mules. They admitted no defeat and no truce. They were anxious to annihilate their ancient enemies.

"As commanding officer," called Maus, "I order you to send the mules."

Lieutenant Shipp's dark side glance noted the Apaches stripping off their tunics for another fight. He yelled: "You're a prisoner of war! I'm the commanding officer and I order the mules to remain." Tom chuckled as the Indians crawled through the rocks closer to the enemy.

At this moment a voice rang out from the rocks behind the Tarahumares.

It was Geronimo's!

For him the sun now shone. Here were his enemies, older than the Americans, cornered between his Apaches and their brothers. It was a royal time to make hay among the hated Tarahumares.

Shipp asked Tom what the Old Roman wanted. Both listened to the booming voice. The renegade begged for the Americans to join with him and wipe out the Apaches' tribal foes. Call a truce for a few minutes, let the Apache factions unite and get all that good pinole which the Tarahumares were carrying.

Shipp and Horn conferred. They realized the irony of Geronimo's request, for, once they let their scouts ally themselves with the old man, they would be his forever. Then, with the Tarahumares gone, who would be next?

Tom, nursing his wound, suggested an intrigue. Shipp approved it. Tom strode out toward the Tarahumare lines holding up his good hand palm outward. He could hear Geronimo's men warning the Tarahumares not to hurt him on pain of awful vengeance. None of the Apaches wanted to hurt Talking Boy if they could avoid it within reason, and except for the blood on the rocks, the fight was like the warfare of children in vacant lots.

Tom shouted to the irregulars that he would give them mules and safe-conduct out of their trap if they would send over enough men to get them. The guileless Tarahumares sent five braves. The moment they reached the American lines Tom disarmed the emissaries and stood them out in plain sight of their friends. His Apaches with cocked rifles stood before them.

Then bounding up, a commanding figure against the sky, Tom stood on an eminence and yelled to the Tarahumares: release Lieutenant Maus and do it "by-Jesusly quick" or see their five friends shot down in cold blood.

His voice echoed away among the cliffs. Almost at once Lieutenant Maus, safe and sound, came out at a dogtrot and the five Tarahumares, elation in their heels, scampered home.

The delay had cooled the passions of the Apache scouts. Maus, Shipp, Horn and Dr. Davis, who had caught up to the expedition, managed to get their savages under control. Geronimo was, after all, their main enemy, so they gave the Tarahumares pack animals for their wounded and sent them away with their blessing.

The Americans retired with the living but unconscious captain— free now from defeats and girls. They camped a few miles away. The officers and Tom sat resting, and talking of Crawford's bad luck, when a renegade squaw arrived with word that Geronimo wanted to talk. The old villain was swollen with oratory and must find relief. Bored with lonely freedom and the company of lesser men, he craved the pleasure of ceremonious debates with important white men.

Maus set a place for the meeting and told Tom to interpret. At the appointed time the renegades filed into camp. Geronimo wore a gay handkerchief around his head like a pirate. He had on a sack coat, stolen only the gods knew where. So small he had to exhale to button it, the jacket seemed shorter than it was, owing to the absence of any trousers beneath it. There was, however, so much dignity in the old fighter's eyes that nobody thought his uniform ridiculous. Behind him came Natchez, Chihuahua and weazened Nana—respectively, hereditary chief, war chief and patriarch of the Chiricahua Apaches. They all sat down, everyone dignified and silent, the air so tense that any sudden noise such as the falling of a dead limb, the coughing of a horse, the yelp of a dog, might startle the councilors into shooting one another.

Geronimo spoke first. Tom interpreted. Maus replied. The pow-wow was long. At last the old Apache agreed to come north and talk with General Crook. When the March moon filled, Geronimo said, he would be at the Cañon de los Embudos, just south of the American border. Maus and Geronimo shook hands. Agreed!

It was a conditional surrender, the sort of arrangement Geronimo liked. For two months now he could enjoy the prospect of another important conference and weighty talk with the head man of the American Army. To insure his appearance at the appointed place, Geronimo gave as hostages to Maus his own wife, Natchez' wife, some warriors and women—and ancient Nana for good measure, evidently glad to be rid of the he-crone who did nothing but complain because warriors weren't what they had been when he was a boy.

True to his promise, Geronimo and his men came to meet Crook in the full of the March moon. Tom Horn was not present, according to the United States Army reports of the affair, but he soon learned all the details of the famous parley. Maus arrived first to prepare the ground. He had become more sympathetic with Geronimo ever since he had, himself, escorted old Nana to the reservation. The venerable hostage had kept pouring into his captor's ears his archaic objections to the younger generation. One minute he drooled about old times, the next he complained because somebody had stolen his squash-flower necklace. He cried when Maus wouldn't stop the cavalcade and search the women for the gewgaw. Then he would forget about it in the dawn of some new criticism of modern warfare, wander off into tributes to his own youth and finally return to the subject of the necklace. He was more bother than any bloody-handed Geronimo.

The Apaches reached the rendezvous on schedule, built jacals or stockade huts with Spanish bayonets and mescal leaves, then waited stoically. The young men sat around camp playing monte with cards made of horsehide scraped thin as a drumskin—muscles flowing under smooth red backs, pythons swelling up and down the red arms as the men flipped the ingenious cards.

A century before, when the American painter Benjamin West had stood before Apollo of the Belvedere he had gasped, "My God, it is a Mohawk."

All Maus and the other white officers noted was that every man and boy in camp wore two cartridge belts, each loaded with metallic cartridges, and that their rifles were all Winchesters, or Springfields that had been originally furnished by the government to its Indian scouts.

Little Indian boys romped around the jacals. One of them had blue eyes and a face as freckled as Mickey Free's. The little girls, dressed in their best, looked at the white soldiers and ran away giggling. A murderous renegade sat pressing a watch to his ear and looking into space with a cherubic smile. Every Apache wore "medicine" of some kind, as did the scouts. These "lucky pieces" were suspended from their necks by the umbilical cords their mothers had saved for them. Some wore a tuft of feathers from the southern cardinal, others the head of a quail, the wings of a woodpecker, the feet of a prairie dog, a button, a piece of glass or a splinter of wood that had been hit by lightning. Tom Horn had associated with the Indians so long that he also shared this habit. To the day of his death he carried certain buttons, fondling them absently. They became a part of him. He fingered them when there was nothing else for his hands to do. But it is doubtful that he shared the orthodox Apache's veneration for such possessions.

When word came that Crook had arrived, Geronimo's squaws rubbed his face with ground galena until it shone like stove polish. Indians set their own value on the prospectors' ore. Next the squaws tied the piratical handkerchief around Geronimo's head. Then he walked down into the ravine with his chieftains. General Crook, a pith helmet on his head and Apache moccasins on his feet, hitched up his blue overalls at the knees and squatted on the ground. Behind him ranged six officers, four civilians, a photographer from Tombstone and four interpreters, each of whom had been coached to check the others for accuracy of translation.

Geronimo sat himself down near the general under a sycamore tree. In the past he had enjoyed powwows but now sweat beads stood on his blackened face like the warts on a Gila monster. He played with a string and argued as businessmen of the cities do when they find it necessary to produce some plausible excuse for having broken a contract.

Geronimo had explained his first runaway as a protest against the bad lands which the government had allotted his tribe. When he ran away the second time he had declared it due to the way corrupt Indian agents had cheated his people. Now he was having difficulty in explaining this third flight.

Crook asked him what he had to say for himself. Geronimo began by describing how happy he had been on the reservation. "I was praying to the light and to the darkness, to God and to the sun to let me live there quietly with my family. . . . I was living there peaceably with my family under the shade of the trees doing just what General Crook had told me I must do. . . ." Then people had begun to plague him, Mickey Free to tease him. Chato and Mickey told him that the Americans were going to hang him, so he left. But now the Earth Mother was listening to him, he wanted peace—everything "rubbed out," his men forgiven.

From On the Border with Crook, *by John Bourke (Charles Scribner's Sons, 1891)*

General George Crook, the "old-clothes soldier." A comrade remembered that he never saw the general in the uniform of his rank until he lay in his casket.

Leonard Wood, when Horn knew him in 1886.

Geronimo acted as though he thought such an explanation would suffice. Swiftly he tried to put Crook on the defensive by accusing him of presenting a grim face.

"It would be better," said the wily Indian, reproachfully, "if you would speak to me and look with a pleasant face. . . . Why don't you look at me and smile at me? I am the same man; I have the same feet, legs and hands and the sun looks down on me a complete man. Look and smile at me."

Crook sat frigid and silent.

Geronimo tried a new tack. "Whenever I meet you I talk good to you and you to me and peace is soon established; but when you go from the reservation you put agents and interpreters over us who do bad things."

Finding that Crook did not respond to this obvious opportunity to lay all the blame on a third party and so establish good feeling between the two principals, Geronimo switched to a different approach. He tried poetry on the hardened old warrior in the funny hat.

"There is one God looking down on us all," said the Indian, speaking like a preacher. "We are all children of the one God. God is listening to me. The sun, the darkness, the winds are all listening to what we now say."

In the midst of this lyric exhortation, Crook cut in with some acrid inquiries as to why Geronimo and forty braves had gone killing, stealing and sneaking around the country like coyotes just because people like Mickey Free had told old wives' tales.

Crook declared that he himself was held responsible for all the people Geronimo had killed because he had let Geronimo escape. There had never been any order to arrest the Indian. "There is no use for you to try to talk nonsense——"

"But," replied Geronimo lamely, "I am a man of my word. I am telling the truth."

Crook called him a liar.

"Then," replied the Indian with the triumph of a debater who scores a swift point, "how do you want me to talk to you? I have but one mouth; I can't talk with my ears."

"Your mouth talks too many ways," answered Crook, but it was obvious that the Indian had scored neatly.

There was some more talk and back talk, with Crook demanding that Geronimo surrender unconditionally or go back on the warpath where "I'll keep after you and kill the last one, if it takes fifty years."

The photographer from Tombstone asked Geronimo to move a little so that a picture might be taken of the assembly. The chieftain was so lost in the delightful game of words that he paid no attention. The argument finally terminated with Geronimo's indicating that he would give a decision at tomorrow's renewal of negotiations.

The next day Chihuahua and Natchez gave long speeches about the happy feelings of men who were forgiven and how they were glad to surrender to so excellent a friend as Crook. Every few minutes in their discourses they got to their feet, shook Crook's hand and sat down again without halting their oratory.

Chihuahua said, "Whenever a man raises anything, even a dog, he thinks well of it and tries to raise it right and treat it well. So I want you to feel toward me and be good to me."

Sentimental, sociable hearts lay paradoxically under the skins of these merciless killers.

"When we are traveling together on the road or anywhere else, I hope you'll talk to me once in a while," said Chihuahua, and shook Crook's hand again.

At the conclusion of the two-day powwow the Apaches agreed to give up and cross the border next day. Crook left for the United States, expecting the hostiles to follow tractably with the white troops. But that night a moonshiner came over from a near-by ranch with liquor and the red men got howling drunk. Geronimo and one of his braves rode the same horse around the jacals, singing and yowling. Natchez shot his wife and lay on the ground dead to the world. Everybody danced and shot bullets at the moon and threw screeches to the stars.

The next morning the soldiers counted the Indians across the international boundary. They found that twenty-two men, thirteen women and six children were missing. Among the missing were both Natchez and Geronimo. The total number of lesser Apaches who came back to the reservation was seventy-nine—a pitiful bag after a whole winter's chase—and from Washington, General Phil Sheridan, Crook's onetime roommate at West Point, criticized him pointedly. Geronimo had shattered Crook's reputation as an Indian fighter. Crook had ridden down Robert E. Lee's horsemen but Geronimo had been too much for him. With a sigh, he asked to be relieved after his eight years' service against the Apaches. Lieutenant Maus closed his winter campaign with a report which contained these words: "I cannot commend too highly Mr. Horn, my chief of scouts; his gallant services deserve a reward which he has never received."

Tom Horn closed the campaign with the belief that he was a great man. Self-confidence had come to add its power to his indifference to death, law and pity.

10

WITH THE SUPERMEN

CROOK, with his mule, his shotgun and birds' eggs, was gone, and the sun began to go down on Tom Horn's great day as a tracker of red outlaws.

General Nelson A. Miles came to the command in April 1886. He dismissed all the scouts, including Tom. Miles reasoned that Crook had failed because he had tried to defeat Geronimo at a game that was the Indian's own. How could the renegades fail to win as long as their chief pursuers were their own brothers and cousins, allied with white scouts who had been virtually adopted into the tribe? Miles knew that scouts like Tom Horn had often become "lost" in mountains whose every foot they knew. Of course these scouts realized perfectly well that their pay would stop the moment the last renegade was killed.

The whole character of the war changed. The Apache scouts, as soon as demobilized, returned to their reservation—or moved into Geronimo's camp. Tom Horn went back to the mine he had claimed at Tombstone and Miles set his engineers to work on maps and logarithm tables.

In Tombstone saloons, Tom followed Miles's preparations as the newspapers reported them. The change of leaders seemed ridiculous. Crook, the fighting West Pointer, who scorned etiquette, was supplanted by a successful businessman whose father had helped him organize a volunteer company to command in the Civil War and who had done well to win his brigadier stars in the regular army fighting Indians in the Northwest, but who was still far from a frontiersman's idea of a soldier. Miles had plump epicurean hands, a fat neck and a thin skin that resented outdoor rigor.

Where Crook's bed was as hard as any private's, Miles's was soft as a Wall Street banker's. Where Crook watched battles from the front line with the wind of bullets waving his scraggly whiskers, Miles read reports in telegraph offices, twirling his fine mustaches with white fingers. Tom read of Miles's campaign, how the general divided Arizona and New Mexico into squares with a cavalry troop in each square and with the whole connected by heliograph stations. If ever the Indians broke out now they would be harried from square to square by the cavalry—a relay race with mirrors flashing signals.

Should the renegades escape this martial gridiron, as they had evaded Crook's scattered army, Miles intended to follow them down into Mexico with picked troops before they had time to rest from their flight across the mirror-flashing squares. These picked troops would be notified by helio as the renegades neared the southern border and would be unleashed for pursuit as soon as the red men were back again in Mexico. Here would be the longest and hardest chase, for there would be no helios in Mexico to relay the white pursuers. General Miles wanted supermen for the final dash in his elaborate game, spick-and-span Nordics, very different from the motley-clad, slouching officers, scouts and soldiers Crook had employed.

He summoned to him the neatest officers, two captains—Leonard Wood and H. W. Lawton—and placed them at the head of his supermen. Captain Lawton was to command, and Wood, since he was a surgeon, was to study the Indians from a scientific point of view. To Wood, General Miles delivered directions, which read:

"We have heard much said about the physical strength and endurance of these Apache Indians, these natives of the desert and mountain. I would like to have you accompany Captain Lawton's command, and as you are probably in as good a condition as anyone to endure what they endure, you can make a careful study of the Indians at every opportunity and discover wherein lies their superiority, if it does exist, and whether it is hereditary, and if hereditary, whether the fiber and sinew and nerve power is of a finer quality, and whether their lungs are really of greater development and capacity to endure the exertion of climbing these mountains than those of our best men."

Tom and his friends heard all these preparations in the cool saloons of Tombstone. General Miles, fresh from the marble corridors of Washington, was a joke to the frontiersmen and scouts. His helio system proved that he was a "looking-glass" soldier, and when Geronimo, sweeping up across the Mexican border, flouted and evaded the tin soldiers in their helio squares for weeks, there was roaring laughter in the bars of western towns.

Reading through the lines of newspaper reports, Tom Horn could visualize what was actually happening—white cavalrymen rushing Indian camps and capturing nothing but willow baskets—red men among the rocks, calling to one another like wood owls while the soldiers cursed in the valleys—Geronimo's men stealing horses from the rear of the column while the soldiers dismounted and deployed to attack an imaginary foe in front—naked warriors patting their rumps as they fled from frantic riflemen.

When Geronimo had enjoyed himself sufficiently among the checkered squares he danced back into Mexico ahead of his pursuers. Natchez, not yet tired of the fun, led another raid all the way to central Arizona.

Miles was furious and the helios flashed like diamonds on the bosom of a hysterical lady. Long lines of cavalrymen, thick dust on their wide hats and blue shoulders, trailed after Natchez, who led the way through valleys of awful thirst and in so doing ruined his horses. When the animals choked for water, the Apaches slit their gums so the blood would cut the dust from their gullets. When the horses fell exhausted racing up steep mountainsides, the naked savages trotted on up over the mountain and down the other side, where they raided ranches and obtained remounts.

This drama was repeated over and over, and even when the renegades reached new squares where they were pursued by fresh troops Natchez soon reduced the relay of United States cavalry to infantry. The white troopers trudged through the scorching desert, drinking from pools of tepid, soapy water that produced vomiting. Some pools had congealed into jelly—stinking jelly. The sun scorched blond Nordic faces, cracked lips, fried the moisture out of Caucasian bodies. The dust, hot as the sun, made thirst unendurable and, according to Miles, some of the reeling men took a lesson from the Indians' horses, and sliced their own arms to moisten their lips with blood.

The helios reported to fresh troops where the Apaches would enter their square but the troopers had trouble puzzling out Natchez' trail, for the Apaches sometimes tied rawhide on their horses' hoofs, and the covering made a fresh track look like an old one.

By these means the raiders got back to Mexico and Miles had no alternative left but to unleash his supermen. Tom Horn and his friends in the cool saloons watched with interest the San Francisco papers that came to the camp a week late. For seven weeks the supermen followed the savages across Sonora before they found Geronimo's camp on the headwaters of the Yaqui River and closing in captured—a few damned willow baskets.

General Miles now realized that chasing Indians was the game of fox and geese that Crook had thought it, and what America needed was Crook's scouts. Supermen might have the strength and the spirit to pursue, but their eyes were not trained to trailing. They were like thoroughbred horses that had reached the end of their picket ropes.

Miles needed a superscout to lead his supermen. Al Sieber was too crippled for the job. Rheumatism and many old wounds had taken him out of the saddle. The officers said that Tom was the best trailer available but that he had lived with the Indians so long he must be watched lest he open communications with the hostiles.

Miles was desperate. Horn was ordered to report. From Tombstone he replied that wealth was coming to him in his mining and he did not choose to go. Miles pleaded. Horn was indifferent to an insulting point. Miles was wont to command. He felt his rank and Tom felt his. Miles weakened and sent Horn a letter naming a salary that could not be refused. Tom rode over to the fort. Miles saw that this superscout was no Nordic blond. He was a brunet, a dark German. The pigment in his skin would not let the sun destroy the vitality in his blood. His lips would not crack, for he carried a plug of chewing tobacco in his overall pocket. Tom did not stand before the general with military alertness. He stood on one foot, leaned against the door casement, looked unkempt, tired, almost sleepy.

Ordered to report to Lawton, who sat with his thwarted supermen in Mexico, Tom rode off alone. Strangely enough, he came upon the trail of the renegades. Was it luck, collusion or, as certain redskins said, the magic of Tom's button amulets? Tom studied the trail for a few miles, then spurred away. Arriving with the news at Lawton's headquarters, Horn found the big Nordics dressed in underwear and moccasins, wasting their strength like baffled hounds babbling cold trails. They had apparently turned into ragged barbarians, but Leonard Wood had not lost his Harvard accent.

Tom looked over Lawton's two jaded troops and twenty-five scouts. He asked his new commander to leave the cavalry behind. Lawton was not ready for such a drastic step. He ordered the entire command to be ferried across the Aros River for the pursuit. The stream was running a flood full of driftwood. Only the tops of the willows showed along the riverbanks. Lawton, Wood and Horn undressed to attempt a crossing. A few strokes in the swift water convinced Lawton that he could not swim the treacherous stream. He came back. Leonard Wood, raised in the Atlantic surf at Cape Cod, struck off boldly through the stinking water. Tom Horn, unused to swimming, but too proud to admit any physical superior, stayed with him. "An exceedingly hard swim," Wood wrote in his diary. "Horn came near going under, as, although a big strong chap, he had not done much swimming in rough water."

A raft was built to ferry the command across but valuable time was wasted. Lawton decided that Tom Horn was right. Red scouts on foot could outdistance horsemen. The cavalry was halted. Wood, Horn and a few picked scouts set off on the final five weeks of the chase. Behind them the main body of scouts followed slowly. The cavalry waited in reserve to come on a run when needed. For the first few days the Indians' trail showed them to be from one to four days ahead of the supermen. Sometimes the droppings from the horses indicated that the fugitives were less than ten hours in advance. It was maddening to Lawton to find the renegades able to close or open the gap at will.

When the red men exhausted their horses, they stopped to raid a ranch or steal new mounts from a mine pack train. Natives of the country told white men about these raids and the American pursuers cut across country and picked up the trail at the smoldering wreckage.

Tom Horn, almost buoyant under the exciting strain, pointed to signs that showed the Indians to be weakening. The cold white ashes of their campfires disclosed food to be scarce. Tracks of their horses in the dust showed heels bumping together, sure sign of near exhaustion. No ranches were close enough now to furnish remounts.

After the third week of the chase, Tom showed Wood bodies of newborn babies by the trail. Geronimo's women and children were slowing down the march. The strain was beginning to tell on all the fugitives. Geronimo's camp had been destroyed seven times in the last fifteen months and some of his best men were suffering from old wounds. Geronimo himself was carrying his arm in a sling. Tom pointed out how the tracks in the dust showed the old warrior to be mounting his horse with one hand. The renegades could not hold up much longer. They were getting no time for food and proper rest.

But the terrific pace was also telling on the scouts. Two-thirds of them had dropped out before the first two weeks of trudging up rocky mountainsides, only to slide down again. Wood had lost over thirty pounds in weight; Horn, the lank frontiersman, strode along as tireless as ever. No remnant of uniform or rank remained; every man plodded on in his hat, underwear and moccasins.

Miles, sitting at the telegraph station, listened to the messages that came out of Mexico, first by runner, then by flashing mirrors, then by wire. He wondered which band would collapse first— Wood's or Geronimo's.

One day Miles read that the Americans would surround the renegades in the morning, and in the morning he heard that Geronimo was ten miles ahead. One evening the general was told that shots had been exchanged and Geronimo was cornered. A few hours later he heard that the renegades had vanished on soft wings that baffled even Tom Horn.

Miles heliographed for Horn to report to headquarters. He had never trusted the man and believed he was betraying the cause. Before the message reached Lawton, there came to Miles a dispatch that took the blood from his face. Geronimo was negotiating for surrender with a Mexican army that had come into the field. United States relations with Mexico were peculiarly delicate. The Hot Trail Treaty and the United States Army's inability to defeat a handful of renegade Indians had convinced President Porfirio Díaz that the *Americanos* were not invincible. He was flirting with England for a defensive alliance and had some assurance that the defeated Confederacy might rejoice in an opportunity to turn against the United States. Miles, in constant touch with the marble halls in Washington, saw the danger both to his own and to his country's prestige. A heliogram ordered Horn to stay with the troops and Lawton, now that the renegade was once more located, to strike quickly before their prey fell into the hands of Mexico.

But the capture was not so easily made. Geronimo, flirting with two governments via squaws for messengers, kept both powers from attacking, lest each one should run him into the arms of the other. Miles won, eventually, because Geronimo wanted to come home— and because he longed for another big powwow and dramatic talk with an American general.

Historians disagree as to which American deserves the credit for receiving the surrendered warrior. Several officers, sent to head off the fleeing renegade, talked with the cornered chieftain near Fronteras, pleading with him to "come in" but refraining from making any hostile move. They knew that threats, light as the shadow of a cloud, might prompt Geronimo and his followers to ooze through their fingers like quicksilver.

Miles always maintained that Geronimo surrendered to Lawton. This made his superman experiment a success. Other officers who were not supermen took the honor upon themselves. Tom Horn insisted that he did the real work. At any rate Geronimo agreed to ride toward the border for a parley with General Miles, and drifted in that direction with his band still armed and glaring suspiciously at the troops who rode on either side and behind.

At this uncertain but apparently successful culmination of events, a large posse of Mexican horsemen rode up to complicate matters and upset the nerves of the Indians. The Mexicans had come with the avowed purpose of massacring all the renegades and attempted to brush aside the Americans to get their revenge. Geronimo appeared delighted. He asked the Americans to stand aside and let him fight it out with the dark-skinned riders in the enormous hats. His Apaches, with their repeating Winchesters, were better armed than the Mexicans who bore only ancient Sharps rifles, shotguns and revolvers. The American officers knew that such a clash would precipitate another affair like the one that had cost Captain Crawford his life. The strained relations between the United States and Mexico were bad as ever. Excited Americans were holding meetings, talking war, shouting with outrage: "Remember the Alamo!" A New York politician, Theodore Roosevelt, who had a ranch in Dakota Territory, had started to organize a regiment of Rough Riders. Only a spark in the Arizona powder house was needed to fire the United States. A pitched battle on the border seemed almost sure to precipitate the threatening war.

Leonard Wood's account of this precarious moment gives Tom Horn credit for riding out in front of the attacking Mexicans and explaining matters to them in such a way that they withdrew, and bloodshed was averted. Tom's self-confidence, courage and indifference to death, once more made him a great man.

The renegades eventually arrived at Skeleton Canyon on the border where Miles came to meet them. Looking at Geronimo for the first time, the general said that he was reminded of William Tecumseh Sherman in his prime. Many were the conditions and stipulations which his savage enemy wrung from Miles before surrendering. Miles had no intention of keeping them, once he got Geronimo behind bars, and made them, as he said, because Geronimo had never kept faith and was beyond the pale of gentlemen's agreements.

The long powwow over, the vanquished red man entered an ambulance for the ride to Fort Bowie where he was destined to be imprisoned. From the door of the ambulance, the old chieftain saw the mountains of Mexico recede—cruel-edged peaks and ridges on which he had suffered and been strong, friendly mountains which had hidden him across happy, murderous years.

"This is the fourth time that I have surrendered," he said to General Miles.

Miles answered that it was also his last.

It was the driver of the ambulance, a muleteer, who boasted loudest, forever after, that he was the man who really brought in Geronimo.

Tom Horn lingered around the fort while the white troops loaded the "bad" Apaches on trains and shipped them to Florida, out of temptation's way. These were terrible trips for the Indians. When one of the trains entered a tunnel all the prisoners hid under the seats. On others three prisoners slipped off their handcuffs and jumped through the glass windows of the moving cars. When resuscitated after his leap, one Indian was asked why he had taken so slim a chance of escape. He replied that he wasn't trying to flee from the white men. He was only afraid of the approaching tunnel which he had seen looming ahead with the distant engine disappearing into the black depths.

"No ride 'im, me," said the Indian. "Train go in his hole."

Tom Horn realized that the scouting days were over. The Indians of North America were conquered at last. They had made their last stand for a lost continent.

Only practice maneuvers occupied the soldiers now. Miles, cutting up New Mexico and Arizona into new helio squares, sent one cavalry troop to chase another in a sort of military scalp dance. Tom Horn looked on such charades with hardly concealed contempt. He saw a young lieutenant arrive, fresh from West Point, to help play these games. Lieutenant John J. Pershing had been learning to kill men by mathematics while Tom Horn had been learning to kill them with a rifle.

Tom looked away to the mountains and, when his discharge came, struck off for a winter's work in the mines.

The long years with Indians and generals had taught Tom that powerful people played with dumb poor people as with livestock. He had, himself, learned that it was sport to kill Indians on the sneak, like game out of season. He had seen Al Sieber kill defenseless prisoners when asked by officers to do so. The officers had made the request as casually as a ranchman asks a cowboy to shoot an old horse. Sieber had put revolver bullets in the backs of the red men while they ate—and Sieber was Tom's first teacher and his hero to the last.

Tom had learned that a man who might be called a stool pigeon in a more complex society was called a scout on the San Carlos reservation. This was the way big men ruled.

Big men didn't kill one another. Miles hadn't shot Geronimo as Sieber had shot those lesser Apaches who cowered like wild animals in the corners of their cells. Miles had only put Geronimo inside a fort with plenty of food and a bow and arrow with which to shoot rats when they came out for crumbs. Wild West showmen came long distances to beg his captors to let Geronimo take part in a circus. Curious civilians paid him money to show them how he could carry more than a dozen pebbles in the battle scars on his old body.

Tom read in the newspaper that the people of Arizona presented General Miles with a silver loving cup for killing the Apaches. He noted that many Indians in the Southwest began to observe a great fiesta called San Geronimo's Day. Padres maintained that the celebration was for Saint Jerome, the cleric. The Indians who took part told Tom that they were honoring the mighty chieftain.

Nelson A. Miles had become a great general. People said confidently that he would become the ranking general in the United States Army. Geronimo, a greater killer than Miles, had become a saint. The more a man killed the more recognition he received from his people. Power, murder and sudden death were the attributes of big men.

Tom wanted to be a big man, always.

11

A NEW CIVILIZATION

WHEN springtime came in 1887, both the renegade Apaches and Tom Horn were unhappy. The red men cooled their heels on the Florida reservation to which they had been sent, and Tom fretted in a mine. The rhythms of life on the plains would not die. But where the Indians could not help themselves, the white man could look around.

Mining interested Tom no longer. He had found pay dirt but not enough to make him independent, so he suddenly sold his interest for three thousand dollars, went back to Missouri and had his tonsils removed. Tom found a childlike joy in being nursed by his sister Nancy, and telling his mother that he could not eat her greens since his operation—the vinegar hurt his throat. At the post office Tom talked about Geronimo to admirers who sat on the edge of the board sidewalk under the awning. Old friends told him that Bennie Markley was running a butcher shop in Keokuk and "doin' fine." Tom smiled. His teeth gleamed beneath his mustache. Saying "Yes" to the teacher had not profited Bennie so much in the end!

A month passed idly. Tom noticed that people were beginning to take him for granted. They no longer asked him about the great generals. He was becoming lonely and bored. The great West began to roll once more in his mind. Out there, he realized, was the only country that was his own size.

By autumn he was in Arizona, punching cows for the Chiricahua Cattle Company near the Mexican border, and legends had begun to gather around his herculean frame. Years later cow hands said of him: "When we'd get ready to turn wild horses out of a corral, Tom would go and hang himself by his hands on the crossbar over the gate, and let 'em run between his feet. All at once he'd drop on a mustang's back and ride 'im bareback."

Presumably it was a killing that drove Tom from the border. A girl, half-Spanish, half-Indian, abetted the fatality by attempting to divide her smiles between Tom and a Mexican lieutenant. At a dance the climax came. The officer, resplendent in his uniform of red, white and green, stood glowering at the big cowboy while the dancers trampled one another in a widening circle. Long afterward, Tom explained what happened.

"When a greaser gets mad he goes blind. I let this one shoot first, for I knew he'd miss me. Then I cut the little bugger in two."

Tom drifted north. At ranch houses he heard talk of a range war in Pleasant Valley. He heard how the Tewksburys were importing sheep to snatch grass from under the noses of cattle belonging to the Grahams. Ominous letters had been exchanged; bullets had dropped around lone riders. Then bands of horsemen had raided enemy camps.

Tom, a soldier of fortune with a long rifle for rent, was apparently the man for such a war, but though he listened, he shrank from enlisting under such small and dowdy banners. It would be a come-down indeed, after years spent in the employ of the United States, "the big rich government."

The Grahams and the Tewksburys were rich enough, it was true, but small-bore. Tom heard that one of the rivals paid taxes on fifty thousand dollars' worth of property but made his wife take in washing, and that the other "mooched" tobacco from the hands who herded his twelve hundred cattle.

Tom started to ride on. But before he escaped the neighborhood, there came to his ears the roar of neutral ranchmen in Pleasant Valley—thrifty and pacific husbandmen, chiefly Mormons—who wanted peace. In later years Tom claimed that he acted as "mediator" in the "war" that cost at least twenty-five lives. Old-timers remember that he was intimate with the Tewksburys. Tom maintained that he was deputy sheriff and "the county coroner begged me to let up until he could catch up on his work." Later, near Willcox, Arizona, Tom said that he killed five train robbers for Bucky O'Neill, sheriff of Yavapai County. He claimed also to have arrested for Bucky many outlaws and bad Indians, whose tribal ways and trails he knew so well. Boasting about killings was Tom's stock in trade when he recounted these escapades. How many men, red and white, Tom killed in Arizona will never be known definitely.

Tom enjoyed a peace officer's work, but there was not enough of it. Between jobs he rode and roped for prizes in Fourth of July "Stampedes." At Phoenix, Arizona, he roped and tied his steer in forty-nine and a half seconds, the world's record. Fifty years later any respectable contestant could do the trick in half that time, but in the late eighties Tom's record was regarded with awe. From rodeo to rodeo went Tom, plagued by only one serious rival—Charlie Meadows, a cowboy whom Tom and his snake-heads had found seven years before, apparently dying, beside burning cabins during an Apache raid. Now Charlie had recovered amazingly. To one of the roping duels came Colonel William F. Cody, hunting talent for "Buffalo Bill's Wild West Show and Congress of Rough Riders." He offered both men handsome salaries to join him. Charlie Meadows accepted and spent years basking in the bright glances of audiences across America and Europe. Tom Horn declined; a Wild West show was only pretense. Tom liked reality. He was no "play actor"; no professional entertainer. He wanted to do things, associate with prominent men and be important to them.

Tom was now in his thirtieth year, with more fame than fortune. He was dissatisfied. It did not suit an ambitious and frugal Pennsylvania German to have to spend his uncertain money as fast as it was made. He wondered what to do, and, while wondering, he met a man who changed the course of his life.

"Doc" Shores, sheriff of Gunnison County, Colorado, had come south looking for a horse thief. Doc was tall and spare with piercing gray eyes. He made money on the side by working for the Pinkerton Detective Agency and, as he looked into Tom's strong dark eyes, he saw the making of a "Pink." Tom had been recommended to Shores as a man who might help him catch the thief he was after. Doc described the fugitive and Tom speedily brought him in. The three men traveled back to Colorado together. Tom and Doc became good friends. They discovered that they were both Democrats. Doc suggested introducing Tom to the Pinkerton superintendent in Denver. James S. McParlan, Doc explained, was the same notable who had spent years gaining the confidence of the leaders of the coal-mining outlaws, the "Molly Maguires," and then brought them to justice. Tom learned that this great detective agency protected the mines, railroads and express companies from labor-union strikers and yeggmen, much as the Army protected the same interests in Arizona from the Apaches. He thought he would like to work for it. In Denver Tom Horn met McParlan. The chief put him on the pay roll and sent him to Salem, Oregon, to get information concerning robbers who had wrecked and pilfered a train—a beginner's case.

Tom rode west on the train, memorizing all the instructions given a new operative. He must always look for a "catch." He might catch a railroad conductor accepting cash instead of tickets; he might catch another Pinkerton man in dereliction of duty. He must mingle with gambling-house crowds. Robbers liked games of chance. Moreover, the man he was after, one Jim McCabe, was reported to be a tinhorn—an itinerant gambler who could not afford a first-rate layout and shook dice in a tin cup or horn. McParlan had suggested that Tom assume the guise of a tinhorn himself, tour the far western fleshpots and try to make a "professional" friendship with the fugitive. Tom understood gambling tricks. In Apache monte games he had learned that the hand was quicker than the eye. On the reservations, too, he and Sieber had mingled with the Indians, learned their murderous designs and warned the whites. Pinkerton work was like old times.

Tom Horn, the border wolf in sheep's clothing, hunted McCabe through 'Frisco—where cowboys called the Barbary Coast the "Barbwire Coast"—Truckee, and finally Reno. In this Nevada town Tom unpacked his clothes in Mrs. Needham's lodginghouse, then set out systematically to visit each saloon. He found no sign of his man and returned to his room to write his daily letter to J. S. Mack in Denver— Mack being McParlan's alias for his correspondents. Tom's letter was long. He revealed himself more of a literary man than a detective. McCabe, he wrote, was not in Reno, but in his opinion there was a man in town who was nothing short of being a real bootlegger hanging out at O'Keefe's saloon, a man with "a rum-blossom and a porous face."

McParlan did not want the whisky-runner, and he did want Tom to move on after bigger game. But before he could send Tom new orders, word came to him that Horn was arrested. This ironic fate had come to the budding detective on the very night that he had written his "rum-blossom" letter, the night of April 9, 1891.

Tom's explanation to his boss later was simple and innocent. He said that he had walked to the post office, dropped the letter and started back to his room. On the return trip he had heard the whistle of a leisurely locomotive preparing to leave town, and decided to depart at once to hunt McCabe at stations down the line. Timing his arrival at the depot very carefully, Tom swung on the train just as the conductor called "All aboard!" This would let the trainmen see that he had no time to purchase a ticket, and it might open the way to bribery and a "catch" for Tom.

Horn sank down on the red-plush cushions, but the train did not start. Instead, four men wearing stars came down the aisle, to press pistols against Tom's head and handcuffs on his hands. Tom asked for an explanation. A constable made the cryptic response, "Al White's a square shooter. Give him back the money, and he won't push the case."

Tom replied that he knew of neither a case nor Al White, but that he would square it if they'd give him a chance. Arriving at the jail, Tom heard what had provoked his arrest.

Half an hour earlier James Conroy and Tim Pollard had been preparing their gambling games in Al White's Palace Hotel. Six hundred dollars in currency was on display to tempt rural lovers of chance. As yet the room had been empty of players, and the drowsiness of a summer night hung over the two professionals as they practiced faro. Conroy dealt. He called each card in a monotone while Pollard kept the rhythm by flicking the beads in his case.

Through the dark doorway they could see the yellow windows of the eastbound train standing at the station. It was changing engines.

"Hands up!" Two masked men stood at the door. "Hands up, quick! Stop that fiddling with the cards, or I'll scatter your brains over the wallpaper." Pollard and Conroy looked at Colt revolvers whose hammers were racked back like snakes ready to strike. The gambling men reached for the ceiling and stood so while the masked men began putting the money in a valise.

Outside they could hear the life of Reno going on as before—men and women and children hurrying down to the train, telling one another good-by, "Be sure to write! Now don't forget."

The robbers backed to the door and were gone. Conroy and Pollard stared at each other.

Placid voices were coming from around the cars, "Bring Mary back with you," "Tell Fred, Lucy says 'nit.' "

Conroy and Pollard had never sheared a cowboy with quicker precision. The silence of Al White's faro room was broken by voices pattering like rain. They called Al White. They called the sheriff. They called the night marshal. Guests at the Palace and bystanders stamped through the empty room explaining just how it had happened. Somebody said he heard a woman scream down the tracks. A few enthusiasts started to run in that direction. A small boy selling 'Frisco papers yelled, "Rubber!" The enthusiasts came back. Several people had seen a tall man run past the Palace to the station. With this information, the officers searched the train and arrested Tom Horn who, as we have seen, pleaded his innocence, but they took him to the justice's court.

The marshal found suspicious articles on Tom, and submitted the evidence to the justice. First, he carried a .45 Colt revolver similar to the ones cowboys carried. Then he had a pocket diary with train times and conductors' and brakemen's names in it. Also he had three hundred dollars in cash—half the sum taken in the holdup. These articles were material but not necessarily incriminating. The thing that mystified and upset the court was the unaccountable presence of several different-sized buttons in the prisoner's vest pocket. Tom's explanation of these buttons was inarticulate. His desire to keep them out of sight and not be questioned about them obviously showed much guilt, so he was put in jail.

The justice of the peace asked Tom when he would be ready for examination. Tom replied, "The sooner, the better." The case was set for April 11, 1891. Tom Horn employed Attorney J. L. Wines to defend him, and Wines, after the fashion of lawyers, asked to have the case put off for a week. This was one of the longest weeks in Tom's life. It was not until July 14 that Tom appeared before the district court for trial. Doc Shores and McParlan came out from Denver. Doc had been apologizing to Mack for three months. An operative's duty was to put other people in jail, not to get in jail himself.

Loafers who dropped into court for entertainment found the first forenoon wasted selecting jurors. At one o'clock District Attorney Julien opened the case formally by drawing a diagram of Al White's faro room on the blackboard, and telling the jury what he expected to prove. Tim Pollard, the case keeper, was the first witness called by the prosecution. He testified that he *thought* he recognized Tom Horn as one of the men who committed the robbery. James Conroy testified *without hesitation* that Tom Horn *was* the guilty man. This identification, the fact that Tom's three hundred dollars was half the sum that had been taken from the gamblers, and the buttons in his pocket made the case look bad for him.

To help the prosecution, the Honorable William Woodburn offered his services. Tom watched him blandly. Woodburn was an orator, more concerned with his political future than with individual justice. Tom noticed that the case was nothing more than a sparring of local wits, with attorneys' reputations at stake. Neither attorney was really trying to give him justice. They were trying to establish who was the cleverer lawyer. To Tom's way of thinking

kangaroo courts were based on justice, while civil courts were based
only on trickery.

Mr. Woodburn's strongest argument for conviction was Tom
Horn's pocket diary. It showed that he was spying on railroad men,
and there were several railroad men on the jury. With didactic and
rampant oratory, Woodburn extolled the high moral character of
his constituents, the ranchmen, miners and cowboys of the western
country, hoping the "day would come when he could write with the
golden pencil of justice in the clear blue above them all, the names
of such heroes, patriots, and philanthropists." This oratory may
have brought·him votes at the next election. It almost convicted
Tom Horn. The Honorable William Woodburn seemed to forget
that legal convictions should be based on evidence of guilt. He
seemed to want Tom Horn sentenced because he was a Pinkerton
operative, one who had "entered upon legalized association with the
criminal element." The fact that Horn left town by walking boldly
down the street, Woodburn roared, was in itself an incriminating act,
in conformity with the actions of a man brazen enough to hold up
Al White's faro parlor.

Lieutenant John M. Neall of the 4th United States Cavalry was
brought into court to testify for Horn. He stated that he had known
Tom since 1885 when he was chief of scouts in Arizona. He had
always considered him a man of sterling reputation and had never
heard anything against his honesty and integrity.

Tom himself testified that he had been engaged in Arizona in
various capacities from bronco rider to chief of scouts, and that he
had gone to work for Pinkerton's National Detective Agency in
Denver in 1890. Tom had had over three months to think out an
explanation for the buttons and testified that he was a bachelor and
carried them to sew on his clothes. Such a palpable lie made the
Honorable William Woodburn guffaw. Tom testified further that
he was worth from twenty-five hundred to three thousand dollars in
real estate and horses, and had a good job, so there was no immediate motive for him to hold up a faro bank.

After four days of this, the judge charged the jury to find an honest verdict in the "tangled mazes of legal equivocations and eloquence." Six of the jurors found Tom Horn guilty, and six found him innocent. His Honor granted a new trial at the next term of court. So ended the first four months.

In September the case was tried again by the same attorneys. Tom Horn had additional defense in the form of a letter from General Nelson A. Miles, citing him for bravery and good character. On the afternoon of the fourth day the case was given to the jury, who returned in seven minutes with a verdict of "Not guilty." Tom was a free man again but he had missed the night train by just six months.

These six unpleasant months made a long groove in Tom's character. They made him ashamed of his connection with Pinkerton's. Was he the sneak some of the first jury and the Honorable William Woodburn thought him? They also made him confident that his military record would get him out of trouble. They taught him, too, the tedious processes of the law courts. Tom began to watch the injustice of involved justice. He noticed that in nine cases out of ten to win at law was to lose, or, as he stated it, "In a suit over a pail of milk the law gets the cow." The long six months taught him another lesson: not to carry buttons. They had "worked" among the Apaches. Here was a new civilization.

Some people in Reno still believed him guilty of the holdup in spite of the fact that twelve men had agreed that there was not enough evidence to convict him. His guilt or innocence did not matter. There was only one thing that mattered to the future of Tom Horn. He saw that these civil courts, like courts-martial, might scold and reprimand, even as his mother had when he was a little boy, only to turn him loose in the end.

12

THE D & R G TRAIN ROBBERY

WHILE McParlan was worrying about getting Tom out of the clutches of the Nevada authorities, a train was held up on the Denver & Rio Grande Railroad in Colorado, near what was known as the Royal Gorge, where Tom and the Quantrill men had fought for the railroad's right of way. Here was a trailing job through the rocks and cedars. McParlan knew that Tom had been an expert trailing Apaches in Arizona, so he turned to his new operative, who, so far, had succeeded in getting nothing but arrested.

With this new commission Tom climbed off the train near the scene of the crime, hired a horse and inspected the trampled sand and cinders along the tracks. He rode in large circles, only to find that the assembled sheriffs had ridden earlier in larger circles. Bloodhounds had proved worthless in the hot sand of early September. Tom was arrested twice in the first two days. He said, "To hell wid 'em," and bought a ticket for Denver. He had failed again.

Doc Shores arrived a little later to take over Pinkerton's campaign against the fugitives, and he asked for the help of the disgraced Tom Horn. So, for the last time, Doc Shores saved Tom from sinking back into the precarious monotony of rodeos and county fairs.

It was now over a week since the holdup, and Doc's first lesson to his hitherto backward pupil was to assemble all the known facts in the case like a true detective, before blundering off down the trail. Shores took Tom to the railroad track at the scene of the crime. Both men noticed that there was a ranch house on the cobble-rock river bottom in plain sight of the robbery. The canyon wall towered above this cabin, allowing but a few hours of sunlight every day.

The smoke from the trains had stained the bluffs and the log house. It was a gloomy scene for crime and poverty.

"It is strange for robbers to hold up a train in sight of a ranch house," said Shores, "unless they stood in with the ranchers." Both men were silent for a moment. Then Doc suggested that they go up to the nearest town, Cotopaxi. The two men put their horses in the livery barn and sauntered over to the grocery store. Loafers slid down from their seats on the counter. Doc and Tom talked to them. One was garrulous, said that the ranch house in sight of the holdup belonged to a man named Dick McCoy—quite a character. A term of court never "set" without Dick McCoy being brought to trial for cattle stealing. He was a Quantrill man from Missouri—Tom became interested—with four sons and two daughters, all night riders but one, and that one, Charles, "run the saloon yender." "Yessir, they do tell, that his ma taunted him onct f'r not butcherin' a neighbor's beef. 'Be a McCoy,' sez she, 'be a McCoy.'"

Doc Shores asked if Dick McCoy could have held up the train recently. "Nope," he was told. "Ol' Dick's in jail down in Canon City. He murdered a stock detective that come to ketch him. Joe, his boy, was throwed in with him f'r helpin' in the murder. Joe broke jail. He's out."

Doc Shores strolled out of the store. Tom followed. The two long-legged men walked over to the railroad depot. "Canon City's only thirty miles from the scene of the holdup," Tom said. "Do you reckon Joe done it?"

Doc pushed his broadbrim hat back on his head. "I don't know. Let's go up to Salida and ask some more questions." The two men bought tickets to the near-by division town. In Salida, Tom watched Shores question the engineer, the fireman and some of the frightened passengers who had peeped at the holdup men shooting along the length of the train. The leader, all witnesses agreed, had a peg leg. He could not have been Joe McCoy. Another of the robbers had worn a derby hat; a third was a gangling willow of a boy with a weather-worn cowboy hat drooping over his face. There was also a woman present, wearing a calico dress whose bottom frill swept the cinders.

Doc Shores led Tom back to Cotopaxi. "A feller must go slow," he said. Tom trailed after him patiently as he had trailed after Sieber. The two men went back to the store. The garrulous fellow was no longer there, but the storekeeper met them on the stoop and offered to talk, "now them fellers is gone." From him the detectives learned that two prisoners recently liberated from the state penitentiary at Canon City had "throwed in" with the McCoys. One of them was a city criminal with a weak pasty face—a whimpering, reforming, backsliding fellow eternally promising to be good. He liked the ladies, wore a celluloid collar, and was conspicuous for his derby hat that bobbed among the sombreros of his cowboy friends. Curtis was his name. The other of the two liberated prisoners was Peg Leg Watson, a powerfully built man, a good horseman in spite of his missing member, and a social fellow who graced every set at the community dance, "bowed to his partner," "chased the squirrel," "balanced all," and pointed his peg leg with consummate grace.

Without doubt these two were in the holdup. The gangling willow of a kid with the floppy hat who had been seen in the gang sounded like young Tom McCoy. The store man said that both Peg Leg and Curtis had disappeared since the robbery. Tom McCoy was still on the ranch.

Shores beckoned Horn with his head and the two walked away. "Peg Leg, Curtis and Joe McCoy are over there," Shores said in a low voice, nodding his head toward the red rocks and cedars south of the tracks, the foothills of the Sangre de Cristo Mountains, a country rougher and more volcano-tossed than any country Tom Horn had ever seen in Arizona. "The kid's taking them messages and supplies. Let's give him an examination."

The two men went to the livery barn, got their horses and rode down the Arkansas toward the McCoy ranch. They inspected their rifles as the horses shuffled along. On the way they met Tom McCoy. They told him he was under arrest and must go back to town with them. Young Tom assented and came with them readily enough. The road led across a ford in the river, now very low in the late fall. The three horsemen splashed into the water. Young McCoy's horse dropped behind, sniffing the surface of the rock-ruffled stream as he stepped gingerly. The boy's captors, picking their own way among the submerged boulders ahead, forgot him for a moment. The boy suddenly jerked his horse around and, with a great splash of water, regained the bank and raced away down the canyon road. The officers, separated from him by the width of the treacherous water, knew that by the time they retraced the laborious ford pursuit would be hopeless.

Tom pointed his rifle at the fleeing horseman.

"Don't shoot," Doc Shores commanded. "We'll get him later." The two men rode off empty-handed. For a week they called at the ranch for young Tom, but he was never at home. Like his father in the good old Quantrill days, he kept a horse saddled in the barn night and day.

The detectives decided that their only chance of surprising the boy at home was to search the house just before daybreak, the one hour in twenty-four when human vitality and watchfulness are at lowest ebb. Capturing dangerous characters at this sleepy time was a professional rule which both men understood. They tried it.

The house was still as death in the ghastly light. Tom Horn stood on guard outside. Doc climbed in an open window and pounced on the boy in his bed. Out came Doc like a giant staghound dragging an unwilling jack rabbit. The two men shook the boy, threatened him, asked him questions. They learned that the calico skirt that had swept the cinders at the holdup had been worn by a certain Minnie, daughter-in-law of a member of the James gang who had accompanied Jesse to Leadville in the same rush for wealth that had attracted young Tom. When Jesse James had returned to Missouri, Minnie's father-in-law had remained as a settler in the mountains.

Further inquiry showed Minnie to be still living in her cabin south of the Arkansas. This clue promised great disclosures. Both Tom and Doc knew that even the worst desperadoes were apt to throw off all caution in their hunger for their sweethearts. The detectives decided to test the old rule on the following night with another stealthy surprise. One of the robbers was certainly Minnie's husband or lover.

It was Doc Shores's turn to stand guard outside this time, and Tom Horn stepped into the cabin. He flashed on his bull's-eye, a small oil lamp behind a powerful lens, used by night prowlers. The circle of light illuminated two blinking figures "settin' up" together. One was Minnie, and the other was a popular and thoroughly respected young man of the community, who certainly was not implicated in the robbery.

Tom had proved himself a ridiculous detective once more. This time nobody but Doc Shores knew, and he himself was also implicated. The two men left the neighborhood as quickly and as quietly as they could. They went south down the San Luis Valley, circling the entire Sangre de Cristo range in which they believed the fugitives to be hiding. At the little town of La Veta on the Denver and Rio Grande Railroad, Doc Shores was acquainted with a man named Frank Owenby who kept a curio store for tourists, operated a moonshine still in the Sangre de Cristo Mountains, and did a little detective work for the railroad. Frank Owenby had killed Marshal Desmond in Pueblo. He displayed in a glass case the gun that he had used, along with miniature canoes, imitation Navaho blankets and silver jewelry for sale. Shores suggested to Tom that they pay Owenby a visit. He might know if the thieves had broken cover in his neighborhood.

The two detectives went into the curio store, stooping a little under the low door. Owenby was cordial; said he knew two men, "Black Bill" Kelley and another range character, who had recently found the robbers' camp in a deep wash near Trinidad. Doc Shores's steel-gray eyes snapped. He offered Owenby part of the reward in case a capture was made. The three men set off to interview Black Bill. In a Trinidad brothel both men were found. They corroborated the story, displayed some false whiskers that they claimed to have found in the robbers' camp, and suggested a small down payment on the reward. This sounded like a frame-up. Owenby and Shores got tough. They called Black Bill and his hangdog companion liars. Both protested and stuck to their story. Owenby and Shores seized them by the collars, loaded them into a buckboard and drove out of town. Tom went along, a willing pupil. Here was a new wrinkle in chasing criminals. Out on the plains Shores told the prisoners that they would be killed if their clue proved false.

Darkness fell before the men reached the alleged camp site. They built a fire and dozed around it. During the night Bill's sheepish companion escaped—never to return. In the morning Black Bill wandered up and down a wash, said it looked familiar, and tried to find the mythical camp.

On the rim, Tom, Doc and Owenby sat in the buckboard. They watched Black Bill in the gully trying to make his dreams come true. Horn and Shores teased Owenby about how gullible he had been. Owenby suggested that they kill Black Bill then and there. Tom knew that Al Sieber would have dealt out justice in this manner, but now there was no United States Army to protect an executioner. He demurred, saying, "Before we do it, let's fix up a good story for the coroner's jury." Shores chuckled and drove away with his companions. Black Bill in the wash was glad enough to scamper away with his life.

Frank Owenby, disgraced with his railway friends, retired to the solace of his still in the Blood of Christ Mountains. Doc and Tom went back to Denver. On the train Shores studied the man beside him on the red-plush seat. Tom Horn seemed too quick on the trigger, always overly anxious to shoot, both at the McCoy kid and at Black Bill. His courage was unquestionable, but for a Pinkerton he bore watching.

The train pulled into Denver at last. The two long-legged men strode up Seventeenth Street toward the office. Doc bought a newspaper. A glaring headline caught his eye. The robbers had broken cover down the trail where Black Bill had pretended to see them. The local sheriff had pursued them with a posse. The outlaws saw him coming, hid in a wash, captured the posse when it came up, took all the men's guns and tobacco, and sent them back empty-handed to Trinidad. Doc Shores stuffed the paper in the side pocket of his coat. "Let's get back quick," he said. Neither he nor Tom wanted to meet Superintendent McParlan.

Shores and Horn found the trail in southeast Colorado. Their chase lasted forty-three days—almost as long as the final pursuit of Geronimo—but this pursuit ranked larger in Tom's destiny, for it ended his friendship with Doc Shores. Doc had found Tom full of nerve and witty stories, good company for an afternoon. Now he discovered that on a long trip Tom was moody and at times quarrelsome. He always wanted his own way, was hard to please and took the best of everything. Doc never asked for Tom on another trip. This would have ended Tom's employment with Pinkerton had not the trip been a success. The two officers caught Peg Leg and Curtis at last in the Indian Territory, and Tom's reputation as a successful operative was established.

13

THE EYE THAT NEVER SLEEPS

WITH one friendship ended on account of his bad disposition, Tom now set out on a trip with men who stated forty years later that he was a companion who entertained them all on a hundred-and-twenty-mile horseback ride, never complained and was always in a good humor.

Tom had come back to Colorado on the railroad train handcuffed to Peg Leg Watson. His prisoner told him that the D & R G train had been held up to get money to hire McCoy's attorneys, Macon & Sons of Canon City, to appeal his case to the Supreme Court. Tom also learned that Joe McCoy had not been a member of the holdup gang, but could be found hiding near the town of Meeker in the northwestern corner of the state. Tom reported the information to McParlan in Denver and was given the case. He boarded the train for Rifle, Colorado, with Sheriff Stewart of Fremont County, where Joe was wanted. Winter had come, with bitter cold, in the high Rockies. At Rifle the Meeker stage left before daylight for the forty-five-mile trip north, taking ten hours with three changes of horses. The thermometer registered thirty below zero. Horn and Stewart shivered in the gloom. A brightly lighted saloon attracted them. Each bought a bottle for the trip. The four-horse Concord stage—one of the last to be used in America—pulled up in front of the hotel. The passengers got in, wrapped themselves in buffalo robes and away they went, the hard snow squeaking under the wheels. Cold cheerless daylight came as the stage crawled up the southern slope of the Divide. At noon the travelers stopped, stiff and cold, at a ranch house for a hot dinner of boiled beef, potatoes, gravy and coffee. Tom noticed the stage driver watching him curiously. He saw something familiar about the man himself but he could not place the face. Then it all came back to him. The driver was Fay Gorham, the man who had hauled him over Mosquito Pass into Leadville thirteen years before—so long ago it seemed like another world.

After dinner Fay climbed up on his box again. The passengers with their bottles got in the coach and the stage crunched off. Darkness came long before the stage stopped at the brilliantly lighted windows of the Meeker Hotel. Tom and Stewart, numb, cold and smelling of whisky, stumbled into the lobby. The proprietor of the hotel met them. She was a charming woman with well-cared-for but irregular teeth, a wry mouth and an elfin smile that melted the hearts of traveling men. She was slim, aristocratic, and spoke with a Southern accent. Rolling the cigar from one corner of her mouth to the other she handed the pen to her guests. Tom felt tipsy and facetious. He had lived in Arizona long enough to acquire a Southern accent himself. Taking the pen in his hand he stooped over the register and signed in the weak trembling hand of a man unused to writing: "T. Hone."

"That's the correct way to sign and pronounce my name," said the tall man, laughing.

"You'll find your rooms up those stairs and down the second hall to the left," the landlady smiled. "A fire is laid up in the little stove in each room. Touch a match to it and it will take the chill off in a jiffy."

Next morning Tom and Stewart hunted up the Meeker sheriff, and explained their mission. A deputy, Sam Wear, was summoned. Sam ran a butcher shop in town and raised thoroughbred horses. He "recollected" that a cowpuncher answering the description of Joe McCoy had been in the county but he had recently crossed the state line to celebrate the Christmas holidays in Vernal, Utah, "near a hundred and fifty mile away." No stage line connected Meeker and Vernal. The detectives employed Wear to guide them on his thoroughbreds. Tom had been on many hard rides in Arizona but none that promised the hardship of this winter trip across the glittering foothills of the Rockies. The hotel woman waved good-by from behind her broad front windows. Tom said to his companions, "We must bring Joe back this way. By God, I'd like to 'brace that skirt."

Had Tom but known it, he was in the second depression of a highly adventurous life. His livery-stable experience had been the preface to his large activities as scout. So now his dull Pinkerton experiences were the step that led to the achievements that made him really famous. As is so often the case, Tom did not realize that his present occupation was a sluggish backwater in his colorful career. Certainly when he stepped into the kitchen of the White River Ranch, twenty miles west of Meeker, stamping the snow from his feet and towering a head taller than all the lank cowboys, his face showed more the marks of success and self-satisfaction than the uncertain questioning of a man trying to find himself. Tom was wearing a United States marshal's star. He had reached the position of Bat Masterson, Wyatt Earp and Wild Bill Hickok. He was wearing the badge of the rulers the boy Tom had been taught to respect at the northern end of the Chisholm Trail. Neither he nor the men who ate supper with him on the oilcloth in the lamplighted dining room realized the eminence and the tragedy that lay so close at hand.

The cold moderated at sundown. A warm winter night followed. Water dripped from the dirt roof, making gutters of slush around the log buildings. The sinister sound annoyed the outdoor men. They slept restlessly. In the morning a warm sun rose in a sky so blue that it was almost a threatening purple. The three horsemen rode out of the gate and headed west. A black cloud was mounting high in the sky. They picked their way across the snow-covered desert where white, sharp-edged buttes appeared to float like icebergs in an arctic ocean. The glittering whiteness silhouetted against the blackening sky made a contrast that hurt the riders' eyes. The unnatural heat made them open their sheepskin-lined coats and their skin prickled.

The storm broke in the afternoon and raged with stinging fury.

Goylothay, Apache medicine man. Mexicans called him Geronimo for St. Jerome, the orator.

Courtesy of the Arizona Pioneers' Historical Society

Council between Crook and Geronimo in the lava beds in Cañon de los Embudos, March 1886. Messrs. Fly and Chase, photographers from Tombstone, came down with the soldiers to take this picture. Lieut. Samson Faison, Capt. Cyrus Roberts, Geronimo, Nana, Capt. Maus, Lieut. Shipp, Capt. Bourke, General Crook, Charles Roberts (ten years old).

The men rattled their feet in the stirrups to keep them from freezing. They put their gloved hands under their saddle blankets. Snow clotted in the horses' manes and tails. The men kept the animals headed into the storm with difficulty. Stewart teased Tom about returning across such a frigid world to keep his rendezvous with the "old girl," but Tom was undaunted—get Joe first, then have a little fun.

The men crossed the state line at the K Ranch. The ranch owner, they learned, was in Salt Lake City visiting his family. The ranch foreman asked them to spend the night and they did so. He was a remarkably frugal man known throughout the country for his western hospitality. A visitor was always welcome here to the best that the ranch afforded and was never charged for the accommodation, but the foreman always managed to steal the price of his guest's bed and board before time to depart.

In the morning the storm had abated and a sharp cold tingled in the western air. The sun rose between opalescent rainbows of frost crystals, and the horsemen continued their lonely way across the great desert country of Utah. There was only one house between the K Ranch and Green River. This ranch was owned by the Royle brothers and was the scene of the writing of a famous play, *The Squaw-Man*.

The riders crossed Green River on the ice and climbed up the butter-colored bank to a riverside tavern, a rambling log house. It was Ma Jensen's, a place accustomed to violence. Fifteen more miles would put the detectives in Vernal where Joe was reputed to be "celebrating." The travelers decided to stop, feed themselves and their horses and get warm.

After dinner Tom smoked and listened to yarns about the ferry that ran in summer at the foot of the front yard. The ferryman liked to tell how a Mormon and his wives had ridden a log across the river just below the landing. It had happened recently when, with Utah's proposed admission to statehood, United States marshals had hunted out all the polygamous Saints who had defied the law forbidding plural marriages. One of these much-married ranchers lived not far from the ferry—a man excessively chivalrous and grandiose. With his flaring mustache, goatee and wide flat hat, the ferryman said that he seemed more Virginia planter than western cowman.

One day the chivalrous fellow heard that the marshals were coming for him. He gathered his wives together and hurried for the ferry, attempting the impossible task of presenting two arms to three ladies. Dignity disappeared momentarily when he discovered the ferry on the opposite side of the stream and the marshals whipping in his rear. Quickly he seized an old cottonwood log, mounted his wives upon it and shoved off, paddling from a seat in the rear. Under their wide skirts, the three women kicked stoutly and the log came to midstream.

There the eddies of Green River swirled like knives, for the water was cut by currents so strong as to become, in reality, rivers within rivers, some back currents racing upstream for a quarter of a mile or more. One of these eddies snapped the cottonwood log in two and carried upstream that half upon which sat two of the Mormon's wives, while the cavalier and his remaining mate drifted downstream. As the bereft pair of wives, screaming inside their sunbonnets, were swept around a bend in the river, out of his life, the husband lifted his magnificent hat in courtly adieu and, trying to bow low, nearly fell into the river. Old Green River had done what the United States government could not do. It had made him monogamous.

Filled with such tales and dinner, Tom and the officers remounted for the half-day's ride to Vernal. They arrived in the dark, hunted up the local officers and learned that Joe McCoy was in town. He ate his meals at Mrs. Colthorp's. The detectives explained that he was a bad man, wanted for murder. The Utah sheriff offered to help make the arrest in the morning. Tom and Stewart went to bed. Vernal was a small town. They hoped that nobody had noticed them put their horses in the barn.

Next morning the officers surrounded Colthorp's log house at breakfast time. Tom Horn opened the door to the living room, strode through the parlor bric-a-brac, burst into the family dining room and said, "Joe, we have come!"

The murderer surrendered without a struggle.

Another storm was threatening. There was a shorter way back to the railroad than by Meeker, and Tom never saw the "hotel lady" again. Whatever Tom's personal opinion of his prowess with women might be, it is certain that he made no impression on this one. When he became famous she remembered him only as a name on her register. The woman with the elfin smile could recall nothing more definite about his personality than she could about another traveler in northwestern Colorado who was also to become famous. This young man had come to study the gold content in desert sand. He signed his name "Herbert Hoover."

Tom and Stewart hired a livery rig, and with Joe in irons drove fast to Fort Duchesne. The 10th Cavalry was on duty there. Tom was among old friends in new surroundings. In the North, he learned, the Indians called Negro troopers "buffalo soldiers" on account of their hair. He asked for Lieutenant Shipp, the dashing cavalier commander when Captain Crawford was killed and Maus was held a prisoner. Shipp, now a first lieutenant, was not at the post, Tom was told.

The storm still threatened, so Tom took no time to renew other old acquaintances. The peace officers hurried on their way toward the top of the Book Cliff, the great southern wall of the basin that rimmed them in. The cliff derived its name from the shale bedrock which at all outcroppings broke in rectangular blocks like books—quarto, octavo, duodecimo. On the Divide, the next day, where the snow packed solid between the carriage spokes, the men looked south over the great warm desert, thousands of feet below. Thirty miles away they could see a puff of smoke: the railway that would take them back to civilization.

The road down the escarpment was steep. Flat rocks shaped like textbooks, dictionaries and dime novels littered the narrow way. In short order the country changed from arctic mountains to temperate desert. The men took off their hats and knocked the snow from the broad brims onto bare ground. At nightfall they spied a ranch and stopped. The cowboys, recently back from town, all had bottles.

The newcomers were invited to drink. Soon all the men began to love one another, but nobody loved Joe McCoy well enough to unsnap his handcuffs.

The next day the officers and their prisoner arrived at the railroad and soon Tom was back in Denver. In four months he had changed from the most-often-arrested of greenhorn detectives to an astute operative.

Superintendent McParlan could not offer the captor of Joe McCoy another trailing job at once, but he did not let Tom go, as Miles had done, as soon as he had made good. McParlan told Tom to mark time at the easy monotony of the "hobo act" until something more interesting developed.

Tom had learned to hide his ignorance of the new civilization. He knew better than to ask the meaning of the "hobo act." Instead he talked with other operatives around the office, learning as a true detective should, without giving himself away. In time he discovered that the act consisted of traveling railroads in the guise of a tramp to discover frauds among trainmen. Tom had noticed that a freight train in the mountains usually contained about fifteen cars. Twenty-five was considered the limit but a train of such proportions was dangerous. The only way that brakes might be applied to the cars was for men to run along the tops of the cars and set them by hand. Each "brakie" was in charge of a certain number of cars and he often claimed privileges that the company did not approve. The brakemen insisted that they had the right to collect fares from hobos, and, when the railroad executives forbade the custom, they persisted on the sly. The Pinkerton men made it part of their business to help enforce the executives' order, to protect the railroads in this minute detail. And this detail was not always so minute. Sometimes a brakeman walking his reeling cars, hunting a hobo, slipped and fell among the roadside cinders. Occasionally a hobo snatched the pick handle which a brakeman carried to turn his brakes, refused to pay and knocked the brakeman into the roaring night. In any case the injured trainman or his family claimed that he had been hurt in line of duty, and forced the company to pay indemnity for his mangled body.

Tom put on a suit of old clothes and set off to do the hobo act. Outside the railroad yards he met some hobos. He sat around their fire chatting with them. Hobos were about as poor as the Apaches. Their living standard in an industrial civilization was about the same as the Indians' in a rural one. Tom gossiped and told stories with them as he and Sieber had done with the Apaches. In the distance a train whistled. The hobos scattered along the tracks, hiding behind tie piles and clumps of bushes. Tom crouched down beside one of his new friends. The locomotive labored up the grade, belching sparks in a great cloud of smoke. She passed. Tom with his companion darted from their hiding place, ran along with the rocking cars, grabbed the first "hand holts" that passed and swung aboard. Out of sight between the cars they rested and talked. Tom learned a new lingo. Hobo transportation was divided into three classes: "laying down," "setting down," and "standing up," with various subclassifications and a separate name for each. Of the first class, Tom learned that caboose travel was the most luxurious and therefore the most expensive. To lie upon the caboose cushions meant that a conductor must be bribed, while to rest on "the rods," those iron bars beneath a car, required paying tribute to a mere brakeman. Often a hobo on the rods could escape a trainman's notice altogether and even when spied he could not be reached by the open palm so long as the train was running. Comfortable as the accommodation seemed, Tom was warned to be wary of the rods. A brakeman or "shack," as he was called, might dislodge and kill a man on the rods if he suspected him of being a Pink doing the hobo act. All the trainmen had to do was to let down a coupling pin on a chain and allow the iron club to churn around between the flying ties and the car bottom until it knocked the helpless detective under the wheels.

Tom learned that "laying-down" transportation could be had in "gondolas"—open-top coal cars—but on bitter nights the stars and the cinder-laden smoke were poor covering for a man. Sheep cars were the best "laying-down" transportation excepting only the caboose. Always there was a little window at the top through which a man could climb. The disadvantage of this accommodation lay in its excessive warmth, for when a hobo emerged he usually caught cold. The "bumpers" and "blind baggage" were warmer and safer than the rods but on them a man could not lie down and was, indeed, better off standing up at all times. Later, when these refuges were altered, the professional hobos felt themselves persecuted by distant rich men in Wall Street. No wonder they sang:

> "Jay Gould's daughter said before she died,
> 'Father, fix the "blinds" so the bums can't ride.
> If ride they must, let 'em ride the "rods"
> And put their troubles in the hands of God.' "

Tom Horn was one of the last Pinkertons to play the hobo act, for soon the air brake's arrival made it unnecessary for a brakeman to spend any of his time on top of the moving cars. The trains grew longer, with more slack and jerk. "Walking the decks" became excessively dangerous, and railroad companies ceased to be liable for employees who were injured by falls from the moving car tops. Hunting hobos could no longer be disguised as a brakeman's line of duty and the detectives stopped watching so zealously for bribe-takers. Eventually the rods were removed and Jay Gould's daughter presumably rested easy in her grave.

The caboose, as Tom learned, was the drawing room of a freight train and here he liked to ride while doing the hobo act. For hours at a time he slept, lulled by the squeaking of the hooks that held up the slat bunks. Now and then during the night there would be a gust of air as a brakeman opened the door. Tom could hear the *chuckety-chuck* of the passing rail ends, like the brisk gallop of a horse; he could open his eyes and see through the rear window the moonlit mountains passing. He would look at the conductor sitting under a kerosene lamp at his desk, and think how angry he would be to discover weeks later that he had taken money from a Pink and earned his discharge.

Sometimes the train would stop with a jerk that piled Tom against the stove. At other times the train stalled and swearing brakies flashed lanterns in his sleepy eyes and rummaged under the bunks asking for "the emergency" or "the simplex."

"If that goddam engineer had to walk sixteen cars on a cold night with a coupling knuckle on his shoulder, he would start his train easy instead of pulling out a drawhead by wracking her tail all the way back and trying to jump a car length."

During the winter Tom turned in a conductor on the Oregon Short Line. Tom's report showed that the fellow had taken money. The conductor was called on the carpet. He said that no such man as Tom Horn had ever ridden with him. The officials wondered and wired the Pinkerton office: Send Horn to Ogden. Let him identify the guilty conductor.

Horn came. His professional honor was at stake. The railroad superintendent took him into a room full of conductors and brakemen waiting for him. Tom walked down the line looking into many hard eyes. Presently he stuck out his hand. "How are you?" said Tom Horn.

The trainmen shouted with glee, as do school children when one of their number, no guiltier than they, is outwitted by the teacher. Tom was slapped on the back. The miscreant conductor was slapped on the back. He had made a good bluff but it had been called. Everybody went downtown and got drunk and told how Horn had picked the guilty man out of a hundred. Of all the strong, happy men the two who appeared to be the most carefree were, in reality, the least happy. One was the conductor, who would be cashiered, and the other was Tom Horn, who had never forgotten the stigma the Honorable William Woodburn had put on all Pinks.

Tom liked these railroad men. Their eyes had the fixed stare he had seen in old scouts. As a boy in the beginning of the railroad era, he had dreamed about being a railroad man himself. Spying on these men disgusted him. With the stubborn singleness of purpose of the boy who had refused to farm or go to school when there were tracks to be followed in the woods, Tom decided to quit Pinkerton's. He belonged to the open range.

The Indians and the soldiers were gone. He could look to Doc Shores no longer. While working for Pinkerton's Tom had met a remarkable group of wealthy men. These men wanted to employ a trailer and killer, even as Crook and Miles had done. Tom's name disappeared from Pinkerton's rolls. The slant of his life was now fixed to its very end.

14

THE BARONS AND THE RUSTLERS

As a PINKERTON, Tom Horn rode many times on the railroad between Denver and Ogden, crossing a country in which for more than a decade forces had been working to set the stage for his greatest performance with saddle and gun.

From the caboose windows Tom had watched the wind sweep pasture land that was far richer than anything in Arizona. Here was water in plenty and a climate mild enough to let cattle roam all winter, eating the grass that had cured on the stem. Unmeasured, the grassland reached from the Union Pacific Railroad to Canada. Tom had seen block after block of it taken from the Indians while he was riding on the Chisholm Trail, years before, and as each new area had been opened, cattle and cowboys filled it as by a clap of magic.

The cattlemen were of three general classes. First came the Texans who knew nothing but cattle, men who had come up the Chisholm Trail with vast herds sometimes netting their owners thirty percent on the investment. Such drovers changed in the course of a decade to grandees of the new grasslands, rulers of pastoral empires. After the Texans came eastern society men and English younger sons, adventurous chaps lured by big-game hunting and the romance of open country. They brought fortunes to the West and quickly doubled them, until there developed a speculation in livestock such as has seldom been seen in Wall Street with less animate stock. This was the Golden Age of the cattle business, an age so glamorous that the second and third generations still cherish its memory.

The foreigners, Easterners and Texans became the so-called cattle barons. In Cheyenne they organized a club that was internationally famous. World travelers were amazed at its ease and luxury, the magnificence of its bar and dining hall, the quiet dignity of its library. Members lived part of the time in New York, London or on the continent. In summer they galloped with their cowboys across the Laramie Plains. In winter they rode to hounds in England or wagered fortunes at Monte Carlo. Cheyenne boasted as fashionable driving horses as could be seen in Central Park in New York.

Prominent club members and great ranchmen of Wyoming included Horace Plunkett, later an Irish peer and noted reformer; Moreton Frewen, haw-hawing British big-game hunter and parliamentarian with investments also in Australia and the Caribbean; Edgar Bronson, the author; Stewart Wortley, the son-in-law of Admiral Schley; Henry A. Blair, president of the Chicago Street Railways; United States Senators Francis E. Warren and Joseph M. Carey; and Governor George W. Baxter—all of them men as charming in the eyes of Tom Horn as Crook and Wood had been.

Opposed to these socialites, modest farmers had come to the country in covered wagons to claim the legal limit of homestead land. The settlers found that their hundred-and-sixty-acre homesteads were little islands in a vast ocean of grass, and this grass was being eaten by millions of cattle—all belonging to distant rich men whose ideas, manners and customs were alien to their humble ambitions.

Immediately trouble brewed between the barons and the settlers. In the eyes of the law a baron with fifty thousand cattle was entitled to the same homestead as a settler and no more, but the cattle baron ignored this fact. The immeasurable expanse of grazing land belonged, he said, to his herds. He was first in the region and priority counted—especially with the men of British extraction. The only limit to a baron's range was the arbitrary boundary established between himself and his neighbor barons. The settlers, with their hundred and sixty acres apiece, did not count.

Living like a feudal lord, the baron surrounded himself with cowboys to ride his boundaries and to keep rival herds from intruding. As the number of settlers increased, depriving him of his range, the exasperated baron was unable to find any legal means of annexing the immense area necessary to his far-flung herds. In a lawless country he naturally evolved illegal means. Looking over the cow hands, he chose the more dependable to take up a hundred and sixty acres nominally for themselves as the law required, but in reality for their employer. The employees filed the proper papers, secured the entry of the desired land in their own names and "proved up" on the farms, then deeded them to the baron. These homesteads, staked out along the available creeks, controlled the dry grazing land on both sides.

But in this system were the seeds of destruction. Twice a year a baron's force of riders was swelled by itinerant cowboys hired to help with the roundup. In the spring the herds were collected and the calves branded; in the fall the droves were gathered again and the steers cut out for market. During the rest of the year these extra cowpunchers loafed in adjacent towns or did chores for their board and keep around the ranches where they hoped to be hired on the next roundup.

It was the very presence of so many bachelor cowboys on and around the baronial ranches that helped to bring ruin to the vast estates. The lonely youths looked with bright eyes upon the settlers' girls—those children whom the covered-wagon men had brought to scattered cabins and who insisted on growing up. As fast as a girl ripened, some baron's cowboy married her and set up a cabin on a hundred and sixty acres of range. When a man quit throwing his big hat at the Wyoming moon and started earning money for a wife, he became an enemy of the baronial system. He dreamed of herds of his own.

A cow baronetcy was so ephemeral that it began to disintegrate almost as soon as it was established. The barons fought over the constantly changing lines of the imaginary boundaries. They fought with one another and with the homesteaders and settlers over mavericks, the most fatal defect in their industrial scheme.

Mavericks were the unbranded cattle that roamed the plains, stray animals whose ownership was questionable if not undiscoverable. They owed their name to a Texan, Samuel A. Maverick, who before the Civil War, neglected to mark his calves. Soon all unbranded animals on the range were known as Maverick's, then mavericks.

The cattle barons' operations were free, easy and expansive. They found it impossible to brand each and every calf born into their herds. The roundups were too careless ever to gather one hundred percent of the wandering and scattered animals.

In the early morning of a typical day on the spring roundup the cook was instructed to drive his wagon to a certain place where the riders would gather at noon. Then the cowboys galloped off in a column of twos, stopping every mile to send one man to gather all cattle in the vicinity and drive them toward the proposed bunch ground which was usually at a watering place. Soon a complete circle of riders was spurring over the hills, squalling like Indians, while cows and their calves ran downhill, the natural direction for them to go when disturbed. As the sun grew hot with approaching midday, the animals drifted toward water, little lines of them like wagon spokes stretching toward a hub.

By noon the herd was bunched, and the riders ate dinner at the wagon. The afternoon was spent by the cowboys, on fresh horses, roping and branding the calves. When two or more barons combined for a roundup, their respective foremen kept close watch to be sure that each calf received its mother's brand.

At dawn the next morning the moving, circling and whooping process was begun again.

As the years passed, cows grew in wisdom and learned to hide with their calves and to avoid the bruises and burns of the branding ground. Furthermore, cowboys were human beings working for wages. A tired rider, seeing a lone cow and calf far up a steep hill, might say to himself, "What's one li'l ol' calf when we got thirty thousand? We'll get it next year."

By the next year these calves were yearlings with no owners. Of course everybody knew that they must belong to the man who owned all the cattle on the range, but if another man's cattle had come onto the range, even in small numbers, the thing became complex, for the outside cattlemen would be around demanding their share of the mavericks.

Mavericks increased amazingly in Wyoming. Barons employed extra riders to scour the country between roundups and to brand mavericks at so much per head. Naturally this produced thievery, for a dishonest cowboy in the lonely hills could burn any kind of brand on a maverick and report anything he liked to his employer.

To protect themselves from this wholesale usurpation of both their grass and their cattle, the barons organized the Wyoming Stock Growers' Association, and appealed as an organization to Washington to abolish the homestead law which, they said, had been passed as a soldier bonus and to facilitate settlement in Iowa and Kansas but was not appropriate for the steppes farther west. However, eastern politicians could not obey western barons against the plain people and the law remained in force.

Next the barons drafted laws to stop the indiscriminate stealing of mavericks. Cattle were to be rounded up only at specified times. No man was allowed to ride the open range with a branding iron on his saddle. This proved of little help. The settler who was a good hand throwing a rope was certain to be employed on the semiannual roundup. Denied the right to carry a branding iron, he might heat one of the cinch buckles on his saddle and tie and brand a calf for himself while he was gathering the baron's cattle. Expert hands could rope, tie and brand a calf in little more than a minute. Was not speed in roping the thing for which the barons and cattlemen's associations gave prizes at fairs and rodeos?

In the 1880's western slang named these fastest of cow hands "rustlers," meaning high-powered men or "hustlers." The term, originating as one of praise, ended as one of infamy because so many of these experts devoted their talents to fattening their own herds even while they accepted the baron's money and ate his food on the roundup. Yet, strangely enough, to the rustlers themselves the name remained praiseworthy.

Great as were the depredations committed by some of the baron's own employees, the greatest havoc was wrought by the settler-cowboys who had already got a start in business and who had established little ranches of their own. Such gentry complained that they were not allowed to ride with the legal association roundup. They openly admitted that rustling was the only way to get even with the big men for carelessly and ruthlessly swallowing up the little man's few cattle during the vast movements of the herds.

The settler-cowboy, trying to keep his small herd close around his cabin all through the year, was in danger every spring and fall, when the whole country was combed by the baron's roundup. When the homesteader saw the roundup wagon unhooked on the horizon, had his sleep disturbed all night by the bells on the cowboy's herd of saddle horses and had his chickens frightened by wild cowboy yells at dawn, he knew that all the cattle in the country were being whooped toward the distance. For after each roundup, spring or fall, the herds were moved miles and miles toward either the summer or winter range.

To rescue ten or fifteen cattle out of the vast dust-disturbing multitude might take a day or two and, again, it might be altogether impossible. Generally, if the settler's cattle once left, their owner would never see them again, for the roundup foreman had no time, admitting that he was honest, to stop and separate petty brands from the immense herd.

When the settler's crop was in, he would be apt to saddle his horse and ride out to revenge himself in silent and devious ways. For instance, the cattle baron, riding the range after the spring calf roundup to see how well his boys had done their work, would notice an unbranded calf standing beside its mother whose udder was swollen and spurting thin streams of milk. The calf would make no attempt to suck.

This was puzzling since the cow was licking and caressing her offspring. It was obvious that the calf was still unweaned. Did the calf have a bad tooth that prevented it from sucking? Quickly the ranchman roped the little animal and ran his hand in its mouth.

Its tongue was split! Unable to nurse, the calf would soon cease to follow its mother. Without a brand, it would then be anybody's property.

Here was a new turn of events. Somebody was *making* mavericks!

As the settlers became more plentiful on the range and the natural supply of mavericks dwindled, this art of making mavericks grew. Sometimes rustlers drove cows and calves into rivers, shot the mothers in mid-current and let their carcasses float away. The calves, emerging safe and sound, would be branded by the rustlers before they were dry.

The cow barons could not be expected to lose their property without a struggle. They did not have a majority in the state but they did have organization. Their only hope lay in a minority insurrection. Force would be necessary to save both their investments and the old order in Wyoming. Many people on both sides saw that civil war was imminent.

15

THE JOHNSON COUNTY WAR

TOM HORN, working for Pinkerton's, read about Wyoming's economic and social chaos with understanding. A democratic government, after all, is based on majority rule and the majority in Wyoming countenanced cow stealing as jocularly as it did the bootlegging of liquor forty years later. Tom had seen three livestock "wars." He knew the signals of approaching danger. In Kansas, Tom had seen battles between the big drovers and the settlers. In New Mexico he had seen the Chisum-Murphy range war with its development of the notorious killer, Billy the Kid. He had taken part in the Pleasant Valley war in Arizona. Tom knew that fighting factions always struggled for the sheriff's office, perhaps elected two sheriffs, and then pursued and executed one another with legal warrants. He knew how the lawless West always liked the semblance of legality. Leadville at its worst had been a bonanza for the lawyers. Range wars were both political and economic. In Wyoming the presence of so many aristocrats made the looming strife assume the proportions of a class struggle.

As might be expected in a civil war, there were some sporadic attempts to regulate affairs with vigilantes—organized dictatorial minorities. The year that Tom Horn first met Doc Shores in Arizona some barons frowned upon Jim Averill's "hog ranch" at Sweetwater, Wyoming. Jim's resort, with his light o' love, Ella Watson, familiarly called "Cattle Kate," was a scarlet blotch on the Red Desert. When a cowboy winked profoundly at the mention of Jim's hog ranch, listeners knew exactly what he meant; they knew that Jim and Kate kept no hogs but that, instead, they ran a log establishment where riders might dismount and spend days swilling liquor.

A hog ranch was the resort of cowpunchers who had no money with which to fall upon Cheyenne and make ta-rah-rah-rah-boom-de-ay till morning. Such riders could pick up a stray steer, lead it to Averill's hog ranch and sell it to Jim for a sum to be taken out in trade. When Averill estimated that the cowboy had spent the value of the steer, the adventure was over.

In addition to being a "sporting gentleman," Mr. Averill was a surveyor. He knew every quarter section in the country and the particular water holes to which the cow barons had dubious title. For a price, Jim located settlers on these choice homesites and if the newcomers were too poor to pay, Jim waited until they had rustled enough cattle to settle their bills.

Jim and Cattle Kate prospered and, as they rose, rustling naturally increased. One day masked vigilantes, with their clothes on backward, came to Averill's and held a kangaroo court. They had forgotten to bring a Bible, but the hog ranch disgorged a copy of Mark Twain's *Roughing It* upon which solemn oaths were sworn and in short order Jim and Cattle Kate—with a rope just above the dust ruffle to keep down her skirts—were swinging from a cottonwood limb, turning slowly in the wind.

A year later some men knocked at the door of a cabin belonging to a man named Tom Waggoner, near Newcastle, Wyoming, a rustler town on the western edge of the Black Hills. Waggoner's wife let them in, fed them, and they rode away. An hour later they came back and took her husband, presumably to town as witness in a trial. When her food ran out and he had not returned, an inquiry was made. Neighbors found Waggoner where he had been hanging for twenty days in a tree. Newcastle said that it had been done on orders from the cattle association. Lynch law seemed to be the newest and surest way to deal with the rustlers. The legal courts showed a record of fifty prosecutions and only ten convictions for cattle stealing. Obviously a rustler jury would seldom convict a cow thief. In some localities, notably Johnson County, the rustlers had thriving communities, with churches, schools, and control of the local government. This created a perplexing situation for cattle barons whose headquarters were in distant Cheyenne in the extreme southeastern corner of the state. Organized wealth, back east, had employed armed mercenaries from Pinkerton's National Detective Agency to protect their property and break the power of striking workmen in factory towns. Would it be possible for organized wealth in the Rockies to smash the Johnson County rustlers forever? The barons discussed their problem with Superintendent McParlan in Denver.

McParlan suggested that they see Tom Horn, who, he said, had had some experience in an Arizona range war.

Tom was called in. He listened to the barons' problem. He had detested homesteaders as stupid people ever since the day they had killed old Shed on the Missouri road. He himself had tried ranching in a small way and had given it up as something fit for dullards. On the trail, in early days, he had served these same range lords, or their prototypes; all the success in his life had come from serving the rich and powerful. Life had made him an instinctive vassal of the vested interests. By no reasoning could he picture himself as a family man, and the thought of a dozen hungry children around a slum cabin in the desert was as distasteful to him as the thought of his own unhappy childhood. The powerful men whom he had always admired, as a class, now were coming to him as had Crook and Miles.

Tom had known the desperadoes of the Southwest who served under Tewksbury in the range war against the Grahams, and his mind centered on them as he sat listening to the Wyoming barons describe their predicament. When the talk was done, Tom struck off for Arizona to have secret conversations with men who lived by violence. Such a trip did not interfere with his steady employment in the hobo act.

By the first of April 1892 his recruits were seen loafing around the offices of wealthy cowmen in Denver. The *Rocky Mountain News* noted the influx and inquired what these hard-faced and bepistoled strangers were doing in town. Up in Cheyenne the editor of the *Leader*, as friend of the settlers, picked up the news note and relayed it to his readers. Its rival, the *Cheyenne Tribune*, organ of the pluto-crats, pooh-poohed all ideas that violence was intended.

The settlers in Johnson County read the conflicting reports in the newspapers and were puzzled. The *Leader* was their friend, however, so they accepted its warnings and prepared to call out the militia. Before it could form, the imperial governor of Wyoming, friend of the cow barons, forbade mobilization and while Johnson County debated what next to do, the plutocrats moved their mer-cenaries from Denver to Cheyenne, thirty strong. There they were joined by thirty more riders, cowboys whom the feudal lords had picked from their own ranges.

Two carloads of saddle horses arrived in Cheyenne and were branded with an unrecorded A—no man was to be identified by his horse. While the sixty men became acquainted with their mounts, another delegation of hired killers, fresh from a range war on the Owyhee Desert, arrived from Idaho.

Had Tom Horn recruited these too? His enemies, knowing that his work with Pinkerton's led him up and down the Union Pacific and across the Owyhee Desert, said "Yes!" His friends said, "No!"

The army complete, the barons hurried it on a special train to Casper, Wyoming, where two wagons loaded with supplies were waiting. Soon, like a troop of cavalry, the hard-faced men were riding north.

In 1892, as well as later, it was customary to believe that business-men were not dreamers, yet here under the Wyoming sun rode an army of mercenaries whom capitalists believed capable of accom-plishing what the courts could not do.

The army had disappeared over the northern horizon before the amazed world realized what was happening. Then the press howled for an explanation. What did this mean in a republican govern-ment? Who were the leaders of such a foolhardy adventure? Specu-lation named governors, senators—all the big stockmen of the West. Wealthy clubmen and Britishers who had presumably left Cheyenne to visit abroad were suspected of being with the little army that had disappeared across the grasslands. It was said that young Van Bibbers in New York who looked at the world through plate-glass windows were as much interested in the expedition as they were in the Harvard-Yale football game. Ladies in Mayfair cooed and fluttered over the affair, saying at teatime that it reminded them of Sir St. George's attempt to conquer the Sioux Indians with his private army. Delicate ears were straining toward far-off Wyoming.

For days no word came. Then two rustlers, riding splendid horses whose nostrils were pools of blood and whose flesh trembled from a long race, drew rein at a telegraph station. The world heard that heavy fighting was going on in the wilderness. An English lord had been captured! The transatlantic cable asked the identity of His Lordship. This detail had seemed unimportant to the couriers and they raced back for the information. Since the days of big-game hunting on the Kansas plains cowboys had never distinguished between English lords and eastern society men. The engraved calling card found in this lord's wallet stated that his address was 1331 Spruce Street, Philadelphia, and that his name was Dr. Charles Penrose—a brother of Boies and Spencer. Milord was incarcerated in the felons' cage at Douglas, Wyoming, charged by the county authorities with conspiracy and murder. Dr. Penrose was a close personal friend of Acting Governor Amos W. Barber of Wyoming, whom he had met at the University of Pennsylvania Medical School. He had come to Wyoming to visit his college friend, and the supply of gauze, lint and ether in his baggage made his captors believe him to be the private army's surgeon. Judge Richard H. Scott, in Cheyenne, issued a writ of habeas corpus and the unfortunate Philadelphian was brought back to his friends. He told the press that he had not intended to do anything wrong. Finally, he disclosed the personnel of the army.

Major Frank Wolcott was in command. Frank Canton led the troop of Wyoming cowboys, and a desperate rider, Tom Smith, led the Southerners. Within a few years legend confused Tom Smith with Tom Horn, on this expedition. Smith, like Horn, was a professional United States deputy marshal, who had been procured with other men of his kind in the Indian Territory. Major Wolcott was a retired officer of the regular army, rabid in everything from Republican party politics to hatred of homesteaders. Brave, blustering, tactless, well educated, a successful cattleman, he was disliked and feared by practically all the "little fellows" in Wyoming. Frank Canton had long been employed as range inspector and detective for the Wyoming Stock Growers' Association. He was the reputed assassin of rustlers Tisdale and Ranger Jones. Canton was a veteran henchman of the barons and claimed, in after years, that the armed movement had been merely a peaceable attempt to remove cattle from a region where rustlers made life impossible for honest capitalists. Canton, like Horn, had been a drover on the Texas trail, a minion of the law and a fearless man to send after toughs and railway-holdup desperadoes. When he died in 1927, Frank Canton was a militia general and dignitaries escorted him to his grave with pomp and honor. Tom Horn had a right to expect the same reward.

It is generally believed that this entire army was in the direct employ of the association, although its president, John Clay, later denied any specific connection between himself and the raid. He said, truly enough, that he had been far away at the time, peacefully fishing in the salmon streams that rise in the Cheviot Hills of Scotland. The records of the time show that, in a public utterance, he said, "I respect them for their manliness."

When the barons' army disappeared over the horizon it headed through the night to attack the first proscribed victims—settlers who had been tried and convicted in secret conclave by barons or their foremen.

Nate Champion and Nick Ray were the first object lessons to the Johnson County rebels. In the night it snowed—a light flurry. The main army, some fifty men, surrounded the doomed cabin in Powder River and waited for dawn. They hid behind the barn and along the riverbank, to cover all doors and windows. At daylight, a man stepped out of the cabin and many rifles were raised. "Wait," said one of the raiders. "That's not Champion."

The man, unconscious of his peril, stretched, yawned and walked to the barn where the raiders pinioned him, only to discover that he was one of two trappers who had chanced to spend the night with Champion. A little later the other trapper emerged from the cabin. He stretched, yawned, looked at the barn, the riverbank, the hills. Seeing nothing, he walked to the barn and was captured.

The raiders waited. Soon a third man emerged from the cabin door, stretched and yawned.

"That's Nick Ray," whispered one of the army leaders.

Nick looked idly at the barn, the riverbank, the hills, then he picked up an ax from the chip pile, brushed the new-fallen snow off the handle and prepared to chop bark from a cottonwood log. He tipped his head back, looking at the buds swelling from the bare branches that gestured in the wind against the Wyoming sky.

A shot knocked him reeling and he crawled back to the cabin through a fierce bombardment that made the chips flip and fly. At the door the giant arm of Nate Champion dragged him in. The siege was on, rifle answering rifle.

At this juncture, a half-grown boy and a man, Jack Flagg, farmer-editor of the rustler newspaper printed at Buffalo, came driving along the road not far away. Flagg's paper had been outspoken about "association men," had preached cowboy organization and strikes for higher pay. More than once he had urged riders with a herd in their possession to demand more money or ruin their employer by turning loose the cattle. Flagg stopped his team when he heard the bombardment. Having a nose for news, he edged nearer to see what was happening. He saw, abandoned his wagon, and the man and boy whipped away on the naked horses, with bullets streaking past them like telephone wires. On the route Flagg cried the news that the "Whitecaps" were coming—Whitecaps being a name given extra-legal "regulators" or vigilantes, a term derived from the sheet-robed Ku Klux Klan of Southern notoriety twenty years before.

All day long Nate Champion held the fifty raiders at bay with Nick Ray lying on the floor of the beleaguered cabin. After a few hours Nick died. A little before dark the raiders took the farmer-editor's abandoned wagon, loaded it with hay, set it afire and rolled it against the cabin. The fire spread to the roof and Nate broke for the riverbank. A volley bowled him over and his corpse was riddled with bullets as he lay in the mud. Nick Ray's body was charred in the burning cabin.

In the late evening the mess wagons arrived. The Whitecaps ate a hearty meal, then swung onto their horses and started up the wet, snowy road for Buffalo, intending to put the country under private martial law. But they had not reckoned with the farmer-editor who had spied them from the road. Ever since that frantic man had come into town on a lather-whitened horse, Johnson County had been arming. Long before the fire had crept high in Champion's cabin, Sheriff "Red" Angus had sworn in the whole male population as deputy sheriffs. And as the raw evening breeze blew across the hamlet of Buffalo, an army of rustlers rode out to meet the oncoming Whitecaps. They camped at every approach to the town.

One of their campfires brought the raiders to a halt. Hiding in the blackness of the night, the invaders watched the flickering blaze. Who lay around it? Was it a sentry or just a lone camper?

In the rustlers' camp a boy, bored with the starless night, was trying to scare his comrades by spurring his half-broken horse over their lolling bodies. The bronco, in white-eyed terror, "swallowed his head and flew to pieces." He bucked his rider's rifle out of its scabbard and an explosion crashed in the darkness.

This was all the Whitecaps needed. They knew that the cat-hop was over. Four men let down the wire fence at one side of the road and, with a thrumming of hoofs, the raiders swerved away. Nothing now to do but hole up and wait for aid. The rustlers, armed and alert, outnumbered them and could easily overwhelm them in open fight.

The next day the invaders barricaded themselves in a friendly ranch, the "T, open A connected" outfit on Crazy Woman Creek, twelve miles from Buffalo. Soon the rustlers arrived in force and besieged them even as they had besieged Nate Champion. Some of the most influential settlers begged the commander of near-by Fort McKinney to lend them a cannon with which to blow the invaders out of the country. They were refused and Sheriff Angus superintended the building of breastworks on wheels with which to approach the buildings.

The siege lasted three days. Before it was over Ray's charred torso and Champion's riddled body were brought to Buffalo to receive a Baptist burial by a roundhead preacher who concluded the funeral by strapping a Winchester on his saddle. Then, quoting Scripture, he rallied a few late-arriving cow thieves and set out to battle for God and Johnson County.

The barons' mess wagons were captured, the beds and baggage rifled. The rustlers reported that Frank Canton's valise contained a list of seventy Johnson County settlers condemned to death.

Governor Barber, in Cheyenne, telegraphed Wyoming's Senators Warren and Carey in Washington. They raced to the White House and persuaded President Benjamin Harrison to order the United States Army to rescue the embarrassed private army and hold it prisoner.

So it was that the raiders passed out of Sheriff Angus' hands and were taken, over his protests, to Cheyenne where, in the days that followed, their trial was postponed and given endless continuances. Much liberty was given the prisoners. Even in jail the "army" observed military rank. Officers ate special food, provided by their friends, at tables separated from the "enlisted" men. In the evenings the aristocratic officers regaled themselves by playing whist while their cowboy employees indulged in the ruder American game of draw. As the guard became more tolerant the captives treated their prison like a free boardinghouse. They climbed out the windows at will to disport themselves in twos, threes and fours, about the streets or in the gambling houses and saloons. Some even roamed as far as Denver. Months went by before they were finally dismissed, leaving an exhausted treasury and a higher tax rate looming.

Again the cattle barons had failed. Neither the law, the kangaroo court nor an army of vigilantes had served their purpose. When next they struck it was with a lone, stealthy weapon, a hired assassin, and that assassin was Tom Horn.

16

"YOU'LL BE NEXT."

As a PINKERTON man Tom Horn was highly eligible for a job as stock detective. The Johnson County war had introduced him to the leading members of the Wyoming Stock Growers' Association. Tom knew the danger of his new work. He had arrested Joe McCoy for killing a stock detective in Colorado. Shortly after the Wyoming war a jury of settlers had tendered a vote of thanks to a man who had killed a stock detective. The judge censured the jury abusively and the case was dropped.

Tom was first employed in this new and dangerous work by the president of the association who had been in Scotland during the raid. John Clay was striving to hold together a baronial estate in the valley of a stream north of Cheyenne called the Chugwater. He was the fox-hunting son of a well-to-do Scotch farmer, and had an instinct for livestock, banking and literature. He enjoyed quoting poetic couplets as he rode "along Chugwater's brimming tide." Free grass brought John Clay out of Scotland, but nothing—not even success—ever brought Scotland out of John Clay. His enemies—and they were remarkably few even among the rustlers—said that his mother packed a lunch for him when he got on the boat at Glasgow and that he still had some of it left when he arrived at Cheyenne. At the age of eighty, with a magnificent home in Chicago, there were only two places in the world where Mr. Clay really cared to be, the Cheviot Hills and the valley of the Chug. The grand old man of the Union Stockyards was something of a hero even to his secretary, whose only complaint was that he was so anxious to keep his desk clear that he threw his letters on the floor as soon as he signed them.

Ostensibly Clay hired Horn to break horses for his Swan Land & Cattle Company, a Scotch syndicate capitalized at four and a half million dollars. As broncobuster Tom could ride around and investigate anything that invited suspicion without causing suspicion himself. While breaking horses, he could study tracks on the range, and discover rustlers moving across it. He watched the ravens and magpies. They led him to the place where a beef had been butchered by thieves. The routine of a cow ranch ignored the activities of a hand breaking horses. Having dozens of horses to ride, Tom could pursue any clue that looked promising.

During the next decade Horn worked in such fashion for most of the established cow barons. Sometimes he cooked, often he rode on the roundup, usually he was given special work to do as a "new cowpuncher" at the ranch where he was sleuthing. Always well mounted, he had a way of turning up suddenly in isolated valleys when all the regular hands were known to be rounding up cattle elsewhere. It was his duty to be in places where people thought nobody would be. Every county in southern Wyoming knew his lonely campfire. Riding for days without a bed, he bragged, "You can always tell my camp when you find it. There will be nothing to eat there but a coffeepot and a pair of hobbles."

A dozen other detectives were riding these ranges for various cattle barons, but Tom stood out from all of them in one particular—his familiarity with death.

In southern Wyoming near the Colorado line Tom camped, campless, for weeks watching the Laughoff brothers. Having been told that they were stealing cattle, he investigated. Finally he caught them red-handed, and brought them in with the cattle they had stolen. Tom was sure that no court could ask for better or more convincing evidence. The case went to trial. Twelve rustlers sat on the jury. The men were not convicted. Tom was as disgusted as was his employer—one of the barons, just which one is not now discoverable. The two men talked it over. There was no use going to the expense of a trial when a conviction was impossible. Tom said that in the future he would save his employer "as many lawyers' and witnesses' fees as possible." He could kill a rustler as easily as he could kill an Apache renegade. The baron gave him a chance.

On Horse Creek, east of Cheyenne, were the homesteads of Lewis and Powell, kindred souls with a reputation for taking liberties with other men's cattle. Powell had but one arm, yet he could, by holding the reins in his teeth, rope and tie a calf with the best of the cowboys. Laughingly he boasted that he never ate his own beef. This proved nothing, since it was a common remark among small ranchers, but Powell's neighbors felt that his utterance was a true word spoken in jest.

"If he stuck to the big KYT outfit and et only KYT beef, it would be all right," they said, "but it's more'n half likely the brand he butchers is just plain FAT."

"Come and see me sometime," Powell would call, "and I'll feed you your own beef," and his neighbors would laugh, but not very heartily. That fall at shipping time, when a neighbor could not find one of his fat heifers, he would be likely to blame Powell rather than a lobo wolf, which would have been otherwise suspected. The settlers distrusted Powell but they also distrusted their own courts. Certainly they had no real evidence that would legally convict him. But they were positive in their own minds, and here and there men said to each other in a manner studiously offhand, "Somebody'll kill that rustler Powell someday." Back in Denver and Cheyenne cattle barons with the same evasiveness said, "That's a bad rustler over on Horse Crick; Powell's his name, and he's a damned nuisance. Somebody'll kill him someday, and it'll be a good riddance."

Such talk, smoldering in cabins on the range and in stockmen's offices in cities, prompted someone's decision to have Powell assassinated. Tom Horn was chosen for the deed. Who hired him to do the killing will, in all probability, never be generally known. All that is known is that he got three hundred dollars for the job. With the promise of that sum, Tom Horn rode up to Powell's ranch one day, found him working in the field, and shot him dead amid his emerald alfalfa. Tom put a rock under the dead man's head and rode away. The rock was his private brand put upon a corpse so that it might prove to his employer that he had earned his pay. The rock also served as a warning to other rustlers that there was a hired assassin in the country.

With Powell dead, there remained Lewis, who bragged that no killer could scare him. One day Horn found him alone in his horse corral. Tom drew his six-shooter and opened fire.

"He was the worst scared son-of-a-bitch you ever saw," said Tom Horn later, laughing over the memory of Lewis' facial expression. "Afterward, I burned powder in five 45-90 shells to make them smell fresh, but the God-damned officers never found them."

It was a fine point in the technique of Horn's art, this trick of killing a man with a six-shooter and planting exploded rifle shells near the corpse to deceive his pursuers upon at least one detail of the crime. There was nothing devious, however, in the boldness with which Tom slipped a rock beneath the dead Lewis' head.

"That's the way I hung out my sign," he said later. "That's how I collect my money. When it comes to killing, I guess I've got a corner on the market." And he had a corner, surely enough, for killing men made no impression on Tom Horn. Life had been hard for him ever since he had fought with his father. Life had been cheap with him ever since he had heard the bloody tales of John Brown and Quantrill, and, under his eyes, it had grown cheaper on the plains. Something of the Apache and Mexican carelessness for death had become a part of him. He could do this killing with light-hearted laughter on his lips as long as anybody was willing to pay him for it.

Six hundred dollars came in blood money for these assassinations, and Horn was flush. He drank hard in saloons and, according to the memories of range riders of the times, boasted loudly of his deeds.

Doubtless the very boldness of braggadocio protected him. In saloons and cabins he made cursing, swaggering brags of what he had done to Powell and Lewis, and of what he would do to anyone else who rustled a maverick. This served two purposes: it convinced many settlers that he was simply telling lies, and it awed others into believing that he was telling the truth. Small ranchmen could now ride close by a big, unbranded "weaner" without feeling any inclination to "dab" their ropes on it.

Tom was not arrested, although the sheriff said he had sufficient evidence for a conviction. Years later, the sheriff explained that he had omitted to make the arrest "because the people didn't want it." In the popular mind, it was believed that Lewis and Powell had got what they deserved. They had not been popular. Western sentiment hinged more upon whether a man was or was not well liked, than upon his degree of guilt as a cow thief. Small ranchers, as well as cattle barons, felt that the country was settling too fast, and that the disappearance of any one cattleman left just that much more range for those who remained. When it occurred to a settler that he might be the next to go, however, his enthusiasm for this summary justice waned. The sheriff said, "Everybody thought 'good riddance' for Lewis and Powell, but they defeated me at the next election because I didn't do anything about it. That's what you get for being a public officer. Everything you do is wrong."

This laxity on the part of the law increased Tom's boldness. He extended his range and became known over half the state. He might turn up anywhere. A settler driving through the hills with a stolen calf in his wagon would be terrified when he saw any rider gallop over the swell of the desert, for that man might be Tom Horn.

A commissioner in Sweetwater County who had a rustler's reputation fell under Tom's eye. Tom believed that the commissioner was changing brands on the cattle of a member of the association, and selling the steers to a butcher in the town of Hanna. Tom laid a trap for him by catching a fat, branded steer, cutting a slit in the hide back of its shoulder and slipping in a two-bit piece. He memorized the steer's image and turned it loose. A few weeks later he met the county commissioner driving a small bunch of cattle to the butcher. The marked steer was among them. Tom inspected all the brands and found that the brand on the animal in question had been changed. He said nothing.

It was easy enough to testify that the brand had been changed, but it would make no difference to a jury. Tom had a better plan. Without saying a word, he turned, galloped into Hanna, collected a few of the most prominent residents of the town and led them down to the slaughterhouse. The commissioner arrived with the cattle, and corraled them. Tom climbed on the fence. "Ain't you changed one of them Two-Bars into a Flying Diamond?" he asked. "That's easy done, but if I was changing a brand I'd be ashamed of a job as coarse as that."

The commissioner replied, "I ain't worked over no brands. Every critter in there I've raised myself. Are you trying to make out that I'm a cow thief? Show me one that has been worked over!"

Tom turned to two cowboys sitting on the fence. "Boys, stretch out that broc-faced two-year-old. I'll show him."

The cowboys rode into the corral and shook out their ropes. With deft throws the steer was snared by the head and hind legs. The ropes tightened like fiddlestrings and the steer went down. The ponies were trained to hold the ropes taut, while the riders dismounted. Tom said, "Now, boys, feel back of that steer's front leg. You'll find two bits under the hide, on the left side."

The boys kneaded the hide in handfuls. "Hell, yes," said one of them. The commissioner himself felt the loose hide.

"Take your knife," said Tom. "You'll find the date is 1889. That was a Two-Bar steer. I put the two-bit piece in there myself."

The commissioner felt the lump and thought fast. Every man on the fence was probably guilty of stealing Two-Bar cattle, but there was not one of them who wanted the others to know.

The commissioner looked up and said, "Tom, you've put a quarter in one of my own steers. Are you trying to job me?"

Tom looked down at him from the fence. "Dave, when that steer is butchered, the inside of the hide will show the old brand and it will be a Two-Bar. You changed it. If there is a man on this corral who thinks I'm lying, let him wait and see the steer butchered. I ain't got time. I've got to be at Rawlins at noon tomorrow, but before I go, I'll just tell you and your friends, if you have any, you're going to be found in the hills with a rock under your head. I'm done with courts and arrests." He turned to the men on the corral. "You boys hear what I say? If he'll steal a Two-Bar, how do you know he won't steal from you?" Tom walked off.

At the livery barn before Tom got his horse the commissioner overtook Horn and whispered an offer of eight hundred dollars if Tom would forget it.

Tom laughed and called the stableman. "He thinks I do business that way. Did you hear his offer? That's a hell of a fine commissioner you've got in this county. I'd vote f'r him if I was you." Then, turning to the commissioner, he said, "Well, you wait. Your time is coming, not this week or the week after, but *you'll be next.*"

Tom rode away, to reappear on the other side of the range in Bates' Hole. Here he pulled up his horse in front of a small ranch house and, without dismounting, knocked with his boot toe at the door. His Winchester lay across his saddle, pointing at the doorway. He said, "Abe, I don't want to find any more beef hides over in the wash. Do you understand? I'm Tom Horn, and I put a stop to that sort of thing." There was no reply. Tom rode off.

He knew he wouldn't be able to use such bold tactics at the Morris ranch. They might shoot a feller. Them boys would fight. It would be better to drop a bullet close to them sometime. That would make them figger out a thing or two.

Willis Workman was another one; a letter signed with a skull and crossbones might quiet him down. Getting rid of Lewis and Powell had put the fear of God into a lot of these rustlers.

Some of the settlers, thinking they were as formidable as Tom, did not scare. One doughty settler said, "Tom Horn threatened my brother, told him, 'You'll be next.' I said to Tom, 'If you shoot Zack, be sure to get us all, because if you don't, I'll shoot you on sight. Do you want to start right now? I believe you're more'n half bluff. You can't throw no scare into me!'"

During the next five years there were settlers in Wyoming who never left their cabins unless their wives or children marched ahead. This put a lure of danger and daring into a monotonous life. Men who had no guilt in their minds and no warnings from anyone, nevertheless went through this dramatic performance as a rite, and bragged about it. When Tom Horn really wanted a man, he got him, whether his wife preceded him or not.

Tom grew proud of his power. He would ride into a ranch saying, "I just killed Tug Wilson. You'll find him at Red Wash, just below the cottonwoods." Search would reveal Tug not dead at Red Wash but alive and well.

Later a notorious character was found dead near Baggs on Snake River, with a bullet in him. Tom Horn said, "I told you I'd get him if he didn't quit rustling, and I *have.*" Then the mail carrier, Zero Lamb, came up from Baggs with the truth. The real murderer had been arrested and lodged in jail.

Such boasting lies were Tom Horn's stock in trade. Always he was threatening to kill people, and claiming that he had killed someone who was still alive. When there was a killing in reality, Tom took all the credit and, at the same time, bragged that in court he could prove that he was two hundred miles away at the time of the shooting. It looked as though the cattle barons were riding to success at last. Tom Horn had the rustlers guessing.

Junction of Bear and Green Rivers south of Brown's Hole.

The broken country where Bear River meets the Green in northwestern Colorado. The rough area at the junction of Colorado, Wyoming and Utah has long been a haven for outlaws.

White River Ranch, twenty-one miles west of Meeker, Colorado. Tom Horn stopped here in January 1892. Theodore Roosevelt rode from this ranch part of the time during his lion hunt in 1901.

Brown's Hole cowboys (with author).

17

A KILLER'S HOLIDAY

Tom Horn's success with the rustlers was like his success under General Miles against the Apaches. As soon as he cleaned up a range the cattlemen paid him off. Usually he could find work on another range, but he lost time between jobs. Looking for work was irksome to his ego. He grew unhappy and felt the old dissatisfaction that had been a periodical annoyance ever since Geronimo surrendered. Even in Tom's scouting days he had sometimes quit when a superior offended him—the curse of the killer's mentality. For all his assurance and boasting he was only a drifter. He would have been farther ahead if he had gone with Buffalo Bill or stayed with Pinkerton's. He was now in his middle thirties and not so prosperous as he had been in his twenties.

Daily he read in the newspapers that war impended with Spain. Here was a new excitement. Orators preached about the patriotic duty to enlist. Tom's past experience with the Army had been successful. He was always ambitious. His knowledge of Spanish might help him get promotion in a war with Spain. He would make new contacts with many men he had known in the Southwest. Chaffee, Maus and Lawton were all generals now. If Tom Horn was not getting ahead fast enough in Wyoming, here was a chance among men who had known him as a great scout. He determined to take a holiday and give the rustlers a rest.

The newspapers screamed for fighting men from the West, men like Tom Horn. The United States was a feeble military country that had turned its attention since the Civil War to the making of money. The small regular army had been employed most of the

161

time fighting Indians on the western plains and mountains. Buffalo Bill with his show, Frederic Remington with his brush, and Owen Wister and Theodore Roosevelt with their pens had built up a great tradition about a western world of happy rowdies—dead shots— with cool fighting tempers. Tom read about a regiment of Rough Riders, interesting enough. The master politician, Theodore Roosevelt, was at last organizing the cowboy regiment he had planned twelve years before. Tom read that his old friend Leonard Wood had been made their colonel. Sheriff Bucky O'Neill of Yavapai County, Arizona, was also one of the officers. There might be boys from Pleasant Valley in the ranks. Here was a good outfit—but Tom did not want to stand in any ranks. He could join a regiment in Wyoming and do that. He wanted to stand out alone.

Tom had no liking for Army discipline. He knew too much about it. He had seen enlisted men trussed for hours with a bayonet between their teeth simply because they talked back to officers. As a scout Tom had been free from such discipline. He could always talk to officers as equals. Furthermore, civilian help was paid twice as much as enlisted men. Would the army have scouts in Cuba? It seemed not!

Tom hesitated. Then he read stirring news. A large pack train was to be organized in St. Louis. Westerners who had had experience as packers were wanted. Tom hurried to the Missouri city and enrolled.

Each pack train contained a chief packer, two pack masters, twenty packers, a hundred mules and a bell mare. Tom started as one of the lowly packers. With luck he might distinguish himself as he had done with Crook so many years ago. It was like old times to be in a government mule corral, to swing straw-stuffed aparejos onto the level backs of the hard black and tan animals, to muscle up bales of hay and lash them in place with looping ropes. Each packer carried over his shoulder a pair of sole-leather goggles to be used as blinders when a mule objected to being packed. A mule that could not see which way to kick was harmless. The goggles served also as a whip when the packers rode beside the bobbing train. Sometimes Tom led the bell mare, an individual as important as the chief packer. Tom understood mules' peculiar instincts. Being sterile hybrids, they are attracted by a mare—call it filial or sexual. Tom knew from long experience that a mule, once it had become acquainted with a mare, would follow her as surely and as closely as though fastened to her by a rope. Mules busy playing among themselves when the cavalcade started would come scampering like school children if the packer rang the mare's bell.

At last orders came for the pack outfits to entrain for Tampa, Florida, the jumping-off place to Cuba. Tom and other old professionals showed grim satisfaction. The young men shouted with glee. The mules were led into stockcars and the men rode in a shabby red-plush-cushioned day coach. In Florida Tom learned that the Army was sending eight pack trains with a hundred and nine packers, sixteen pack masters and eight chief packers to Cuba. Tom became one of the sixteen pack masters—a distinction that he appreciated.

His promotion and the chaos of Tampa gave Tom sardonic pleasure. Politicians arrived with volunteer regiments, scrambled to be generals and to be the first to go to Cuba. The regulars cynically shouldered the volunteers aside. Each commander struggled for possession of the transports that rode in the bay waiting to take a small number of the fight-hungry patriots to war.

Tom saw General William R. Shafter, a stout man with a leonine mane, sitting on the veranda of the Tampa Bay Hotel among bevies of charming girls in long skirts and ostrich-plumed hats. He heard the girls shrieking in happy terror and holding their pompadoured hair from falling down when the rumor came that the Spanish fleet was approaching. This rumor was quieted, and Tom Horn found himself with his pack train cooped on board a transport, smelling rancid bilge water. Through portholes he spied other transports and warships, admired the sea gulls, listened to soldiers playing mouth harps and joined in when they beat on their mess kits with their spoons and sang, "Just Because She Made Them Goo-Goo Eyes."

The cowboy packers were not used to seeing so many men together and were shy, but they smiled at the songs.

Days and days of the boredom of crowded passage—men standing on the decks, thick as cedars on a mesa—Colonel Leonard Wood standing on the bridge looking out to sea—Lieutenant Colonel Theodore Roosevelt on his bunk below, reading Thackeray's *Vanity Fair*—military men saying, "Teddy should be studying the manual of arms"—yet he returned the hero of the war.

Wood had planned to sail to the Klondike with Theodore instead of down to Cuba. One day Wood appeared on deck wearing a golf cap. A cowboy who had never seen a body of water larger than the Gila said, "The colonel's hat blowed into the crick."

More days of boredom, then "Land"—mountains coming up out of the sea—white sand where the waves broke, palm trees—Cuba! The mountains floated on an azure sea exactly as the Arizona mountains had floated on an azure mirage. Tom watched from a porthole deep in the bowels of the ship where the mules were stalled. He heard men climb down the side of the ship and jump into boats. He saw them row shoreward. Mules and horses were shoved off to swim through the breakers. One mule swam out to sea by mistake. Cowboys waved their hats at it, screaming, "He's goin' back to ol' Missouri. Whoopee!"

Tom, years after the war, would maintain that it was he, the mule master, who showed General Shafter how to unload mules. He had told the general just to shove 'em off and let 'em swim. Theodore Roosevelt gave himself credit for the suggestion.

There was also the much-mooted question of which American had first stepped on Spanish soil. Forty-seven men in later years claimed this distinction.

The beach at Daiquiri, where Tom landed among the troops, looked like an Arizona anthill. Companies were in fragments, each portion organizing and marching to join the main body only to find that the main body had moved out of sight. Tom was busy catching the mules as they came ashore. Nobody recognized his own mules, for they looked so unlike themselves sopping wet, with their ears hanging sideways from their heads. Tom Horn, the mule master, saw Major General Lawton standing under a tree with his staff, smiling as he watched the confused recruits weave themselves into a pattern on the beach. He saw his old sheriff, Bucky O'Neill, a captain now. He heard that Shipp, a lieutenant still in the 10th Cavalry, was over yonder where the colored troops were forming. Some men had not improved their ranks like Lawton and Leonard Wood. Jaunty cavalier Shipp, who had commanded for a brief period after Captain Crawford had been killed in Mexico, always looked like an officer. Why had he not advanced like them?

Amid the confusion Tom ran face to face into Colonel Leonard Wood. Twelve years had increased the colonel's waistline. Tom Horn was slim and active as ever. The two men shook hands. Wood said, "So you're in the pack train! That's fine."

"Yes," Horn replied, "I'm pack master but I'm acting chief."

Recalling Arizona days, Wood asked, "Do you remember when we were climbing up that canyon together after deer in Sonora and the renegades shot so close that it sprinkled dirt into our mouths?"

"You bet I do," replied Horn. Then the colonel, with the assurance of rank, dropped his familiarity and walked away as though Tom Horn did not exist. Surely Tom would be remembered and made chief! They had slept in the same blanket together many a time. As cowboys say, "They had licked salt together down in Arizony." Tom looked forward to promotion.

Twenty-four hours after landing, the troops had disappeared in the jungle and a mule corral had been improvised. Out of it the packers led the animals to be loaded for the journey on the soldiers' trail. Along the black mud trace Tom went with the train, hearing the faint rattle of musketry in the forest ahead, and the soft cooing of wood doves in the trees at hand. Spanish sharpshooters, sitting in trees, cooed like doves, Tom was told. "That's the way they signal to each other."

Men with loathsome bullet sores on their bodies staggered back past the advancing muleteers. Others, limp in death, were being carried by their comrades, and among them Tom saw Captain O'Neill, shot down just after boasting that no Spanish bullet could kill him. Tom had seen another captain killed in the dripping Sierra Madres. This was war. The pack train brushed by the soldiers. In a clearing vultures flew up from a corpse. The young packers gasped. Tom scoffed at them. He had seen such things often in Arizona. A little farther along, a dead man sat against a tree with a ring of land crabs whetting their claws around him. Tom Horn jerked his mule to a standstill and caught his breath.

At length the train came to the front, unpacked its supplies and trotted back to the beach. It was good to get out of the hot, poisonous jungle into sea air.

Tom was occupied in work like this when the Rough Riders, and other regiments less favorably publicized, stormed San Juan Hill. Tom himself saw no fighting, but boasted to his friends in Colorado and Wyoming that he had met Colonel Leonard Wood and Lieutenant Colonel Theodore Roosevelt as they were walking into the decisive battle of the war, and that he had given the two great men the mules which they rode in the historic charge that followed.

Military records show that Horn probably did lend Wood and Roosevelt some mules a few days after the fight, but both men rode their own horses in the battle of San Juan Hill, Roosevelt abandoning his at a barbed-wire fence to continue, on foot, the charge that ended in the White House, a charge that might have ended in fiasco except for the support of the 10th Cavalry—the "buffalo soldiers" with jaunty cavalier Shipp, who was killed in the action, still a lieutenant.

After the war, Roosevelt denounced the cowardice of the packers and pack trains. "The mule packers stampeded, turning loose their mules," he said, and again: "The packers with the mules were among those who ran." Officers of the quartermaster's department testified, "The packers didn't care to be shot at," and "The packers were on strike."

However it might have been with the muleteers as a class, in the fighting which swept the Spaniards to ignominious defeat, it was not like Tom Horn to run. On the plains of the United States he had given too many proofs of his deadly courage to make it likely that he would have fled from the Spaniards whom he despised. As late as 1930 cowboys in Colorado who remembered Tom Horn were saying of him, "Tom could kill a man and laugh about it, but if there was any runnin' goin' on, somebody else was furnishin' the legs."

Three weeks after the mules swam ashore at Daiquiri the war was over, with only twenty-three officers and two hundred and fifty-seven men killed. Then came the wave of fever and dysentery—all the usual sicknesses of military camps, all the unusual sicknesses of the tropics, all the ills caused by wearing winter uniforms in Cuba and summer uniforms when the soldiers returned to a northern winter. The final casualties amounted to a hundred and thirteen officers and twenty-eight hundred and three men: one per cent of the soldiers under arms.

By mid-July half the packers were down with fever. On August 1, Tom was promoted from pack master to chief packer, in charge of one of the eight trains. This was the top in his branch of the service—as high as a mule packer could go. His salary was a hundred and thirty-three dollars a month and board. Twenty-two men, a hundred mules and a bell mare were in his charge—on paper at least. The legend in the West has always been that Tom Horn was Shafter's "Master of Transportation" with pay equal to that of a colonel. Perhaps he was able to save more money than a colonel, but chief packer was his highest rank, a responsible position requiring both stamina and special skill. Tom's glory lasted but a short time. Fever forced him into a hospital and he came home watching the sky through a porthole above his pillow. Weak and wan, with his service ended, he applied to Pinkerton's New York office for help to get back to the plains of Wyoming.

The big city baffled him. He did not care to wander about and stare at its foreign—its seemingly hostile—civilization. New York was no place for him. A lonely man, he looked at the crowds. This was a different world from the great cool mountains, so silent, so contemptuous of all this bustle and fluster.

Tom boarded the train for Wyoming. A lodginghouse keeper nursed him back to health. His friends, the association men, had not forgotten him. He could have his old job back whenever he wanted it.

Tom Horn had emerged from the war more definitely than ever patriotic and loyal to the great men of his country. A powerful, rich and intelligent United States had pulverized a weak, poverty-stricken and almost helpless Spain. America and American capital had made the United States the greatest nation on earth. Tom was proud, in his rough way, to be allied with the men of wealth who had created such a nation.

18

THE MYSTERIOUS TOM HICKS

It was as "Tom Hicks" and sometimes as "Tom Curtis" that Tom Horn rode northwestern Colorado at the close of the Spanish-American War, looking for cattle rustlers. Rumor had it, ever after, that he was working for Ora Haley, the Wyoming cattle baron. No one, in all probability, will ever know just who his employers were, for when Tom floated into the world of myth and legend the men who had hired him locked their secrets in their own hearts.

By tradition Haley had come to Laramie, Wyoming, one year before the Union Pacific Railroad had reached town, having walked his way across the plains. As a carpenter he had gone to work, toiling for eleven days at a dollar a day and having, when he quit, eleven dollars, a hammer and a saw. Later he was proprietor of a butcher shop, became a shrewd judge of cattle and soon owned a ranch. His stock multiplied and Haley prospered. It was said that he could count his own cattle so swiftly, as they were driven between riders on the range, that when the last tail had passed he had the number of two-year-olds, threes and fours all classified in his head. Cowboys gaped at him, tallying the different classes of cattle on his fingers as they trotted by. The total number of cattle in his herds, at his heyday, is a matter for fabulous guesses. He sold out for nine hundred thousand dollars in 1913.

From herds so immense and so loosely scattered, it was to be expected that he would lose many cattle to thieves. His beef seemed as wild and free as the deer and the antelope. Through this region it was a standard joke to say, "Out here when we say grace over our vittles we put it, 'Thank God f'r the bread and Haley f'r the meat.'"

Respected and liked by his business acquaintances, Haley was hated more intensely by the settlers than any other cattle baron of his time. It was a hatred grounded on terror, for it was believed that Haley hired professional assassins to kill off some of the rustlers and intimidate the rest. Many settlers declared that they were not cattle thieves, that Haley's foremen only spread such tales about them in order to bully them into giving over their little ranges to the larger herds. They said that Haley's riders stole their cows, sweeping them from their usual ranges during his roundups, and that when they retaliated they were marked down as rustlers.

And, said the rumors in 1900, this Tom Hicks (or was it Curtis?)— whoever he was—could be nobody in the world but one of Haley's killers. So keen was this feeling against Haley that when he died, years later, the small towns on his old range celebrated the event as joyously as the Fourth of July. Ball games were played, horse races run and powder fired from anvils.

The roughest and most desolate part of Haley's range, where Colorado, Wyoming and Utah cornered, was known as Brown's Hole. Immediately south of it a diabolic nature had let Green, mother of all western rivers, sink two thousand feet below the swelling plain, and Bear River rushed through a cross canyon, to meet the Green. Hundreds of side canyons and box canyons cracked the whole region, and made what was, and probably always will be, the haunt of shifty men. Little ranches in these canyons changed hands at many times their real value because they made excellent bases from which to prey upon the surrounding big outfits. For Tom to become acquainted with all the cracks and crannies in the rocks that harbored doubtful men, to drink and joke with them, as he had with the Apaches, to learn their brands, their suspicions, their ambitions and their secret trails, was not the work of a few days but of hungry, sun-baked months.

Fancying himself a Sherlock Holmes of the hills, Tom Horn determined to clean up this vast area by ferreting out the worst offenders and either killing or driving them away. Tom's Pinkerton boss, McParlan, had gained the confidence of the Molly Maguires. Now

Tom set out to gain the confidence of the Brown's Hole settlers. Their chief pleasure was dancing. Tom attended several Brown's Hole dances. Whole families, from gran'ma to the baby, in wagons and on horseback, attended these celebrations. The boys hid their bottles behind fence posts in the dark and stood bashfully around the door. They parted to let the girls go inside to take seats demurely along the ladies' row. Tom's business was to judge the merrymakers, even as he danced with them, and mark the worst for death. He studied the women as well as the men.

That was "Berthy" Hall with the wildcat skin around her neck, the gift of a trapper friend and still smelling like a dead animal.

That frail little girl with the delicate features and the well-chiseled nose was Wanda Dudley. She would be pretty as a spring flower if it were not for her eye—knocked out by her angry father's quirt when she was a toddler.

That other girl was Kelma Young, short-backed and sturdy, her merry head as round and black as a huckleberry.

That girl beside her was sprightly Josie Bassett, and there sat her queenly sister Ann, who had just returned from St. Mary's Academy at Salt Lake City.

Tom could not find out the name of a strange girl who thought she was cute. All the boys were scraping their wings around her. Joe Davenport had brought her from a cabin over on the Red Desert. Joe felt sophisticated, Tom learned, because he and the son of the Sweetwater County superintendent of schools had stolen a bunch of Haley's cattle to get sufficient money to attend the World's Fair. Those boys might have to pay the penalty for such bragging, but Tom was cautious. He studied the other dancers.

A tall Negro was playing a mouth harp behind the stove. A white boy accompanied him with a guitar. Dust rose from the floor as the Brown's Holers swung their partners to the tunes. The tempo grew hilarious. The dancers shouted and stamped their feet. The Negro's face flashed like a black diamond. His jungle blood throbbed with the music. He liked being too hot, behind the stove, when it was too cold outside. He liked to see everybody happy, to have them speak to him and call him by name. He liked to hear their talk, half-soled with oaths.

It was strange for a Negro to be in this far-off valley. Perhaps he was hiding from some crime. Certainly he would bear investigating. Tom learned that "Nigger Isam" Dart and a white man named Matt Rash had come to the country with a Texas trail herd. When the herd had been sold, they had not drifted southward with their companions, but remained to take up homesteads. Isam had gravitated to the Bassett home in Brown's Hole, for Mrs. Bassett, being Southern, understood Negroes. Mr. Bassett had been a Union soldier from Illinois, who had met, wooed and won his bride while marching under Southern pines. The Bassetts petted Isam, let him sleep in the shed and eat back of the stove during his frequent visits. Often he rode and worked with the white Bassett boys, outdoing them—and all the neighboring riders—in horsemanship.

Desert suns and Wyoming's arctic gales had changed his complexion from the velvet black of his race to one spotted and traced with arabesques of pink and white. Southerners called him a "yaller nigger," and Westerners knew him as a "pinto" or "painted nigger" or "calico coon."

The variety of color on his face and hands could not compare with that in his clothing. His leather cuffs were unusually large, elaborately embossed. On his hand he wore a topaz ring, traded from the Indians. A gay silk muffler draped his shoulders. Nigger Isam always wore a rattlesnake skin for a hatband and the brim of his sombrero drooped around his ears like the headpiece of a nomadic sheik. Some Arabian blood may have flowed in the veins of his forebears who crossed the Atlantic in an ancient slave ship, for he sat his horse like a true son of the desert. On the open range, with a good horse beneath him, he was a dusky lord. When he dismounted at Bassett's ranch he became a grinning coon. An expert cowboy, an adept with a rope, "the Nigger" thought Haley's far-flung herds Providence's chicken coop. Isam was the kind of victim Tom was looking for—except for his color. Would the violent death of a Negro intimidate the white settlers of Brown's Hole? This was

Tom's problem as he studied the situation further. Matt Rash and the Nigger were as inseparable as a Texan and a Negro could be. Did they work together rustling Haley's cattle or was it Matt's interest in Josie Bassett that kept him constantly at the Bassett ranch? Tom decided to get more details before he acted. He "throwed in" with Matt, camped and rode with him for days, but Matt was tight-lipped. He never suggested working a brand with his new friend or even killing a calf for "camp meat." From all Tom could learn, Matt was a capable young settler with a small herd of a few hundred cattle and generous social habits that made him well liked in the community.

Then one day something happened. . . .

Tom and Matt were riding up a gulch when suddenly the Nigger met them with a Winchester in his hands.

"Don' come no closah, Matt," he said, with a guilty grin on his big mouth. "If you do I'll sure nuff have ter shoot."

Tom turned to his companion. Matt was looking at the Nigger the way a born Texan looks at a black man. He replied, "What you-all up to? Nothin' good, I reckon." The cowboy touched his horse with the spur and started forward. Tom followed.

"Now don', Matt," expostulated the Nigger as the cowboys rode by him. "I'll have ter shoot. Hones'." His pleading voice trailed after the horsemen.

A dead bull lay in the gulch close at hand.

"Isam, you've done killed Sam Spicer's roan bull," said Matt, dismounting the better to examine the carcass. "You hadn't ortah done that."

"I knows it, Matt. Wha's I gwine do now?"

"This is what you-all goin' ter do. Buy that bull off'n Sam befoah he finds out you-all killed it."

"Yes, Matt; dat's right."

"And, Isam, I ain't goin' to say nothin' about this, you black niggah you, but, you'd better leave me that sorrel hoss thaih, or I'll sho' enough tell Sam what you-all done."

Isam kicked the carcass absently, mumbling, "No sah, you-all cain' hab dat sorrel hoss." The Nigger had raised the sorrel on a bottle. He loved it like a friend.

The next time Rash passed through Dart's meadow, he roped the sorrel and took it away, announcing to the countryside that he had traded for it. The "calico coon" said nothing, but the wrong glowed in his black heart. He appealed to Tom and told him all the "stealing scrapes" in which he and Matt had taken part.

This was all the evidence Tom needed. But before killing Matt Rash, Tom gave him a chance. A note tacked on the cabin door warned him to vacate the country within sixty days. The notice came soon after Matt and Josie Bassett had decided to marry, and the prospective bridegroom had this additional reason to remain. Furthermore, he was too full of vital sap to run from threats. And then, such warnings might always be nothing but practical jokes. Joe Davenport had received such a note when he came back from his eastern trip, and nothing came of it. Matt laughed about the affair, and announced, "I'm goin' to stay where I goddam am."

Tom was still living with Matt when he made this decision. It would have been suicide to kill him at once. Had the Texan been murdered at this time, the stranger bunking with him would have been immediately suspect.

After a week Matt's guest departed, announcing that he would look for work at Haley's ranch, some forty miles away. Matt went to Rock Springs, Wyoming, to celebrate the Fourth of July. Tom Hicks faded from his mind; the world was full of tall, cow-faring men who searched for work they hoped never to find—horseback hobos riding the chuck line.

After the Fourth, Matt put his bed and grub on a pack horse and, mounting Isam's sorrel, rode to his summer camp on Cold Spring Mountain to watch his seven hundred cows and their calves. Arriving at his hill fastness, Matt took a great swallow of spring water to cool the fever of celebration whisky in his belly.

Meanwhile, down at Haley's ranch, Tom Horn, still masquerading under the name Tom Hicks, rode away, telling his hosts that he must be in Baggs as soon as possible, and that it would take him two days and a half to ride it.

He waved good-by and rode out of sight; but when he had passed the mountain's shoulder, he turned from the Baggs road and spurred for Cold Spring Mountain, riding along creek bottoms and gulches, avoiding sky lines.

Tom rode to within ten miles of Rash's cabin, shot a rabbit, picketed his horse in a little gulch out of sight, built a fire and roasted his meal. After eating he put his saddle beneath his head and lay among the wild flowers that made a carpet under the aspens. He lighted a cigarette and gazed with connoisseur eyes at his horse. To-morrow his life would depend on the fleetness and stamina of that animal. The gelding had big flat bones unlikely to bruise in a burst of speed through the rocks. He had a short back and wide heart girth indicative of strength and endurance. His sloping pasterns gave spring to his gait and kept both horse and rider from tiring. A well-rounded "bread basket" beneath his flank reassured Tom that the animal could make a long journey without eating. Tom turned to his saddle. He untied his sweater from behind the cantle and took out a handful of fancywork, hair embroidery that the Indians had taught him to do.

In recent months he had spent more and more time on this delicate handiwork, and found it increasingly diverting as time went on. While he worked he ate the rabbit and thought of many things: of the food on the transports going to Cuba, of Roosevelt and how men who ate with him said that he liked five cups of coffee or seven glasses of milk at a meal. Tom knew a man who once saw Teddy guzzling at a table while he expounded on international politics. Near by sat a cowboy who understood nothing of the monologue, but who finally blurted, "I ust to know a feller who always set the water bucket on a chair beside him when he et." Tom remembered other great men: how General Crook and General Miles had talked; Miles's words had raised blisters, Crook's words had drawn blood. He remembered how Buffalo Bill had loved the ladies! He remembered the hotel lady in Meeker who had called him, "Oh, Mistah Hohn," always like that.

Birds of solitude sailed over the gulch while Tom sat making lace from horsetails.

Tom remembered how empty the streets of New York had loomed that Sunday morning when he walked to the station, Wyoming-bound. He remembered how Geronimo had talked to Crook about God. He recalled the faces and faults of the women who had loved him. . . .

The rocks above the aspens pinked with the late sun. Tom took his six-shooter and walked to the spot where the sagebrush came nearest to the seep of the spring. Here, as he expected, sage chickens came to water; he shot three. His marksmanship satisfied him.

Then he changed his horse to new grass. Tom watched the animal move—no sign of lameness. He rubbed the horse's legs—not a blemish. He rebuilt the fire and stripped the skin and feathers from the sage chickens, then set the birds before the blaze on spits. The dark meat browned and blistered and the stars came out in silence on the sky awning over the gulch.

Tom ate a chicken, wiped his mouth on the back of his hand, put on his sweater, picked his teeth with a bitter aspen twig and lighted another cigarette. Steeped in mountain scent he drowsed, the women who had loved him walking in the half dreamworld, doing silly, delightful things.

Tom woke shivering. He smelled very cold water and little mountain flowers. Rising to his feet, he shook himself, ran his hand inside his overalls to rearrange his shirttail. Then he moved his horse to fresh grass. Next he gathered dead wood, snapped it across his knee and built up the fire. For something to do, he cooked and ate another sage hen. He practiced Apache counting, and saying all the words in German and Spanish that he could remember. He recited cowboy songs to himself, until he dozed in the darkness. In an hour he woke again. He blew the ghost ashes for little rubies and raked them together, covering them with bark straw. A thread of smoke arose. Tom lay on his stomach and blew into the eye of the smoke needle. A little flame ran up the smoke. He put twigs on the flame. Many little fingers came through the twigs, casting patterns on the white aspens. He took a glowing twig, leaned back on his saddle, and lighted a cigarette of satisfaction. He thought up homespun epigrams that he would shoot at Haley on his return. Then he dozed again. He took fatigue and hunger as the animals did. There was the uncomplaining calmness of the rocks about Tom Horn. This was his life.

When the east paled with dawn, he led his horse to the spring and watched the small ears pump with drinking. Then he saddled up and led him back to fresh grass. The horse appeared rested and well filled. His hair gleamed with health. Tom planned to reach Matt's cabin at noon, in time for dinner, so he lay down for another snatch of sleep, but the sun was getting hot and the flies bad. At ten o'clock he watered the horse again, slipped the bit into his teeth and swung aboard. Horse and horseman climbed out of the gulch onto the carpet of swelling tableland. At the top of the mountain the horse paused to inhale a deep breath. Then Tom started straight for the cabin where Matt Rash camped. Luck was with Horn. When he looked over the ridge above Matt's cabin, he saw a small man-figure walk into the distant door. Only one horse was tied to the aspens in front of the cabin. In a minute Tom saw the fresh white dinner smoke come out of the chimney.

There was no window in the cabin, so Tom circled around and came to it from behind. He knew it would take Matt half an hour to get his meal. Tom stopped, dismounted, pulled off his boots—an Apache trait—tied them behind his saddle, remounted and rode on a fast walk down toward the cabin. Matt's horse, tied to the aspens, watched him silently. Behind the cabin Tom dismounted, let his reins fall to the ground, slipped his revolver from its holster and walked noiselessly across the chip pile to the open door.

In a second's flash he saw Matt's face come up from his plate on the table, his arms spread out holding knife and fork, his mouth drooping open in astonishment—food showing inside. Even as he saw the picture, Tom fired at it, and Matt fell to the floor.

There was a crash from the aspens behind, and the barefoot man jumped into the shadowy cabin. With revolver poised, he peeped out of the dark doorway. Matt's horse had broken loose from the aspens at the sound of the exploding cartridge and was trotting up the hill through the trees, stirrup leathers flapping.

Tom turned back to the room.

Matt's white face was coming up over the table. His numbed arms and shoulders were weaving, shaking, as he pulled himself upward from the floor.

Tom's revolver was as much a part of him as the hand that held it. There was another deafening roar and when the smoke cleared away the face was gone. Tom walked around the table. Matt was dead. Tom rolled the body over and noted that the first shot had been too high, missing the heart. Then Tom went to the door. No one in sight! He turned to Matt's bed, a rude frame built in one corner of the cabin, a mattress of slough grass with quilts on top. Tom threw back the upper quilt and tossed the corpse into the bed. He pulled off Matt's boots and hung his six-shooter on the bedpost. In the dead man's pockets were twenty-four dollars in bills, neatly rolled. These Tom stuck in a chink in the logs over the dead face. Then he pulled up the quilt, walked to the table, drank a cup of coffee, munched some bread and meat and stepped outside. The brilliance of outdoors hurt his eyes. He untied his boots from his saddle and pulled them on. He mounted and, riding across Matt's horse pasture, hunted out Isam's sorrel and shot it dead.

Now, when Matt Rash was found, people might say that Nigger Isam killed him in a fight over the animal.

The killing of the sorrel completed, Tom rode off along the rim-rock summit of the hill where his own great horse's hoofs would leave no track. After a half mile of this progress, he turned toward Baggs and leaned forward in the saddle with the grace that came from a quarter of a century of riding. He must go it like the wind, to reach Baggs in time to prove his alibi.

19

TWO FIGHTS IN A BAGGS SALOON

In the West there live two tales of Tom Horn's entrance into Baggs. One is the story told by his friends, the other is the story told by his enemies.

The first is set down here as it was given on a certain September night, beside a campfire in Echo Park where Green and Bear Rivers join. A bent and twisted veteran of the range was talking. All day he and his companion had ridden that tumbled country while Bear River ran like a dog at their side. Behind them now the moon was rising, throwing shadows of cliffs upon the canyon wall. Carved and creased by the years, the eroded cliff looked like a row of stupendous, sculptured Indians sitting motionless, and the black shadows were like buffalo robes across their knees.

The rivers roared and wailed, coyotes howled, stars burned on top of gashed and mangled walls.

"Yes, sir," drawled the old cowpuncher, "the gods had a hell of a wrastle here when the world was soft, didn't they?"

Silence—the black shadows slipped slowly down the canyon walls—silence for a quarter of an hour.

"Say," came the old man's voice from beyond the little cedar fire. "You were talking this afternoon about Tom Horn. Well, the day after he killed Matt Rash he rode into Baggs. He was dirty and he smelled tired, and you could tell that his horse was all in by the way it poked its nose too deep into the horse trough. Tom went into the Four-Ace Beer Hall—it was painted white and its doors opened up the whole front of it so's a man could ride his horse in and have a drink in the saddle. After a long ride the damp floor in there felt good to a man's feet, and there was a whole lot of cowboys there drinkin,' when in walks Tom, and rings a silver dollar on the bar and says, 'Give me a pair of overalls.'

"The barkeep sets out a bottle of Overholt's and two glasses. Tom drunk 'em both and then walked over where there was a poker game goin' on.

"A feller named Newt Kelly was there and he'd had just enough likker, so he looked at Tom and said, 'Men in the country I come from would be kangarooed f'r takin' a drink alone.' He was shorter than Horn and thicker and, when Tom took him up, he said he wouldn't fight fists nor pistols, but knives.

"'That suits me,' says Tom, and everybody watchin' leaned their elbows on the bar and put their backs against it while Tom and Newt took off their shirts. These two men's faces and hands were sunburned so red it made their bodies look as white as the grass you see when you raise up a board.

"Newt got out his knife and then he put one end of a bandanna handkerchief in his teeth. The barkeeper came out and as he put a knife in Tom's hand he whispered, 'If you hear me say, "Here comes Bud Wilkins," you turn around and look behind you quick.' Then in a loud voice he says, 'Air you ready?'

"Both men grunted with the handkerchief in their teeth.

"'All right then, *go!'*

"Newt hit Tom in the stomach with his left fist so Tom would double up and give him an opening for the knife. But Tom jumped in close to Newt and the knife missed his throat and ripped him from the shoulder to the point of his chin. Then each one caught the other one's knife hand and they froze there, strainin'.

"Damned if they didn't look like dancers waitin' f'r the music to start.

"The boys crowded closer to see and one of 'em felt a hot spray on his face. He wiped it off and seen it was red. Then he seen there was a quiet little spray comin' from Horn's neck.

"All at once Newt's arm gave away with a jerk as though it worked on a spring and Tom's knife hand was free at Newt's back.

"Both were breathin' and gurglin' like a buck that's been shot through the lungs. Tom didn't want to kill Newt, so he just swiped the blade up and down Newt's back to show who was boss.

"Just then the barkeep sings out, 'Here comes Bud Wilkins,' and Tom whirls Newt around like a feller turns his partner in a dance and he sees one of the men in the crowd pointin' a .45 Colt. They stand like that from then on, you bet. Tom didn't give Newt's friends a chance to shoot him in the back.

"It made the boys kinda mad to have their attention drawed from the fight to a feller pullin' a gun, so they made him put up his .45 after a while.

"Tom's eyes stuck out like oysters trying to look down over Newt's shoulder to see how much damage he was doin'. The blood was clottin' where Newt's drawers rolled up over his waistband.

"Then Newt folded up like a trap and his knife rattled across the floor. The barkeep tied up Tom's neck. Wounded as he was, Tom loped sixty miles to Rawlins."

The story Tom's enemies tell comes from a sage and venerable sheepherder who recounted it one summer day on Baldy Mountain. His sheep dotted the green slopes above timber line as plant lice dot a rose leaf. He was building a fire from the skeleton of a wind-twisted spruce. As his hands worked, he talked.

"That Tom Horn was an overbearing bully, but he got his onct. After he killed Matt Rash he got into Baggs on a fagged horse. He was dirty and tired and you could tell his horse was all in by the way it poked its nose into the waterin' trought. It was a hot day, so hot that the lizards carried little boards with them to lay on every little bit so that they could blow on their toes. It was durin' the first cuttin' of alfalfa and nobody was in town.

"Tom walked into the Bull Dog saloon and rung a dollar on the bar and asked for a pair of overalls. The barkeep folded up the *Rocky Mountain News* and put it back of the Budweiser picture of the plump lady on the feather bed and set out two glasses and a bottle of Overholt's.

"A freckle-faced kid was lookin' in the door and Tom said, 'Hey, kid, shut your mouth and take my horse to the livery barn.' The kid just stood and stared. Tom was out of kilter and abused the kid. The kid's face began to swell and get dark red. He blubbered bad names at Tom and Tom slapped him and the kid run off bawlin', 'I'll get my Pap to tan you good and plenty.'

"Horn walked over to the gamblin' table and wanted to play seven-up. People who say he tried to play poker only prove they wasn't there when they say a thing like that, for there was only one man in the saloon beside Tom and the barkeep and he was Jim Davis.

"While Tom and Jim played seven-up, who should come in but the kid's older brother Newt, who had been to Shafer's to borrey a sickle bar and had stopped in to get a glass of beer before goin' home?

"Tom looked up and saw what appeared to be a bigger annex of the kid and says, 'Have you come to take it up?'

"Newt said, 'Take what up?' and Tom told him what had happened and Newt said, 'If you feel fresh, I'll accommodate you.'

"Tom run for his gun behind the bar where he'd left it. Newt weighed only a hundred and twenty-five pounds but he whipped out his pocketknife and jumped on Horn like a weasel and started to whittle him down to his own size, so's the fight would be even. The first slice he got Tom from the shoulder to the chin and then both rolled on the floor with Tom twistin' the knife outa Newt's hand. The big and little men lay spraddled out, strainin' and reachin' for the knife. Tom's fingers were about to get a hold of it when Newt give it a kick and it went rattlin' clear across to where Jim Davis picked it up and put it in his pocket.

"Horn dropped Newt to see about his own shoulder and Newt run and got Tom's gun and went away with it. He left it on a fence post within sight of the saloon. Horn sent for a doctor and was in bed at the hotel for six days. Then he rode to Rawlins."

The first of these stories is the version the cattle barons and their henchmen spread in the days when Horn was serving them; the second is that developed among the farmers, and other enemies of the feudal lords.

There was beyond any doubt a Newt Kelly in Baggs at the time Tom Horn arrived immediately after the death of Matt Rash. The Newt Kelly remembered in later years was, however, no famous knifeman, nor sturdy farmer; he was, instead, a loafing drifter, a little horsejockey of a man with an Irish face, who never worked and seemed welcome without money among the covered-wagon gypsies who camped along Snake River with a bottle and a woman or two for sale.

It is also certain that Tom Horn had a fight with Newt Kelly and was cut by his opponent's knife. All accounts agree as to the slicing of Tom from shoulder to chin and the rattle of the knife across the floor.

All accounts agree also that the horse thrust its nose too deep into the watering trough. Even Tom Horn's very different explanation of how he got his chin-and-shoulder scar carried the detail of the weary horse and the water. Tom's story was that he was shot by cattle rustlers while pursuing them between Wamsutter and Tie Siding along the Union Pacific. He had stopped at a water hole and was whittling a toothpick with his knife while his horse buried its hot nose in the spring. A shot from the sagebrush knocked him out of the saddle. He crawled into the cedars, bandaged his neck with his shirt and lay there three days, creeping down to water after dark. At the end of that time, feeling sure that his enemies had fled, he escaped to safety, but the scar was always on his chin and shoulder.

NIGGER ISAM'S LAST CAKEWALK

On July 9, 1900, two boys, riding casually across country, stopped at Matt Rash's cabin for dinner. They spurred their timid, snorting horses on to the chip pile in front of the door. One of them yelled, "Hello!"

No answer.

The other boy said, "Somebody must be home; the door's open." Dismounting, he stepped into the dark cabin. Soon he bolted out, his face the color of fresh chips on the pile. Together the two boys whipped to Green River and spread the news—Matt Rash was dead! For miles in all directions ranchers loaded their families into wagons and rattled away to Cold Spring Mountain. Whole families came on horseback with pack animals bearing their food and bedding.

The Bassetts came, bringing Ann and Josie, who sat apart from the bevy of girls in their white starched party dresses. Iron resolve was in their girlish faces.

The menfolk stepped into the cabin as soon as each family arrived. They came out grim and solemn. All evening the women cooked supper over the fires. Little boys, soon recovering their spirits, played loudly on the outskirts of the crowd. The men argued and reargued the question: Who killed Matt Rash? Some thought another of Josie's suitors had shot Matt; some wondered if the cow barons hadn't really sent that warning two months ago, the note that Matt had laughed at. Nobody suspected Tom Horn or Tom Hicks, if indeed any of them thought of that passing cow hand in this connection.

The neighbors stood around their fires talking late into the night.

Next morning the boys went after their horses. They came running back to say that Nigger Isam's sorrel was dead there in the pasture. "He's been shot, too!"

Instantly many voices fixed the murder on the calico coon—"Isam and Matt quarreled when Isam come after his horse; Matt shot it, and Isam shot Matt!" For a few minutes this seemed acceptable; then a Southerner drawled, "No, the Nigger never done it. You notice Matt's boots were pulled off? Well, no coon's ever goin' to monkey that long around a corpse; let alone a corpse he's made his own self."

So Matt's murder went unsolved. The community buried his badly swollen body and retired to gabble over the affair. His aged and feeble father came from Texas. Charles Neiman, former sheriff of Routt County, was appointed to administer the Rash estate. He drove down from the county seat to Brown's Hole—two hundred miles—with old Mr. Rash. It was necessary for the administrator to gather the Rash cattle and sell them to the highest bidder. Charlie Neiman hired every cowboy he met to help with his roundup. On the road they ran into Tom Horn and offered him a job. Tom agreed to come to Cold Spring Mountain in a few days and help. The murderer and the murdered man's father separated.

Both parties moved toward Brown's Hole, one by a northern and the other by a southern route. Neiman and the old man left a trail of parallel wagon tracks in the desert sand. Tom's trail might have been made by an Apache renegade.

As Neiman and Rash continued their peaceful drive they did not know that a small ranchman named George Banks dashed into Craig reporting that he had been shot from ambush at the head of Big Gulch, twenty miles west of town. The bullet came from a long way off and only tore his shirt. Banks declared that he had been shot at because he had overheard Tom Hicks and Ora Haley's foreman, Hi Bernard, planning the Rash murder. Nobody knew which way Tom Hicks had ridden, but it was not long before more evidence of his mysterious route came into town. Fifty miles west of Big Gulch another ranchman, "Long Horn" Thompson, heard the crack of a rifle and the zip of a bullet as he rode along Snake River where he owned a ranch that joined Haley's headquarters. Long Horn spurred his horse through the willows and, wallowing through muddy water and quicksand, he escaped. Soon both he and George Banks were boasting that the barons' executioner couldn't get them. And for the following fifteen years, Long Horn bragged upon all occasions that he was the one and only man whom the notorious Tom Horn had missed. By that time Long Horn Thompson had many rivals for the honor. Merely to have been shot at and missed by the fiendish Tom Horn was to be a celebrity.

When Neiman and Rash unhooked their buckboard on Cold Spring Mountain a few riders had assembled for the roundup but Tom Horn was not among them. Neiman saw that he was going to be shorthanded, so he sent word to Nigger Isam and the Bassett boys to bring two more men and come help with the work. Neiman never suspected how he was entangling the lives of persons already connected by the tragic skeins. He had known Nigger Isam some years before, and liked him. Dart, at that earlier time, had been riding and camping with two white desperadoes who were arrested for burning a ranchman's hay. The white men had convinced the Nigger that his only hope of escaping the noose was to admit that he alone had burned the hay and that his friends were innocent. The poor fellow had complied and had lain in jail on a short sentence while the liberated rascals stole all the cattle he had accumulated.

Neiman had been sheriff during Isam's incarceration and told, in later years, how the other prisoners had liked the calico coon. He added, "I never knew you could have so much fun with a Nigger; why, he was the life of that jail."

Neiman proceeded to gather the Rash cattle as rapidly as he could, shorthanded. Old Mr. Rash, too feeble to ride, stood around the campfire all day with a drop on his nose and his overcoat trailing in the mud. When riders brought in bunches of cattle, he rode out to examine them.

The few cow hands worked hard to cover the wide range over

which Matt's cows were scattered. Neiman wished that Isam and the Bassetts would hurry to his camp.

The Bassetts planned to go, but they were delayed gathering fresh horses to be used in the work. They lost more time getting the two extra riders. At last they set off. On October 5 they came to Isam's homestead with their horses, turned them into the pasture, and settled down for the night. Tomorrow would put them at Neiman's roundup.

In after years, one of the Bassetts told how the wind moaned over the cabin that night after supper. The boys moved closer together around Isam's stove, their cigarettes glowing in the dark. The Nigger, in sympathy with the mournful night, kept saying, "Somebody's goin' ter git me. People think I got Matt, but I never. I didn't kill dat sorrel neider, hones'! I'se afraid I'se goin' to be nex'."

The Bassetts knew Isam's fears to center not on any killer of the cow barons, but on friends of Matt's. Isam seemed not to know or care about the vague rumors that had risen concerning the mysterious executioner, Horn.

But through this night of October 5, Tom Horn was riding toward the Painted Nigger. Tom had noticed that the killing of Matt Rash had not stopped the rustling in Brown's Hole. Haley's foreman, Hi Bernard, reported that there was no cessation, and that the execution of Matt had proved no lesson at all to the community. In fact most of them scoffed at the idea of complicity by the big cattle interests and went ahead, insisting that Nigger Isam or some rival for Josie's affections had done the deed.

Tom Horn had decided that somebody else must die, and that this somebody must be so obviously a rustler that there would be no question as to why he was killed. Isam was to be the man. Everybody knew that he was reckless in his stealing of Haley's steers.

Dawn came on the morning of October 6 with the wind, which had scared Isam, blowing higher now than ever. The Nigger got up, put shavings into the stove and thrust a match beneath them. The wind whistled down the stovepipe and blew out the match. Bad luck! Isam struck two more with trembling fingers before the fire started. Then he stepped out in the morning twilight. The wind whipped him right and left as he walked to the corral where he saddled the night horse and rode it out over the sagebrush range to bring in the main band of horses. Isam drove them inside the pole corral, put up the bars and went in to breakfast.

The wind grew worse with daylight. It blew chips from the woodpile. Acres of sagebrush waved like wheat. The men finished breakfast. Two of the white boys set to washing dishes. Sam and George Bassett and Isam started for the corral to saddle up. As they emerged from the cabin the wind struck their rears, flattening their hatbrims around their necks, and sending them forward as though they were doing a dance very popular at that time, the cakewalk, in which the dancer leaned far backward and lifted his knees high as he advanced. The furious gale blew the bridles out from the men's shoulders like pennants.

Nigger Isam lifted his left hand to fix a strap end on his right leather cuff. George Bassett watched the mottled fingers adjust the strap. His boy's heart admired those extravagant cuffs. A shot came on the wind. George thought it far off, but he saw Isam snatch at his shirt front as if to tear a hot coal away, then topple back into the wind and onto the ground, heavily like a sack of oats. The tempest prevented the boys from halting for a step or two. When they hove to, they stood bending into the wind and staring across Isam's body at the cabin. Had the shot come from there? They saw two startled faces peering from the door, and knew that the assassin was elsewhere. Then they realized that the rifleman was down near the horse corral somewhere, and that the wind was taking them to him. With that, the Bassetts tossed their bridles into the gale, and with the motions of boys fighting bees, they burrowed back desperately through the gale toward the cabin. With the wind holding their hatbrims over their eyes, they missed the door and went entirely around the cabin before they found it. For years afterward, campfire talkers would say that Sam Bassett never did find that door, but that he kept going until he joined the Klondike gold rush. It was true that he was still living in Alaska as late as 1932.

A coroner's jury assembled, after the boys, daring to come out, had got their horses and ridden away with the news. They had seen no man depart, but the jurymen found the spot where the assassin had hidden, and from which he had run to his horse. One juryman said, some years later, "I stepped the distance three times from where Horn hid to where the Nigger fell, and it was a hundred and ninety-six paces."

Within a few days the community was sure that Tom Horn had done it. Two men, in after years, claimed that they had seen Horn on his two-hundred-mile ride to safety. One was A. G. Wallihan, the wild-animal photographer, who had set his camera near a desert deer trail. Waiting in his carefully constructed blind, he saw a man on a buckskin horse appear on the sky line, pause a moment and look back, then spur down the trail and pass in front of the camera. The little photographer murmured, "Why, that was Mr. Hicks, the great stock detective." Two days later Mr. Wallihan heard about the shooting of Isam Dart.

A few hours after Hicks passed Mr. Wallihan's camera a long-legged man rode up to a corral on the MacIntosh ranch thirty-six miles away. Two boys had just corraled some horses and remembered the incident.

"It was Horn, all right; we learned that later. His horse was limber, so I knowed he'd come a long ways. He rode up, never said hello, how-de-do, go-to-hell or nothin'; just glanced at us. I don't ever want to see a man look at me that way again. Tom had a raw-hide lariat—like the Arrowzony hands use—and he built him a small loop and tied onto a half-broke sorrel on the fer side of the corral. We knowed that horse and what he'd do, but we didn't dare say a thing. Tom screwed his saddle down on the bronc' and swung aboard. The last I see him, he was headed east, the bronc' still turnin' handsprings and Tom whippin' and scratchin' every jump.

"I said to the cowwaddy settin' on the corral beside me, 'You've been tellin' all summer about killin' bad men. Why don't you stop that desperado?'

"The 'waddy had a harelip and he answers, 'Iah don' minth killin' the houtlaws you read about in magazines, but that sommabix looked like a *real* houtlaw.' "

Tom's ride was a duplicate of that which put him in eastern Wyoming so soon after the Rash murder, and quickly he was boasting that he had killed Isam, but adding that if it came to law he could prove an alibi. As a matter of fact, men would have to swear that Tom was seen in Laramie too soon after the killing to have had time to be on the scene of the murder.

Tom hung up his saddle with satisfaction to wait for winter to pass. The terror of his name had penetrated the most remote recesses of the range. The "medicine" he had worked was beginning to have effect. All over Brown's Hole men could be seen riding past mavericks without a single look of longing or one solitary watering of a mouth.

21

WILLIE NICKELL OPENS THE GATE

IT WAS in the spring of 1901 that Tom Horn, gravitating ever toward important men, came to the ranch of John Coble, north of Laramie, Wyoming. Everything about Coble commanded Tom's loyalty. Coble's background was aristocratic. He was graduated from an exclusive school at Chambersburg, Pennsylvania. His mother planned to send him next to Lafayette College. But John Coble, like Tom Horn, was a problem to his mother. So when John's cousin, Matthew Stanley Quay, United States Senator from Pennsylvania and czar of the state, got him an appointment at the United States Naval Academy, young John started for Annapolis. When he reached Baltimore, the fickle lad suddenly yielded to a fever that was then burning on the seaboard—cowboy fever. He mounted a train for Omaha, and arrived at the time Tom Horn was chanting bed-ground songs to cattle along the Chisholm Trail.

The range cow was king. Fortunes were being made everywhere. Young Coble telegraphed his mother for ten thousand dollars, received it, went into partnership with Harry Windsor and, within two years, paid his mother back with interest. As the Indians were driven from the ranges farther west John moved his herds from Plum Tree, Nebraska, to Powder River, Wyoming, where with his old partner and Sir Horace Plunkett, then an Irish youth of twenty-five, fresh from Oxford, they established themselves as the Frontier Land & Cattle Company, and were wiped out, with all the big outfits of the region, in the cruel winter of 1886-1887. Sir Horace journeyed back to Ireland and a political career. John Coble moved down to Iron Mountain, Wyoming, where he started a horse ranch, coaxed

Frank Bosler, a friend from Carlisle, Pennsylvania, to purchase an adjoining ranch, and then, as part owner of this second outfit as well, and manager of both, emerged as a power in the region.

Although it was as a stock detective and guardian of the range that Tom Horn came to Coble, a great friendship soon developed between the rich man and the itinerant rider. Tom admired Coble and found life with him the best he had yet known. After a day's ride, he liked to slump into an easy chair and either read newspapers and magazines or talk with his employer and the many important men who visited the picturesque ranch.

John Coble was a member of the Cheyenne Club. An Easterner of means, he enjoyed "western atmosphere." From his pastures came Old Steamboat, the greatest rodeo-contest bucking horse of his time. Once on a spree in the Cheyenne Club, John Coble shot at a picture of a member's bull, and missed—the bull's eye, not the picture. With enthusiasm for the "wild and woolly," John Coble viewed Tom Horn with romantic eyes. He liked to have the tall, bronzed horseman stop at the ranch. He liked to introduce him to his Cheyenne Club friends, and listen to his thrilling experiences as a scout, Indian fighter, champion broncobuster and all-round adventurer. Tom was moody at times, but when he felt talkative he told a story well. His humor was provocative. He delighted Coble when, at the newspapers' announcement of General Lawton's death in the Philippines, Tom Horn related to the ranch guests vivid experiences with Lawton in the Apache chases. Tom set the visitors guffawing when one brought out a popular book entitled *Wild Animals I Have Known*. Tom said that the author, Ernest Seton Thompson, had been arrested over in the Meeker country for chasing deer with hounds and killing game out of season. The authorities had quashed the proceedings, said Seton Thompson could not be guilty because he loved animals.

Tom found Coble's employees as congenial as his guests. The foreman, Duncan Clark, listened to him with respect. Crack cowboys like Pink McCoy, Otto and Albion Pflega, all but worshiped him. Tom sat many hours in the bunkhouse, playing, joking, listening. In the office he discussed how to guard the range. From a distance

John Coble, wealthy ranchman from Pennsylvania. Famous bucking horses came
from his range.

Joe Lefors. His testimony convicted Tom Horn.

Ora Haley, the poor boy who became a
cattle king. "Thank God for our bread
and Haley for our meat," rustlers murmured before meals.

Soldiers prepared to keep the cowboys from freeing Tom Horn.

came other representatives of the neighboring barons: Henry Mudd, foreman of the Swan Land & Cattle Company for which Tom had worked after quitting Pinkerton's; Stubb Biggs, wagon boss of Ora Haley's northern empire; and Hi Bernard, who managed Haley's southern provinces.

They all had theories of just who were the most annoying of the rustlers, and just how the small settlers could be prevented from crowding in on the open range. What they determined definitely, or how often they assembled, was never known, but whatever they did decide, Tom Horn knew it.

During the spring Tom radiated, on seemingly pointless rides, about the Coble-Bosler range. He was enigmatic, chatting leisurely with the settlers while they built fences around their hundred-and-sixty-acre homesteads which ate into Coble's kingdom. Tom made threats against rustlers, and ate meals in small cabins, boasting meanwhile of the murders he had committed. It was in this capacity that he first drifted into the Miller homestead where he met an odd little schoolma'am who attracted him mildly.

The girl was a stranger to the hard ways of the West. The previous summer when the Iron Mountain School Board advertised for a teacher, they had received a letter from Missouri, written by a certain Glendolene Myrtle Kimmell. Her photograph which accompanied the application was that of a round-faced girl whose eyes protruded somewhat and slanted enough to make the examiners wonder if she were a Jap, a Chink or what.

This curiosity spread, a little later, when Miss Kimmell was employed as a teacher and arrived in the district. She chatted pleasantly in a deep voice, but her skin was sallow enough to make some observers think her part Mongolian. Hawaii had been her place of birth, she said, and her ancestry German. She taught well and was so full of resolve and good manners that the community soon abandoned its initial wonderment about her race. Her sincerity was appreciated. She was too honest to wear a "rat" or a "switch," and her pompadour usually parted miserably and lay flat on her head.

She did not hide the fact that one reason she had left Missouri was to see the cowboys of whom she had read such romantic tales, and that in the Miller household, where she roomed and boarded, she was disappointed, since the Miller boys were only farm hands on horseback.

Then one day there rode into the Miller yard the knight of Glendolene's imagination—Tom Horn, with his straight, lean back, his brown, lean face, his sweeping mustache and his sidelong glance under a rolling sombrero. On his saddle and bridle were the accouterments he had acquired in the Southwest—decorations that Mexicans, in their turn, had found on the horses of Cortes, and which the Spanish Crusaders had copied from Saracen saddles around Jerusalem. The accouterments had changed shape and form somewhat, with the centuries, but they were as calculated to charm the eye of a schoolma'am in 1901 as of a European peasant girl a thousand years earlier.

Glendolene Kimmell forgot all about her new school when, after supper, Tom Horn tipped back his chair and talked to the Miller men while the Miller women washed the dishes. He made it clear enough that he was not only a king on the Laramie Plains but a man who knew his way about in New York, San Francisco, St. Louis and Havana. He said that he had traveled all over the United States, Cuba and Mexico; he spoke several languages for the Millers to hear; and he told anecdotes of Shafter, Crook, Roosevelt, Leonard Wood and many other great men of whom Glendolene had only read.

Tom noted the girl's interested eyes; he liked the quick eagerness with which she laughed at his sallies and, in the weeks that followed, he paid her more attention perhaps than he had intended. While engaged in this diverting dalliance, Tom Horn learned all the harrowing details of an ancient feud in the neighborhood. For almost twenty years the Millers had been quarreling with a neighbor, Kels P. Nickell, an erratic, red-haired Kentuckian. Nickell had been first into the country and resented the arrival of the Millers. Nagging each other over their respective rights to the range, the heads of the clans had gone often to law; then, when that method had brought its usual dissatisfactions, they took to carrying firearms strapped to their saddles.

Both Nickell and Miller expressed indignation at the entrance of John Coble into the region. Tom realized that an acquaintance with the schoolma'am might further his employer's interests just as his acquaintance with squaws had worked to the interests of the United States Army in Arizona.

In the past the Miller clan had "taken it out" on Coble with sullen hatred, while Kels Nickell had openly challenged the rich man for "usurping grazing land most lawlessly." Coble had met Nickell once for argument and in the resulting quarrel had leaped back just in time to escape a mighty swipe of Nickell's knife. The blade had slit Coble's vest, trousers' top and shirt, leaving an angry line across his abdomen. The wound was slight and prosecution was not expected, but Coble had Kels arrested. Pleading self-defense on the ground that he was a constitutional coward apt to grow hysterical in disputes, Kels went free.

From a distance, Coble, as well as the other barons, was known to hope that the feud between the Nickells and Millers would sooner or later eliminate both families from the range. Rightly or wrongly, the barons believed both clans made free with beef not their own.

Hope grew with the barons when news came that the two disputants had gone to court again to settle their ancient grudge. When the case went against him, Kels whipped out his knife and went for Miller as he had gone for Coble. This time he got his knife into his enemy's body, but not seriously, for Miller quickly recovered. Thereafter Miller never went without a shotgun with which to protect himself. Tragedy soon followed this decision, for as Miller jogged along the road one day, the gun slipped from his wagon seat, went off by accident and killed one of his own sons. Promptly Miller swore that only the death of a Nickell boy could now even the score. He reasoned that Kels was responsible for his carrying the gun in the wagon, and so guilty of the death.

Shortly thereafter Miller, while accompanied by another son, aged seventeen, met on the road Kels's son Willie, aged thirteen. Miller shouted to his boy, "Knock him off his horse with a rock!" Willie escaped by wheeling his horse. He galloped away hurling back oaths through his tears.

As the country settled, poverty trailed Kels Nickell. His family increased and his herd dwindled. Eventually he took it into his red head to brave the unwritten law of the cow range and to import sheep. Having leased a band, he put them out on the hills and stood over them, gun in hand, glaring defiantly at neighbors who rode past with black scowls. He knew that he now had scores of enemies where earlier he had none but Coble and the Millers.

Vengeance soon descended. On July 18, Mrs. Nickell told Willie to ride over to the sheep camp and see how the "woollies were making it." She added that Willie might stay all night. Eagerly the boy donned his best cowboy togs and rode away, glancing out of the corners of his eyes at the magnificent shadow his big hat made on the ground beside his horse.

From the doorway, Mrs. Nickell watched his little figure disappear down the road toward the gate less than a mile away. Twenty minutes later two shots came from afar on the wind, but no one in the Nickell house paid any attention.

The night passed, and in the morning two smaller Nickell boys set out down the road both on one horse to look for the milk cows. They decided to hunt around the gate through which Willie would have ridden last evening. Perhaps they might meet him coming home.

They found Willie, rightly enough, but not coming home. He lay dead in the dust at the gate, and the July sun had already begun to do horrible things to his small body. Shrieking and weeping, the urchins whipped their barebacked mare to the house, and told the news.

The wireless of the range—galloping riders—sent word far and wide, and before sundown settlers and their families were at hand. Dozens of eyes peered into the dust and read the record....

After going through the gate, Willie had taken a cutoff among the rocks and in so doing had surprised a man hiding near by. Willie had spurred for home, only to be knocked from the saddle by a bullet.

Dazed, the little boy had struggled back to the wire gate, let it down and then run twenty paces when another bullet had knocked him down to stay.

The assassin had come down from his ambuscade to view the body, treading gingerly in stocking feet. Then he walked back, mounted his horse which had been tethered among the rocks, and rode away. The trail disappeared.

Everybody asked, "Who did it?" Neighbor women, forgetting all their recent hatred of "them sheep-stinkin' Nickells," put their arms around Willie's mother, washed her dishes and fed her babies. Men, milking Nickell's cows for him, asked one another, "Who does Kels lay it to?"

Kels, circling and gritting his teeth, finally blurted out, "Tom Horn will get the blame for this, but he never done it." Soon through the crowd went the whispers, "Victor Miller is the guilty man."

A coroner's inquest was held. Many of the settlers wished to blame the crime on Tom Horn but it was proved that he was on the railway train between Laramie and Cheyenne on the day Willie was killed. Next Victor Miller's guilt was considered. Miss Kimmell defended her hosts by testifying that Victor was in the ranch house at the time Willie was shot. The Millers were called on to testify. Loud and obstinate, they maintained that Tom was the murderer. Soon after, the schoolteacher reversed her testimony and on second thought remembered that Victor Miller was *not* at home at the hour of Willie's death. This resulted in nothing more than throwing Miss Kimmell's testimony out of court, and the settlers loaded their families into their white-top spring wagons and went home. But the thing preyed on them. They imagined their own little sons' bodies swelling in the dust. They grew angrier. Soon the county commissioners offered five hundred dollars' reward for sufficient evidence to convict the murderer, and the state doubled it.

A few days later Willie's dazed and mourning father was shot as he and his little daughter walked to the milk-cow corral with a bucket. Two bullets broke his arm and as he lay fuming and fretting in his hospital bed news was brought to him that masked men had come in the night to club some of his sheep to death. Discouraged at last, the oldest homesteader south of Iron Mountain decided to move to Cheyenne, where he opened a steam laundry.

The thousand-dollar reward offered for the murderer of Willie Nickell attracted to the Iron Mountain section one Joe Lefors, United States marshal from Cheyenne, a medium-sized Southerner, a re-assuring sort of fellow. The marshal looked at the blood still drying on the Nickell gatepost. He talked with a quiet voice and gentle drawl to the Millers, to Glendolene Kimmell, to Coble's foreman, to everybody, and in his talk he did not conceal the fact that he was an old acquaintance of Tom Horn's. But he could find no employee of the barons who would make any admission other than the general one that it was cheaper to kill rustlers than to waste money on vain prosecutions under the law.

Before he left the region, Lefors stopped at the Iron Mountain post office to consult the postmaster, "Windy" Edwards, who was suspected of holding every letter to a strong light in the hope of satisfying an idle but avaricious curiosity. After an hour with Windy, Lefors departed in a high state of confusion, for he had heard enough, in this brief span, to convict not only Victor Miller and Tom Horn, but some forty other residents of the county.

Lefors drove out of the community, Laramie-bound, and as he did so, Glendolene Kimmell sat down and wrote a long letter to Tom. She said that she was sure Lefors was plotting against him and he should be careful. When this letter, after being forwarded and unclaimed at several addresses, finally reached Horn, he was in no mood to appreciate it; he was in Cheyenne where he had gone from Denver to spend his money on a woman whom he afterward referred to as "the big blonde." He was sure that the schoolma'am was seeing spooks. He didn't want to be rescued by her. He remembered her with the casualness of a man recalling a collie pup who had once fawned upon him. The big blonde promised more entertainment.

The only effect the letter may have had was to keep Tom from re-turning to John Coble's ranch. After a summer in Denver, Tom had planned to go back to the one place where he had been happiest. Autumn weather was always the best of the year in Wyoming. Coble would have new books, the hay would be stacked, the thoroughbred colts showing their blood. Tom wanted to sit a horse again, to ride with Coble and look at the fat beef cattle as the hands gathered them for shipment. He and Coble could hunt antelope, shoot ducks and geese in the streams, and race after coyotes on fast horses while gigantic and elastic wolfhounds streaked ahead of them.

Now Tom could not go because the schoolma'am was waiting for him. The Terror of the Range was himself in terror of the girl with the slanting eyes. She bored him, and boredom was horrible to a killer.

So he stayed in Cheyenne. The details of his summer's experiences were fresh in his mind. Certainly it would be hard to implicate him in the Nickell-Miller mixup. True, Nickell's death would have been a benefit to Tom's employer, but Kels had too many other enemies to make suspicion point exclusively at him. Besides, Tom could prove that he was on the train between Laramie and Cheyenne on the day Willie was killed. At the time Kels Nickell had been shot at while going to milk the cows, Tom could prove that he had been taking a load of outlaw horses to Denver for John Kuykendall, who was staging a rodeo performance for Denver's carnival. After delivering these animals at the stockyards Tom had said, "I'm going now to have me a good time"—and had disappeared up the crowded streets where electric signs, BALTIMORE RYE and WILSON WHISKEY—THAT'S ALL, flashed brightly.

"THE DIRTIEST TRICK I EVER DONE"

THE electric-lighted Denver that Tom saw on his holiday was eight times larger than the kerosene-lighted town he had first visited in 1879. The wooden sidewalks and the stores with their false fronts were gone. The city was no longer in a turmoil about mines. Now it was bicycles. The two-wheeled vehicles had become a national means of locomotion. Tom, a horseman at heart, stood on a street corner with jaw adroop as herds of cyclists pedaled past him. He drifted into a saloon on Larimer Street, a labyrinth of mirrors and mahogany. From men along the bar Tom heard about another anti-horse craze that was sweeping the city—horseless carriages. They were crimson and otherwise resembled fire engines in their use of brass honk-horns, shining like bells. Tom heard men in saloons say, "I rode in one and liked it, but they will never be used except by millionaires."

In the Curtis Street Theatre, Tom watched actors in voluminous dusters, with goggles, and veils over ostrich-feather plumes, singing the song that was eclipsing bicycle ditties:

> I guess I oughtn't auto any more,
>   Oh, I guess I oughtn't auto any more,
> For there're seven doctors busy
>   Taking splinters out of Lizzy,
> So I guess I oughtn't auto any more.

So popular was the song that within a few years the public had transferred the auto heroine's name to small automobiles in general. Slowly Tom awoke to the fact that Denver had changed, the world had changed. He stood on the street looking at the sign DANIELS & FISHER over the most elegant of the city's department stores. He remembered when that sign had hung over a shack in Leadville—full of red woolen undershirts, gold pans and miners' candlesticks. He had heard how within a year the shack changed to a store selling lingerie finer than in any city west of New York, lingerie for the fabulous bawds who dug for gold in rich mineowners' pockets. Now Tom saw in Daniels & Fisher's display windows wax models of gentlemen in derby hats, pointed shoes and peg-top trousers, bowing to wax ladies who resembled inverted Burgundy glasses. Tom strolled into another saloon, spoke familiarly to the barkeeper, told him that Daniels & Fisher's store yonder was managed by a boy he had once known—Charles McAllister Willcox—the little boy who had, with his father, the general, caught him killing Mexicans, one February day nineteen years before. Tom, always proud of his acquaintance with men of wealth and distinction, repeated the story about the scolding the general had given him. He remembered that in the end it had amounted to nothing. That was the way big men ruled. Tom emptied his glass. Along the bar he overheard a voice berating the murderer of Willie Nickell. The voice sounded as angry as General Willcox had been—and the general got over it. Tom ordered another drink, gulped it down and drifted away through Curtis Street's gleaming mahogany world.

The Willie Nickell case glared at Tom from the newsstands. It roared in his ears in the saloons. Little bootblacks ran past him with their polishing boxes, shouting about it. Drinkers at the bars around him said that nobody would have complained if old Kels had been shot, but a boy was different. No kid could deserve that.

Tom Horn, the disciple of Al Sieber who had taught him that papooses grew into renegades, that "nits make lice," awoke to the grim fact that the killer of Willie Nickell had transgressed against the new civilization—bitter medicine for his ego.

Mortified and unhappy, with jaundiced eyes Tom watched Denver drift past as if he were nobody. He had been accustomed to adulation in saloons. Now he saw that the day of the frontier peace officer

had passed—in Denver at least. Barroom crowds were not talking
about marshals and outlaws. They were not even interested in the
carload of bucking horses he had brought to town. They were talking about Joe Gans, "Gentleman Jim" Corbett and the past glories
of John L. Sullivan. Prize fighters, not cowboys, were the demigods
here. Tom Horn looked at himself in the barroom mirror, a magnificent figure of a cowpuncher standing almost seven feet high in his
big hat, a slim isosceles triangle from his broad shoulders to his
high-heeled boots. He was the picture of everything the boy Tom had
hoped for when he first looked into the saloon mirror at the railhead
in Kansas twenty-six years ago. Yet to the sports of the Denver half-
world he was nobody, a range-hand yokel.

A waiter and bartender in the Scandinavian Saloon on Blake Street
revealed months later that Tom Horn broke out against this lack of
notice which Denver visited upon him. The waiter said that he had
noticed Horn's physical splendor when the fellow first said, "Bring
me whisky." He noted Tom's high forehead, and thin, receding
hair. He watched how Tom got drunk, and swayed uncertainly
between the tables, his eyes bloodshot, his voice calling thickly for
more liquor. The waiter said that he had seen eyes like that in the
zoo. He watched Tom settle at a table and announce, "I'm a detective myself. I'm the best shot in the United States—yes, or any other
goddam states, by God! I can hit a dime at thirty paces. Waiter, fill
'em up again."

At length Tom rose and came weaving to the bar to cash a check,
which was too large, the barkeeper said. Tom leaned against the
mahogany muttering to himself, "I can hit a dime at thirty paces."
Then the bartender heard him say, "That goddam Nickell shot was
the best I ever made." Tom's eyes finally focused on the check. He
picked it up with fumbling fingers and said, "Le's go down the street;
I know a son-of-a-bitch that'll cash it." He staggered out.

From bar to bar Tom drifted, looking at himself and his companions in saloon mirrors. Old faces dropped out from the train that
accompanied him, new faces appeared. Some of these faces Tom
liked, others he hated. Weazened, suspicious faces grew thicker as

he progressed into the lower groggeries, faces broken and rebroken in prize rings and saloon brawls, broken and reknit into twice their original strength. They weren't the kind of faces to be hanging around an Indian fighter and a friend of Geronimo, the Apache.

Tom decided to show these rats who he was. Dimly he saw a fist flash out and land among the features of a head whose hair was clipped. He realized it was his own fist. He heard a chair crash on somebody's head. He saw billiard balls flying across the room like bullets through the chaparral that time he and Captain Tupper had gone after the Indian pony for Tupper's little girl.

The room whirled around, the floor came up to meet him. Was this the dewy soil of the Sierra Madres in his mouth again? No, it was wet sawdust. The roar was dying away. . . .

Tom woke up in his room at the Windsor Hotel. Who had carried him home, he didn't know. The proprietor of the hotel had called John Kuykendall on the telephone to say, "We've got a man laid out in his room with his jaw broken. There's a letter in his pocket addressed to you. Do you know him?"

"Yes," said the wealthy transport and rodeo man, "that's Tom Horn. I'll be right down."

Kuykendall walked down the large, gloomy corridor of the Windsor and into Horn's room. Tom lay with his mouth open, unable to speak a word. He could only fix his eyes on Kuykendall. The rodeo man hurried Tom to St. Luke's Hospital where physicians found the lower jaw broken on both sides. Investigating, Kuykendall discovered that Tom had, in his drunken wanderings, collided with a great prize fighter of the day: "Young" Corbett who, with his managers, sparring partners and trainers, had been frolicking in the mirror-and-mahogany world. Corbett's "pugs" had practiced on big Tom.

As Tom recuperated, Kuykendall visited him occasionally. The wealthy man was interested in western history; he had known Generals Miles and Crook and the buffalo-killer William F. Cody in the Northwest. He liked to hear Tom tell about Army life in the Southwest.

While he waited for his jaw to knit, Tom braided for Kuykendall a pair of hobbles with rawhide decorations so intricate and delicate that experts, examining them years afterward in the historical society museum at Denver, wondered that human eyes could have vision sharp enough for such work.

Delicate as filagree, more jewelry than harness—horse hobbles from the hands of a killer—a curious Cellini touch to Tom Horn!

Tom's brother Martin had been working in the railroad shops in Cheyenne all summer. He read in the paper that "Tom Horn" had been injured in a Denver saloon. Martin thought this man must be his brother. He came to the hospital. The two had not seen each other since they had left the Missouri farm. Martin told Tom that their brother Charles lived with his wife at near-by Boulder. He was driving a brewery wagon there. Tom had not seen his old partner of Horn & Horn's Livery Stable for twenty years.

Finally the hospital discharged Tom. He journeyed to Boulder and stayed a month with his brother. Together they attended the Frontier Days celebration at Cheyenne. The Willie Nickell case seemed to be forgotten. Tom moved to Cheyenne and received the school-ma'am's unwelcome letter telling him to beware of Joe Lefors.

Tom knew Joe, and wasn't afraid. What he did not know was that when Lefors drove away from the Iron Mountain neighborhood he had headed straight for Laramie where he made an interesting discovery. On the day Willie Nickell was killed, Tom Horn had galloped into town on a steaming horse. He had visited a cobbler's shop and left a blood-stained sweater there, then he had mounted an eastbound train.

With this garment in his possession, Lefors had returned to Cheyenne, and learned that Tom had gone to Denver with bucking horses for the carnival. Joe kept his secret all summer, weighed the problem carefully and planned to set a trap for Tom. When he learned that Horn had returned to Cheyenne from Boulder, Joe hired Leslie Snow, a deputy sheriff, and Charles Ohnhaus, the district-court stenographer, to help him. Together they made ready.

The three men all knew Tom Horn. Snow had a grudge against

him. Horn had insulted him recently. The stock detective had registered at the Inter-Ocean, close by the Cheyenne Club, the best hotel in town, where the great cowmen came and went continually. Tom had commenced to drink and cut up as soon as he got to town. One day Leslie Snow walked past the Inter-Ocean with his giant wolfhound, thirty-two inches tall at the shoulders. Tom, in fun, lassoed and threw the hound, as dexterously as he would have caught a calf on the range. Snow resented the insult, but what could he do? Overbearing, laughing Tom Horn was too big to whip. Joe Lefors' proposition to spy on Tom Horn appealed to Les. With Snow and Ohnhaus ready and waiting, Joe Lefors sauntered down to the Inter-Ocean, nodding pleasantly to his friends. The bellboys said Tom Horn was not in. "Go try the saloons, Luke Murrin's, perhaps!" They were not enthusiastic about hunting for Tom Horn. He had been entertaining the guests by lassoing the boys as they ran to answer calls. An expert with a rope, Tom could call his shots and snare either foot of the most nimble runner.

Joe drifted along affably into saloon after saloon. Finally he found Tom and suggested a drink. The two men stood up at the bar. Joe turned the conversation to the condition of the range in Montana. He said he knew that the Wyoming range had been well cleared of rustlers but that "two-legged wolves" were pretty bad up in Montana. He said that some friends of his, rich cattlemen in Omaha, would pay well to have the rustlers cleared off their Montana range. Would Tom like a job of that sort?

Horn said that he would, and took the address of the men in Omaha. Joe and Tom parted, to meet the next day. The morrow came and Lefors was nonplused, for Horn had struck off during the night on a train for Omaha. Joe was bothered, because of course there were no such men in Omaha. He had merely invented them to start a conversation with Tom.

Horn reached the Nebraska city and looked vainly for his new employers. When he did not find them, he telegraphed Lefors for instructions. That night he got drunk, missed whatever message Lefors sent him, lost his saddle and blankets and, in disgust, threw up the whole affair and returned to John Coble's to spend the winter. Hiding in the great ranch house, not so much from any man as from the near-by schoolma'am, Tom soon received a letter from Joe Lefors, saying that the cattlemen had missed him in Omaha and were now awaiting him in Cheyenne. Would he return at once? Unsuspecting, Tom borrowed a bed and saddle to use in Montana, and drove across the snow-locked plains to Laramie. There he found the train late. He retired to a saloon and began drinking to his new job. When he reached Cheyenne, he needed more liquor and obtained it. For several days he was elated over the prospect of earning money once more, and he was too busy at the bars to settle down to a conference with Lefors who followed him about, urging him to meet the imaginary employer.

Lefors kept patiently at his job. In a room behind the marshal's office he kept Leslie Snow and Charles Ohnhaus waiting for Tom's appearance.

Finally, in the back room of a saloon, Lefors found Tom asleep in a chair. He shook him and said, "Come on over to the office, and we can talk without anyone overhearing us."

Obediently Tom arose and went along. As they crossed the street, Tom said, "Joe, I'll bet everybody who sees us is saying, 'I wonder who those sons-of-bitches are goin' to kill next?'"

They entered the marshal's office. Ohnhaus and Snow heard them. In the adjoining room they lay on a buffalo overcoat near a crack in the door. Ohnhaus had a pad of paper and pencil at hand. Snow was to be the second witness to everything that was said.

Horn and Lefors sat down.

The hidden men heard the chairs squeak. Tom began: "God, this is slick as a whistle. When a man meets a feller downtown he has to stand up with him at the bar." The stenographer started to copy each word. "Standing almost kills my feet," Tom continued. "I like to ride in boots but they're hell for walking. A man my size has no business wearing a boot with a heel the size of a dime under his instep. You know even a high heel don't make my number nines look exactly dainty. Now about this job? Will shooting be allowed?

Ever since I brought in the Laughoff brothers with the beef they'd stole and couldn't get a conviction I've tried to save my employers as many lawyers and witness fees as possible, but I shoot too goddam much. You've got to protect your employer in a job like that. Nobody ever got in trouble who hired me. But it's a hard graft. I sometimes get so hungry riding that I could kill my own mother for something to eat."

Horn sat with his long body far down in a chair, his feet on the marshal's desk. "The schoolmarm warned me against you, Joe. Sent me a letter as long as the governor's message; said that you were not all right and that you were trying to find out something. I don't put much stock in her; talks too much. She's quarter-Jap, half-Samoan and the rest just German. Jim Miller's got it in for you too. Said he would kill such sons-of-bitches as you if God would let him live long enough. The Millers are an ignorant set of jays—too ignorant to even appreciate a good joke."

Joe brought the conversation around to casual killings. Tom said, "I don't count Indians or Mexicans. I killed my first greaser at a dance when I was twenty-six years old. Cut the little bugger in two."

Joe turned the conversation to more recent times.

"Don't you have difficulties collecting your money?" he asked.

"No, a man has to pay for a job like that. I'd kill my own mother for beating me out of a dime that I'd earned."

Joe countered with the suddenness of a skilled cross-examiner: "Was there any agreement signed in the Nickell killing, Tom?"

"No, I do all my business through Coble. He's the whitest son-of-a-bitch a man ever worked for in a job like that."

Joe wanted a direct confession of the Nickell murder, so he sparred with, "I know all about it. You got six hundred dollars apiece for killing Lewis and Powell, didn't you, Tom? You were paid three hundred for the Nickell job! Why did you cut the price?"

Tom took a bite from a plug of tobacco, and returned it to his pocket. "I got twenty-one hundred for killing three men."

"How much is that to the man?" asked the soft southern voice.

"Twenty-one hundred dollars for killing three men and shooting five times at another."

Tom was trailing away from the subject again, so Joe brought him back with, "Tell me about Nickell, Tom."

"The old man? You ought to have seen him run and yell like a Comanche Indian. I'd have hit him, but the sun was on the gun sights."

"Tell me about Willie, Tom. I want to know about that. What kind of a rifle did you use?"

Tom replied that he always carried a 30-30 Winchester. Lefors asked if a 30-40 did not shoot farther. Tom said that was not important. He liked to be close to his man.

"I shot the kid at three hundred yards. It was the best shot and the dirtiest trick I ever done. Killing is my specialty. I look on it as a business." Tom's jaws moved contentedly.

"You're the best man to cover up a trail I ever saw. I found no trail in the Nickell killing and I'm a good trailer."

"Sure you didn't." Tom's mouth was getting full of tobacco juice. "I pulled off my boots."

"You always pick up your shells," Lefors added.

Tom mumbled, "You bet your goddam life."

Next Joe risked the question that most concerned him. "Why was Willie Nickell killed? Was he marked or did you have to do it?"

Tom raised up out of his chair and sluiced the cuspidor. "He saw too damned much." Then Tom qualified his confession: "I *think* that it was this way. Suppose a man was in the big draw at the right of the gate; you know where it is—the draw that comes into the main crick below Nickell's house, where Nickell was shot. Well, suppose a man was in that draw, and the kid came riding up to him from that way. And suppose the kid started to run for the house, and the fellow headed him off at the gate, and killed him to keep him from going up to the house and raising a hell of a commotion. That's the way I think it occurred."

The conversation drifted to other experiences but Joe Lefors always brought it back to Willie Nickell. He intended to give his hidden witnesses as much evidence as possible. "Tell me about the Nickell killing, Tom," he urged again.

"Wait until I get back from Montana," Tom replied. "It's too fresh now."

Joe bandied his victim for half an hour, then the two men parted. "I'll see you in the morning," said Joe. Tom Horn suspected no hidden meaning in the remark.

Marshal Lefors swore out a warrant and gave it to Sheriff Smalley to make the arrest. Ed Smalley was the youngest sheriff Laramie County had ever elected. He was a soggy-built youth with a likable personality and a remarkably steady eye. Ed wanted to be a successful peace officer as much as Tom Horn ever had. He would have traded his chance of salvation for one of the long-horned mustaches fashionable among western marshals of the time. Frank Canton's mustache was a thin black line that curled like a wicked smile. Joe Lefors' mustache bowed down and back like the handle bars on a racing bicycle. Ed Smalley's upper lip still looked like a fretful porcupine.

Ed knew Tom by sight and reputation. This was his first important arrest. He was not afraid of death but he realized that it would destroy his cherished plan to marry a certain young lady in Cheyenne. Ed looked first to his revolver. Next he consulted his two deputies: Leslie Snow, who had acted as witness behind the door, and Richard Proctor, a big man almost as tall as Tom and a veteran at this work. Proctor's forehead was bald and his magnificent peace-officer mustache drooped down like the tusks of a walrus. Pompous and dignified, Dick Proctor resembled a high priest of the county jail. He and Snow both looked to their revolvers; then the three men walked around town looking for Tom Horn. They found him in the lobby of the Inter-Ocean, a usual haunt, where he could meet and talk with important cattle barons.

The officers did not want to make any disturbance in the lobby. They consulted briefly outside, then stepped in the door. Each knew his part. Snow walked to one side of the room and turned casually, his hand near his gun. Proctor stopped at the door, folded his arms and stood ready, looking at the unsuspecting Horn over his mustache with monstrous melancholy eyes. Sheriff Smalley stepped quickly up to Tom with his cordial manner and shook hands. As he held Tom's right hand, he reached for Tom's pistol with his left, and told him that he was under arrest. Tom showed no surprise, and went readily to jail beside the youthful sheriff with the two deputies pacing behind them. This was like working for Pinkerton's again.

The arrest was unbelievable. Consternation ruled among the wealthy, both in Denver and Cheyenne. Suppose Tom Horn told all he knew? Conjecture said that the heads of men high in the political machinery of the nation might start dropping into the basket. If Tom Horn talked, there was no telling where this thing might end. And Tom Horn was a free and easy talker.

A strange little woman who taught school at Iron Mountain was sure that a terrible injustice had been committed. Her Gabriel was in irons. She was in youth's time of high enthusiasm, and could not realize that the man of her romantic imagination had been born and reared in feud and violence, had seen only the bloodshot entrails of life. She knew his friends were the rich and influential men of the great West but she did not understand the secret dread and fear that haunted the cattle barons in Wyoming, nor could she foresee the baffling undercurrents of self-preservation and greed that flowed to hidden pools of treachery. All she knew was that, when Tom Horn rode away from Miller's ranch that summer morning, her eyes had seen a glint of armor.

THE TRIAL

Tom Horn's preliminary hearing was held in Cheyenne. Justice of the Peace Joe Reed bound Tom over for trial by the district court. He refused to accept bail and after the hearing told friends that he was certain of Tom's guilt but was willing to bet a new Stetson hat that he would be acquitted.

The Tom Horn case appeared on the front page of the Denver and Omaha newspapers. The press was at first in his favor and influential men backed Horn. Major Wolcott, leader of the Johnson County raid, said, "Show me a man who is against Tom Horn and I will show you a cattle thief." Then the Denver papers changed their friendly attitude. The editors sensed that Tom Horn opposed the will of the common man. Suddenly he was blamed for every unsolved killing in the last ten years. Small ranchmen, the majority at the polls as well as at the newsstands, crowed exultantly. Tom's arrest, they said, ended their troubles. Some unhappy women announced that Tom Horn must have killed their runaway husbands.

Tom Horn's trial, called for May 1902, was postponed until October. Everyone knew that the trial was bigger than the man Horn. It marked Wyoming's Fall of the Bastille, the test of organized wealth and the old Bourbon order against the mob. The cattle barons employed a battery of attorneys headed by John W. Lacey, general attorney for the Union Pacific Railroad. Judge Lacey was a small man with a quick, twinkling eye. He had come from Indiana to the territory of Wyoming, in 1884, to be Chief Justice. Judge Lacey knew the problems the large owners faced to succeed, and the problems the small ranchmen faced to exist. He had a large corporation practice and was a suitable man to defend the big interests.

Tom appeared confident that the barons would save him. The courts had never convicted him in the past. His position as chief of scouts had freed him from the holdup charge in Reno. His military record would probably get him out of this scrape also. All summer he whistled and sang, braided hair ropes and hackamores. Tiring of this, and of reading newspapers, Tom wrote an autobiography. It covered five hundred large-sized letter pages, and, aside from one chapter on his boyhood, and four pages about his Pinkerton experiences, was devoted to his Indian exploits. He wrote as he talked, like a modern Captain John Smith, with himself the hero and savior of every crisis. His affection for Mickey Free and Crook and Sieber seemed genuine. He made no references to his years on the Chisholm Trail, nor to the sod homestead and the livery barn, nor to Leadville. He probably thought those years unimportant. He did not mention the Spanish-American War or his Reno arrest. One was a holiday, the other was a disgrace, and Tom was writing to save his life, as General Miles's citation had once saved him from imprisonment. In his story Tom told of a relationship with Bucky O'Neill which could easily be proved false, and he omitted to mention the greatest exploit of his life—the day he averted the skirmish which might have led to war between the United States and Mexico—a deed easily proved true. Fluent with dates that were generally wrong, and names that were generally right, Tom's autobiography demonstrated him to be a self-appreciative storyteller with an imagination unhampered by facts.

Tom's trial by the district court was on the second floor of the old courthouse on Ferguson Street in Cheyenne. The building contained also the jail and the offices of the county clerk, assessor and treasurer. A hundred and fifty witnesses were subpoenaed. The county was paying these fortunates to see the great show. Less fortunate settlers were obliged to spend a cow or two to attend. The case was one for the children to remember. The settlers brought little girls with their hair stretched back and tied with ribbons so tight that it hurt to close their eyes, and little boys, clean at breakfast, dirty by noon.

"Baby" came too. Mother hoped that he would not cry when the best testimony was being given.

City reporters beamed with appreciation of the quaint rural costumes. There were little derby hats, too small for heads used to sombreros; men dressed in suits that still had size tags on them; men with their shoes polished and a three days' growth of beard; men neatly shaved but with muddy run-over cowboy boots; men with celluloid collars big enough to go over their heads, and with no neckties; and men with collarless shirts, and ready-tied neckties strapped around their wrinkled leather necks. A man in a tuxedo and flowered madras shirt was pointed out as the man who had overheard Tom "talk" in the Scandinavian Saloon, an important witness.

One settler laughingly told his friends that he couldn't afford to come to town but he saw everybody else spending a year's work for a holiday, so he decided that he would come if it took every cow Ora Haley had.

On the morning of October 12, 1902, opening day of the trial, Cheyenne was thronged with strangers. The hotels were crowded and many of the townspeople were taking in boarders. Saloon men looked to their supply of beverages, and footpads and pickpockets came from Omaha as though it were Frontier Day.

A motley array of passengers got off the ten o'clock train from Denver. Among them was a small, slant-eyed woman. The big blonde might weep at home; the schoolmarm had come to crusade for her knight. She was wearing a short tan jacket with big sleeves. A red tam was pinned to the knot on top of her head. Reporters interviewed her on the station platform. Miss Kimmell said in her deep voice that Tom Horn was not being treated like a Spanish-American War hero whose ingenuity and energy had supplied ammunition for the battle of San Juan Hill. "Let any thoughtful, fair-minded person reflect upon the possible consequences if the chief of the train had not insisted upon immediate landing, and then with tireless zeal, kept his hundred and more packers at work through the long, tropical night," she wrote later for publication.

Miss Kimmell walked to the courthouse, and up the steep wooden steps to the courtroom. She found it crowded. Every seat was taken. Overcoats were piled on the sills of open windows and on an old organ at the back of the room. A tall rusty stove stood before the bar. The rickety pipe was wired to the high ceiling. A half-dozen attorneys sat around two baize-covered tables. In the audience Miss Kimmell recognized John Coble, Victor Miller, Kels Nickell and Windy Edwards, the Iron Mountain postmaster. Behind the elevated bench Judge Richard H. Scott sat between two bronze, gas-burning candelabra. He was reputed to be a military man, the kind who had always protected Tom Horn. Judge Scott had been graduated from Annapolis, not West Point, and he had served as an officer in the Navy. He had been a member of the Wyoming bar since 1886, had known Wyoming in the days of the big outfits, and had watched the little men crowd in. He had seen the impossibility of getting a conviction for stealing, the futility of individual hangings and the failure of the Johnson County raid. It was Judge Scott who had issued the writ of habeas corpus to free Dr. Penrose from the rustlers. Miss Kimmell hoped that a judge who had sympathized with the barons' destroying army would protect their private detective. Other people wondered if the barons really wanted to protect their killer. He knew so much. Miss Kimmell was too young and honest to understand.

"Bring Horn into court, Mr. Sheriff," Judge Scott ordered. A side door opened and Tom Horn strode in with Deputy Leslie Snow, the wolfhound man who hated him. Sun-scorched necks craned to see the famous prisoner. Homesteaders who claimed to have seen Tom Horn before now really did see him. His bronze face had paled to a barkeeper's pink. The inactive summer had softened Tom. He was not the lank, stringy man of six months before, who rode for days with little food, and dozed and shivered while waiting for the dawn. Tom bowed to his attorneys, then with catlike grace sat down. His athletic movements were not hidden by his best dark suit. Tom Horn was as calm before these hundreds of eyes as he had been when he and Lieutenant Maus were surrounded by Geronimo's Apaches. He appeared to be sure, as were most people in the room, that he would be acquitted. Moreover, he had the high spirits of good health. Tom twirled his little mustache and looked steadily—"stared insolently," some called it—at the audience, the homesteaders he had abhorred all his life.

The whine of a fiddle playing a quickstep country jig came in the open windows. Idlers in the courthouse yard were singing whisky-flavored cowboy songs and sentimental frontier ballads. Judge Scott ordered the windows closed to keep out the noise. The selection of jurors commenced. The air became bad.

Thirty-six jurors had been impaneled instead of the usual twenty-four. Oddly enough, Kels Nickell was among them. Judge Scott dismissed him without waiting for him to be challenged by either the prosecution or the defense. The remaining panel seemed to have few qualified jurymen. Professional cowboys did not want to serve. Blustering fellows from the range, who talked fearlessly around the pot rack behind the mess wagon, whispered their answers to the examining attorneys as bashfully as schoolgirls. A few poor homesteaders who had not been in town for a year spoke out like orators, enjoying the limelight of the witness chair, and withdrawing reluctantly. Finally twelve men were chosen who did not know enough about the case to be prejudiced either for or against Tom Horn, or said they did not. Of the twelve, one was a butcher—a tradesman not permitted usually to sit on murder trials—one was a drayman, one a porter, one a professional cowpuncher. The rest were small ranchmen or homesteaders, a class who might be expected to convict Tom Horn except for a deep-grounded fear of his vengeance. In case the settlers overruled their fears, the professional cowpuncher would be certain to hold up the verdict. Tom had gained a point there.

The prosecuting attorney was Walter Stoll, another military man. He had been graduated from West Point in 1881, had known the Army officers who admired Horn in the Southwest, but had his own ambitions to further in Wyoming. Stoll had been three times elected district attorney on the Democratic ticket, and Tom had voted for him every time.

Tom had had enough experience to know that man-baiting was the trait that elected district attorneys in the West. Other candidates might be elected on account of their popularity, but district attorneys were chosen to give the populace free drama. It was said of Stoll that a prisoner once committed suicide rather than face him in court. Stoll did not deny the compliment. If Tom thought that this man might bawl him out in public for murder, as an officer had once done in Arizona, only to conclude with, "Now let's go and get a drink," he was much mistaken. Walter Stoll, with all his military background, did not have a military make-up. He was a large, studious, bald-headed man, somewhat untidy in his dress. Either his personal opinion of himself or the weight of his paunch bowed his spine forward so that he held his head back and looked down haughtily. Stoll was a bold orator, and the Horn case was inexpensive campaigning for the November election. If Tom Horn were convicted, the small ranchmen would surely return Stoll to office. Tom's friends hoped that they could drag the case along until after election, when a less vigorous district attorney might lose the case.

The opening scene of the drama was staged with consummate skill. Unimportant people were the first to be put on the witness stand. These conscientious citizens wished that they had not been sub-poenaed. They obviously tried to tell the truth as abruptly as possible and get back to work. The ex-sheriff was called to testify that Horn had killed Lewis and Powell. John Coble took the stand to make a few fearless remarks in favor of the accused. On account of his wealth he was respected by the attorneys, and hated by the small ranchmen as keenly as was Tom Horn.

The Miller sons, Gus and Victor, both testified that Horn had stayed at their father's ranch for several days, and had ridden away on the day before Willie was killed. They had had target practice with him twenty hours before the murder. Then, as though planned to instill a little humor into the performance, and to get the audience in a frame of mind to enjoy the melodrama of the afternoon, Windy Edwards, the Iron Mountain postmaster, was called.

Edwards was not disappointing. He told everything that he knew, or thought he knew, or thought someone else knew. Unable to understand the impropriety of hearsay evidence, he was harder to stop than he was to start.

Tom gave the same look to his friends, when they came to the witness stand, that he gave to his enemies—a straightforward curious appraisal. Attorney Stoll soon saw that his own eloquence was not so persuasive as Tom's dull eyes, crowfooted at the corners from looking long distances. Vigorous examination of the state's witnesses got only reluctant answers in front of that drowsing eagle. Many witnesses forgot the things they had told Stoll in the security of his office.

Recess came as a pleasant respite. The audience went down the stairs lighting their cigarettes. On the sidewalk in front of the courthouse a card game was being played. The courtroom crowd tarried, then went on to the restaurants and lunchrooms. In the afternoon "Dunk" Clark, foreman of Coble's ranch, was called to the stand. Tom's face turned white as alkali. The spectators noticed him and leaned forward, sitting on the edges of their chairs. If Tom Horn had conferred with any man as to which rustlers should die, that man was Duncan Clark. Tom knew that his quondam friend, Joe Lefors, had set a trap for him. Could Dunk Clark be in the conspiracy?

Up to this point in the trial many witnesses had shown deafness in the ear next to the questioning attorney. Walter Stoll had shouted his queries often. Duncan Clark proved to be very hard of hearing in both ears.

Tom Horn noted the witness' ailment, and the color came back in his face. Court adjourned for the day without further spectacular disclosures. Tom, back in the quiet of his cell, could hear the flag rope flapping against the pole. It sounded like the rigging of the transport when Cuba slipped past the bow. Somebody said, "It's going to blow up a storm."

The second day of the trial the rain came down in torrents. Girls got spots on the starched frills around their shoulders. Mud was tracked into the lobbies of the hotels, and the barrooms. Nobody seemed to mind. The trial engrossed everyone. Kels Nickell walked importantly from group to group. He had failed in the laundry business and now made his living as night watchman at the railroad yards. This gave him liberty to attend every session of court. As he walked up to a knot of men they would suddenly become silent. As soon as he passed, someone would say, "There he goes. Did you hear about him stabbing Taylor for contributing money for Horn's defense?" or, "Wasn't that a good one about his being paneled as a juror?" And, "There goes Kels; I guess it's time for us to go back to the courthouse. I want to hear Willie's mother testify today."

Mrs. Nickell took the witness chair with modest dignity. She was a comely woman with large appealing eyes, a Kentuckian, like her inflammable husband. Stoll laid Willie's bloodstained shirt on the baize-topped table in front of her. Tom Horn lowered his eyes—with chivalrous deference, his friends said; with shame, his enemies whispered. Mrs. Nickell identified the shirt in a soft, calm voice. Then she recounted every detail of her son's departure. She told how Willie had worn his new white hat, and freshly washed overalls, and new boots that he was so proud of, and how he had ridden away on his father's horse. She had heard shots, she said, but had thought nothing of them until the next day when Freddie came back from hunting the cows.

Her brother, a laborer in Cheyenne, also testified. He told how Willie's spurs had made tracks in the dust as he dragged himself to the gate. He too had heard the shots and was sure that they were fired from a smokeless-powder 30-30, instead of a black-powder 45-90. Judge Lacey tried to tangle him on the sound of these reports, but was unsuccessful.

Experts were called to testify for both sides. Plenty of educated men had been found who would give diametrically opposite testimony for a hundred dollars a day. One of them testified that the bullet holes in the corpse were made by a 30-30, Tom's own gun. Another expert, equally as reliable, testified that the wounds were made by a 45-90 black-powder rifle. Both experts were physicians with military experience and admitted that they knew all about gunshot wounds.

Finally the barkeeper and the waiter from the Scandinavian Saloon in Denver were put on the stand. Both men swore that they recognized Tom Horn as the man who had said, "That Nickell shot was the best I ever made." A livery-stable owner from Laramie testified that Tom had ridden to town and dismounted at his barn with a lathering horse a few hours after the murder, and a shoemaker said that a man who looked like the defendant had left a bloody sweater in his shop on the day Willie was killed.

Tom did not seem down-spirited. Could he possibly have an adequate answer for all this evidence?

Saturday came. Everybody knew that the state was going to play its trump card: the reading of the confession. Court opened and there was a noise at the door. Judge Scott looked up from the papers on his desk. The school children of Cheyenne filed down the aisles of the courtroom, their eyes sparkling in anticipation of the best Diamond Dick yellowback they had ever read. The judge ordered them cleared from court. Their places were immediately taken by adults. Overcoats were piled in the window casements. Men and the smell of horses filled the corridors. At ten o'clock Tom Horn came in, followed by five attorneys. He showed no nervousness, but his cheeks were flushed and his eyes roamed around the room. He looked at Kels Nickell, the Miller family and Joe Lefors, among the spectators. John Coble gave him a reassuring glance. Entering the bar, Tom shook hands with his attorneys and sat down. Had John Coble and the Millers known what was on the program they probably would not have attended Saturday's entertainment.

The first witness was Kels Nickell. He walked to the stand nursing his elbow which had been shattered by the mysterious bullets a year before. Kels had brown eyes and an Airedale-brown mustache. He twisted in his chair, and could not turn toward Tom Horn, who studied him closely. Tom had asked that Nickell be allowed to sit on the jury, it was said.

Both attorneys pumped Nickell. Then they extracted some unimportant testimony from a surveyor who had stopped for the night at Nickell's ranch. The deputy sheriff and others who had come to investigate the dead body added a few words. The coroner testified to seeing the imprint of a gun butt behind some rocks near the road. Tom leaned forward in his seat, with sudden interest. Two very deep red spots glowed on his cheeks.

At last came the moment for which the crowd was waiting. . . .

Attorney Stoll leaned back in his chair and called over his shoulder, "Mr. Lefors, take the stand, please." The two red spots vanished from Tom's cheeks and he fidgeted in his seat. The small, pleasant-voiced Southerner with the handle-bars mustache, sat in the witness chair. Three plain-clothes men moved up front with their hands on the guns in their pockets. The state was taking no chances on losing this witness.

Tom Horn and Joe Lefors looked straight into one another's eyes for a full half minute. The court was silent. Everyone knew that it would be death at first sight for one or the other of these two men if Tom was acquitted. Joe Lefors' face flushed. He started to testify haltingly. Then his voice steadied. Without faltering he explained how he had set the trap by putting Charles Ohnhaus and Leslie Snow behind a closed door, and how he had brought Tom Horn into the next room and talked to him.

Tom Horn sat up, aggressively staring his onetime friend out of countenance.

Leslie Snow and Charles Ohnhaus were both called upon to corroborate the Lefors story. A pad full of shorthand notes was entered in the court records as an exhibit. Then Tom was put on the stand to deny or admit each sentence of the confession as Ohnhaus read it.

Tom admitted saying that he had been unable to get a conviction for cattle stealing in the most flagrant cases, and that he had laughed about killing the Mexican lieutenant on the border. He admitted telling about the hardships of a stock detective. Stoll asked, "Did you not say, 'I sometimes get so hungry riding that I could shoot my own mother for something to eat'?"

Tom's face turned purple, but he nodded. Yes, he had said it.

"Did you not say, 'The Millers are an ignorant set of jays—too

ignorant to even appreciate a good joke'?" The audience roared with
laughter. John Coble, with an amused, indulgent smile, glanced
across the courtroom to see how the Millers were taking it.

Next the stenographer read, "Coble's the whitest son-of-a-bitch
a man ever worked for in a job like that." The whole freckle-faced
Miller tribe stared back at Coble to see how he was taking *that*.

Ohnhaus continued reading: "I don't put much stock in the
schoolmarm. She is quarter-Jap, half-Samoan, and the rest just German." The prisoner who had never understood women leaned back
in his chair and laughed toward the water-stained ceiling. Yes, he
had said that, too.

Leering eyes focused on little Miss Kimmell. "And you said," Stoll
interrupted, "that you received twenty-one hundred dollars for killing three men and shooting five times at another. . . ."

There was a stir in the courtroom. Kels Nickell, with firebrand
eyes and one hand in his pocket, slipped from the back of the room
to a front chair. He had always accused Jim Miller of shooting at
him five times. Now he seemed unconscious of his movement in
his eagerness to catch every word. Kels slipped next into a seat near
the reporters' table. Then, still unnoticed, he moved forward and
sat in Tom Horn's own armchair. The attorneys at the near-by baize
tables did not like the look of Kels's arm in his pocket. One of them
beckoned to a deputy and Nickell was moved to the far side of the
room and kept under guard.

Tom admitted all the confession except the sentences in which he
stated that he had killed Willie Nickell, but after the first hour of
cross-questioning the strain began to tell. A recess was called. The
spectators stepped out, scratching matches for their cigarettes. Tom
was led out of the room. At four o'clock he was back in his seat. The
prosecuting attorney came in. Tom took a deep breath and stretched
his arms. The grueling continued and before adjournment Tom
was showing something like fear.

At last, Saturday's testimony was completed. The foreman of the
jury stood up and asked the judge if the veniremen might attend the

Presbyterian Church on the morrow, as they had gone to the Methodist Church the week before. Tom watched the foreman casually and smiled when his request was granted.

During the Sunday recess people told one another that two officers were in town from Routt County, Colorado, waiting to arrest Tom Horn for the Rash and Dart murders if Laramie County freed him. People also pointed out John Coble, employer of Tom Horn. Coble packed his valise and set off to his ranch. He would rather have gone to Denver to see a good show—Francis Wilson or Anna Held, but he was much concerned about his friend Tom Horn. The attorneys followed him, enjoying a hunting trip in the name of business. They talked of the Horn case and other interesting cases while they waited for mallards to fly over the slough.

To roundup camps and settlers' cabins throughout the West a wild rumor spread: The citizens of Wyoming, having heard Tom's confession, had taken him from the officers and hanged him to a telegraph pole—a palpable error. The citizenry had gained confidence in the law and spent Sunday reading about themselves in the newspapers and enjoying Tom's reference to the Millers.

On Monday Tom took the witness stand to defend himself. He appeared almost jaunty, sat with his knee in his hands, talked easily and with confidence. Some thought that he acted conceited, and said afterward, "Tom Horn tried to be funny." He insisted that the shorthand notes of his confession had been garbled in order to satisfy Lefors' hunger for the reward. Tom said that he would have talked just the same if the two men hiding behind the door had been in the room. As for the Scandinavian Saloon men's testimony, they were mistaken in his identity. (Mistaken identity had saved Tom in his Reno trial.) Tom said that he was a stock detective and that he rode through the huge public pastures, to see that cattle did not stray in or out of the "drift" fences, and that the settlers in these enclosures were not stealing cattle.

Tom Horn admitted that he had ridden the Two-Bar pasture—an enclosure twenty miles wide and fifty miles long—and that he had gone to Miller's ranch to see whether Nickell's sheep were trespassing on Coble's patented land. The prosecution cut in, "Do you take your orders from Coble?"

Tom, evidently mortified at the reference to Coble in the confession, replied, "No, I take orders from nobody. I just ride around looking after Coble's interests."

On these trips, so Tom testified, he generally carried bread and bacon tied behind his saddle and made it his business to drop into small ranches and tell what a killer he was. This intimidated the homesteaders and rustling stopped. Tom said it was all talk, for, in reality, he had never killed a man in his whole life—an odd statement in the face of his recent autobiography, not yet published.

Tom testified further: On the day Willie was killed he had hidden his bread and bacon in a cedar near Mud Springs, and, as he did not go back that way, he had shot a jack rabbit for supper. He preferred to travel without a packhorse and bed, as grass was scarce, and, by sleeping cold, he would be forced to get up every hour. He could then repicket his horse on fresh grass and thus keep him fat and strong. Tom said that he was scouting along the Sybille, fifty miles from Nickell's ranch, when he first heard of Willie's death.

Here was the ancient alibi that had always saved him. Tom stepped down from the witness chair. The defense called up Albion Pflega next. He testified that he had seen Tom on the Sybille on the day in question.

This was not enough. The defense had two more witnesses and the spectators turned in their seats when they heard the swish of heavy leather-skirted chaps and the ring of belled spurs on the wooden floor of the courtroom. It was Thornton Biggs, nicknamed "Stubb," and Henry Mudd, in all the leather and strap ends of cowboy regalia. Their skin was the brown of chap leather and cracked like their boots. Henry Mudd came from John Clay's Swan Land & Cattle Company ranches on Chugwater. Stubb Biggs was wagon boss for Ora Haley's vacuum holdings.

These quaint horsemen had ridden out of ranges and townships of western scenery to testify for Tom Horn, but Attorney Stoll would not let them do so. All that he would permit them to say was that

Albion Pflega was a man known for his truth and veracity. There were just as picturesque ruffians as Henry Mudd and Stubb Biggs, who were willing to testify that Albion Pflega was not known for his truth and veracity, so their testimony got nowhere.

After the dusty gentlemen had abetted the Pflega boy's verification of Tom's fifty-mile-away alibi, Tom himself was called to the stand for his final cross-examination. Stoll asked him about the bloody sweater in the Laramie cobbler shop. Tom answered, "It must have been left by a man who looked like me." (The Reno mistaken-identity defense again!) "It could not have been mine, because I never wear a sweater in summer—just a vest."

"You did come into the Elk Horn Barn in Laramie on a sweaty, trembling horse about three hours after Willie Nickell was killed, did you not?" asked Stoll. "And is it not about three hours' hard ride from the Nickell ranch to Laramie?"

"When I got back from riding the Two-Bar pasture, I went to Coble's ranch and put on some clean clothes and told Mrs. Coble that I would pay for my laundry as soon as I got back, as I had some money coming. Then I got a fresh horse and went to Laramie."

"Is it so, as the livery-barn man says, that your horse was sweaty and trembling when you got into Laramie?"

"I was riding old Pacer. He wanted to go and I couldn't bear to disappoint him."

"That's all."

Walter Stoll closed his case before a third of his witnesses were called. He summed up the evidence in a five-hour speech, basing his case on Tom's bad reputation; on the fact that he was employed as detective by John Coble, who was an old enemy of Kels Nickell; on Horn's having been at Miller's ranch the day before the murder; on Willie's having been killed by a smokeless 30-30, such as Tom carried; on Tom's having left a bloody sweater at a shoeshop in Laramie a few hours after the murder; and on Tom's admission in the Scandinavian Saloon, and again in his confession, that he had killed Willie.

During the oration Tom sat with his head in his hands and looked almost ill. The corners of his mouth twitched whenever there was

Tom Horn in Sheriff Smalley's office.

Photograph by W. G. Walker, Cheyenne, Wyoming

"That ain't Tom Horn. That's a hobo the sheriff hung instead." (Charles Horn third from left.)

any reference to the boy. Stoll told the jury that secret murders were brought to light by Almighty God. He neglected to give any credit to John Barleycorn. Tom might have thought that he was in Reno again, listening to the Honorable William Woodburn. Stoll, in his final appeal to the jury, referred to Willie Nickell's bloodstained shirt on the table before them. The prosecuting attorney turned it over a time or two, hunting the bullet holes. Kels Nickell saw his hesitation. He came to the table eagerly, pawed the garment, stuck his fingers through the holes and disgusted the jury. Tom had won a point there.

John W. Lacey closed the defense by reminding the jury that the prosecution's case was based on circumstantial evidence and Tom's confession—a boasting joke. He showed by hospital records that Tom's jaw was broken before the saloon men claimed to have heard him brag about killing the boy. Lacey produced the Laramie livery-stable books and proved that Tom had not come to town until two days after the murder. "I ask you to consider every single fact," Lacey said. "Certainly not one of the state's points has been proved beyond a reasonable doubt. It will be to you a pleasant duty to give to life and liberty the protection allowed by law. I thank you, gentlemen."

The jurymen retired a little after eleven o'clock on October 23, 1902. Sheriff Smalley locked them in a room for their deliberations. A few minutes later he heard a knock on the door. Smalley opened it and stuck in his round, boy's head. The foreman said that one of the jurors was ill.

Would the whole case have to be tried again? If so, Tom Horn had won, for the county was bankrupt. The case had cost over thirty thousand dollars. A similar situation had ended the trial of the Johnson County raiders. Smalley called a physician and stood anxiously at the door. Before long the doctor came out with his satchel. He reported the juror's health restored. Smalley locked the door again and reported to Judge Scott, who gave a great sigh of relief.

In the saloons and gambling houses books were opened and bets were placed on the jury's verdict. All the odds were against conviction. A hung jury was considered probable. The bartender at Harry Hynd's Faro Parlor sent word to Tom that he had a bottle of wine on ice to drink over the bar with him as soon as the jury brought in its verdict. The proprietor of the Inter-Ocean Hotel said he intended to ask Tom Horn to be his guest as soon as the jury made up its mind to his innocence. Joe Lefors, Charles Ohnhaus and Leslie Snow debated what they must do in case of an acquittal.

In front of the stores the witnesses packed their wagons for the ranch. They were leaving over five thousand dollars of the state's money in stores and saloons where they bought groceries wholesale and filled demijohns with liquor for the long trip home. At noon the jury marched down to dinner at the Inter-Ocean Hotel, then back to the room it had occupied for just two weeks. The ranchmen continued their trading. A Denver newsman was amused when a settler purchased a dozen pairs of cotton work gloves with the remark: "Them Democrat gloves are the thing. They keep your hands warm and you don't need to pack no handkerchief."

News that the jury had reached a decision fluttered down the street like a breeze across bluestem. Ranchmen hurried from the stores smoking cigars given them for paying cash and scampered up to the courthouse. The courtroom, halls and stairs were packed. Members of the jury filed in and took their places in the mahogany-railed jury box. Joe Lefors was in the audience with a .45 Colt showing under his coat. Several other witnesses had made up their minds what they would have to do if Tom was released. The door opened from the sheriff's office. There was an expectant silence. Tom Horn entered with a quick step. His jailers followed. Tom looked anxiously around the room, then took his seat. He saw Joe Lefors, Leslie Snow and other unfriendly faces. He could not see his best friend, John Coble. Finally Tom's eyes brightened. He saw Duncan Clark, Coble's foreman.

Judge Scott ordered the roll call and said, "Gentlemen of the jury, have you arrived at a verdict?"

"We have, your honor."

"Give me the verdict, if you please."

A paper was laid on the desk. Judge Scott read it to himself with a perfectly impassive face. The paper trembled as he passed it to the clerk, saying, "Read it aloud, Mr. Clerk."

The clerk began: "The people of the state of Wyoming, versus Tom Horn, indicted for the crime of murder in the first degree, as set forth in the charge. We, the undersigned jury, impaneled to try this case, do find the defendant guilty of murder in the first degree, as set forth in the charge."

"Is that your verdict, gentlemen of the jury?"

"It is, your honor."

Tom Horn did not blanch or give any sign that he had heard it. He turned and walked out of the courtroom and back to his cell. On the way he smiled to a friend. The jury was discharged and the crowd melted away.

That night one of the jurymen said to his wife, "The first time we voted it was nine to three. I was sure that cowpuncher and one other of them three would hang the jury. We voted six times and the last time even the cowwaddy wanted to hang Tom Horn. He said, 'It was hard to go against a man I have known and liked. But what could I do? . . . I did my duty.'"

Tom, in his cell, knew all about the delays of involved justice, appeals, remands and writs of error. He believed in the power of the cattle barons. As a last resort he might save his own life by telling the names of his wealthy accomplices. Tom had been arrested on January 13. His trial began on Friday. Court was in session thirteen days and he was convicted on Friday. So far so bad. But Tom held an ace up his sleeve that would fool them all.

"TOM HORN HAS ESCAPED!"

TOM looked at the barred windows at the end of the corridor as he exercised in jail. "I'm not a dead man yet," he said. The petty criminals heard him and wondered what he meant. The cattle barons in their city offices did not hear him, but they realized their only hope lay in Tom's spoken word that "nobody ever got into trouble who hired me." However, they would rest easier when Tom's mouth was stopped with death. As things stood now Tom might make them join him trotting between the iron cages, and they were afraid he would if he suspected duplicity.

Tom had been allotted a second-story cell formerly occupied by Kinch McKinney, a cattle thief whose attorney had smuggled him a revolver with which, for fourteen hours, he had held the whole jail at bay. Tom was not allowed to talk with the prisoners but he talked and joked with his jailers as they watched him exercise in the corridor between the cells. Trains going east, west and south carried the news of his conviction to his brothers and sisters, who kept the news from his ninety-year-old mother. Sheriff Smalley saw Tom Horn's furtive look at the barred windows. Tom was his first important prisoner and the youthful sheriff was nervous. He stroked his pincushion mustache in meditation and determined not to let his prisoner escape, no matter what it cost the county. Cautiously he increased the number of his deputies.

Tom's spirits were still high on the first Sunday after his conviction when many of the prosperous citizens of Cheyenne reluctantly followed their wives to St. Mary's Cathedral across the street from the jail. Tom heard the chugging of their bicycle-tired red autos. It seemed a sacrilegious way to go to church; the women in the machines thought it was a good way to get their menfolks to go. As soon as the cars coughed to a standstill, the churchgoers could hear whistling notes from the convicted man's cell. The tune was, "Good-by, My Honey, I'm Gone."

Glendolene Myrtle Kimmell did not hear it. She was on a train headed for Denver. She knew, as well as Tom did, that hope was not gone.

While Tom was amusing himself in this manner, waiting for his cattle friends' next move, his old acquaintance Buffalo Bill opened the Irma Hotel at the gateway to Yellowstone Park. The hostelry had an antlers-decorated barroom and pictures in the halls said to be worth ten thousand dollars. With him still was Charlie Meadows, filling the job that Tom had turned down.

The ranchmen who had attended the trial were reaching their distant cabins, and inspecting the corrals that had been deserted for several weeks. They wondered who broke the gate, and counted the chickens to see how many were missing—a terrific headache after their spree. Their wives swept out the cabins, unpacked the groceries and medicines. They put bottles of Peruna, Swamp-Root and Hostetter's Bitters along the wall where a log bowed inward to form a shelf.

The day after the conviction, a newspaper printed a cartoon of a fat cattle baron, wearing a William Jennings Bryan hat and Cossack's boots, running out of town with a suitcase marked "Conviction." The real barons went home on the trains talking to one another in quiet anxiety.

Their first move to support Tom's courage was to have Judge Lacey plead for a new trial on the ground that new evidence had been found. It was rumored that the defense would bring in the real killer of Willie Nickell. Tom was taken into the courtroom while his attorneys made their plea. He had followed the concrete testimony at his trial with interest, but he was now baffled by the abstract trail of the law, and went to sleep. When the hearing was over, his jailer woke him and took him back to his cell. The barons gained their point when the court took the plea under advisement. Judge Scott said that he would give his answer on November 12, 1902, the day set for Tom's sentence. Tom, however, seemed none too confident and still looked at the barred windows as he took his exercise. Young Sheriff Smalley again warned his deputies to be on guard.

The people of Cheyenne speculated on the barons' game; delays seemed dangerous and some cried for summary justice. Lynchings were common in the isolated parts of the state and the strain of watching Tom, who wanted to get out, and the mob, who wanted to get in, began to tell on the youthful sheriff. The sympathetic young lady he had been courting noticed his haggard look, consented to become his wife and move into the sheriff's house adjoining the jail, where she could comfort her new lord and master. Gossips whispered that she did not take the step, however, without exacting a promise from the bridegroom that he would shave off his outlandish mustache. Tom Horn's incarceration affected even these domestic trivialities.

On Halloween night the sheriff's friends decided to "chivaree" the newlyweds. The harassed young officer heard the crowd moving quietly up an alley toward the jail. He feared it was a mob coming either to save or to lynch Tom Horn. Smalley sounded the alarm, called out his deputies, mounted guard; and the thwarted merrymakers slunk back down the alley.

Election day came. Tom watched the voters walk up Ferguson Street to the polls. Walter Stoll was re-elected district attorney by an overwhelming majority—without Tom's vote. The people of Wyoming thus registered their appreciation of the man who promised to end the rule of the rifle.

Tom's high spirits changed as the motion for a new trial hung in the balance. To this was added one of the periodic illnesses, or fits of bad temper, to which he was subject. The rich men in their offices worried about what Tom might say in his despondency. Their attorneys, trying to cheer him for the ordeal of hearing his sentence, promised him that if Judge Scott, the barons' friend, did not see his way clear to grant a new trial, the defense would file an appeal to the Supreme Court.

Local politicians trying to build up a clientele among the settlers saw this move and said, "It's clever, isn't it, the way they always have another hope all ready for Tom before he gets each disappointment? They are teasing him along and when he is not looking they will snuff him out."

Came the twelfth of November, with Tom wondering what answer Judge Scott would make—Judge Scott, the military man, the old-timer in Wyoming who knew all the cattle barons by their first names and had seen them grow from cowboys with a future to businessmen with a past. If the court could not help the barons' private killer, times had certainly changed since the Johnson County War. The courtroom was not crowded. All spectators found seats, Sheriff Smalley on the front row. Tom came into the room with two deputies. His face was gray from his recent illness, but he showed no sign of nervousness other than an occasional chewing motion with his jaws. Once he started to bite from a plug of Horseshoe tobacco, but he returned it to his pocket untouched.

Judge Scott leaned forward in his swivel chair and looked down at the attorneys around the baize-covered tables. New evidence, he said, had been submitted to him in a plea for a new trial. He had examined it and found that it had been available all the time. It was therefore not adequate cause for another trial.

Suspicious spectators had anticipated this. Would Tom see the ruse? Tom remained impassive and gray in his chair. Evidently he suspected nothing. The Judge continued: "Nothing remains now but for the court to pass judgment. The court has no discretion in the matter. The duty is as unpleasant to the court as it is unwelcome to the attorneys for the defense. The defendant may stand up."

Horn rose with a spring, took two steps forward, then stopped and straightened, as he had when Generals Sheridan and Crook had inspected him with his scouts. His head was tilted high on a rigid neck, his chest protruded and his heels were together at attention. His hands were clasped behind him, and where the fingers gripped, white spots appeared. He tried to keep his eyes on those of the judge but failed. Several times he glanced hurriedly aside. The only other sign of emotion was a constant swallowing.

It is doubtful which was the more moved—the judge who was about to pronounce the sentence of death, or the man who was to receive it. Judge Scott's voice trembled. Never before in his twelve years on the bench had he sentenced a man to death.

"Horn, have you anything to say why judgment should not be pronounced against you?" Judge Scott's voice was soft.

"I don't believe I have, sir," came the clear reply without a quiver.

"Then it becomes the unpleasant duty of the court to pass judgment. It is ordered, adjudged and decreed, that you, Tom Horn, be taken from hence to the jail of Laramie County, and there confined, until Friday the ninth of January 1903; on which day between the hours of nine o'clock in the forenoon and three o'clock in the afternoon, you will be taken by the sheriff of Laramie County to a place prepared by him convenient to the jail, and there hanged by the neck until you are dead. And may God have mercy on your soul."

The stilted phraseology of the penal sentence ceased. Tom did not move, but remained erect, motionless, staring through a window to the judge's left. He saw unimportant people walking down the street. A woman ran out of a gate to grasp a toddling child by the hand. For perhaps a minute he stood, and everyone waited. Then Judge Scott noticed him and said, "That is all."

The words startled the eyes that stared out of the window. Tom turned abruptly. Without a glance at the sheriff and his deputies he rushed from the room. Young Smalley half suspected that a bolt for liberty was being made. He called softly to his deputies, "Hurry, watch out now!" Tom strode down the flight of stairs two at a time, with the deputies at his heels. In the hall below he halted and tried to enter the sheriff's office—the way to the jail. The door was locked so he turned and waited, saying, "I'm locked out, Mr. Sheriff."

Tom showed no despondency that day, but appeared confident many things could happen in the two months less three days that were given him to live. First he could appeal to the Supreme Court. There, three days later, he appeared before the judges, and listened to Lacey as he argued his case. The outside air was iron-cold and the zest penetrated the courtroom. Tom felt good. His rich friends were certainly fighting hard to save him. When his attorneys had completed their argument, Tom did a jig step, and laughed with Sheriff Smalley as he was led from the room.

The appeal was denied and still Tom was gay. Had the association promised Tom an escape by violence? His good humor engendered a perpetual anxiety about the jail. Smalley realized that his big prisoner was probably to be the first man he would have to hang, an unpleasant requisite of his office he had not considered during election. Ed Smalley, a friendly fellow always, visited Tom Horn in his cell. He thought it might be a good way to discover what made Tom so gay. The prisoner taught the young sheriff to play cooncan and the two men spent many hours together. A rumor spread through town that the barons had offered Smalley twenty-five thousand dollars for Horn's escape—or were they just making Tom think that they had? Busybodies discovered from the county records that John Coble had recently mortgaged his ranch. Coble explained that he needed the money to complete a twenty-thousand-dollar reservoir on the Sybille. Rumor insisted that he was raising his share of the bribe to release Tom Horn.

Smalley heard the rumor. His naturally sociable young nature, as well as his desire to keep in close touch with Tom, had prompted him to too much intimacy. He saw his mistake. He notified the press that henceforth he would keep two deputies all night in the sheriff's office next the jail, one sleeping while the other sat in the dark doorway listening for any sound. Under such vigilance escape would be impossible, Smalley reassured his constituents. Frankly he had learned to like Tom Horn. He did not want to hang him—but business was business.

All day Tom, in his second-story cell, whistled and braided hackamores and did his exquisite hairwork. Killing as a business had grown on him gradually. He had not realized at the time Willie was killed the heartlessness of the deed. Would he rather die than confess a disgrace? In any event he was not a dead man yet.

Judge Lacey called. Tom was brought down to the sheriff's office. Lacey told Tom not to worry about the fatal ninth of January, because his cattlemen friends intended to wait until a day or two before, and then file a petition in error with the Supreme Court, which would be obliged to order a stay of execution. Irrespective of their final ruling the hanging would have to be put off until July 4, 1903.

Was this another of the barons' promises? Tom went back to his cell grim and gloomy. His patience with legal proceedings seemed exhausted but he was not yet ready to tell on his accomplices. He had a plan of violence more to his liking and wrote to a friend, "To hell with my lawyers, I must get out of here or I will be hung."

A well-planned plot was progressing two weeks before Judge Lacey got the Supreme Court to postpone the execution.

In the middle of December a boy named Hubert Herr was arrested for stealing a saddle and sentenced to the Cheyenne jail. The officers did not suspect that Hubert Herr, with his thirty-day sentence, was employed by Horn's friends to deliver a message to the prisoner and to bring out Tom's plans for escape. Sheriff Smalley assigned the boy to a cell in the jail but let him spend much of the daytime tending his horse in the jailyard.

Tom wrote the details of his plot on toilet paper which he rolled into tight balls and hid in his bunk. The cold December weather moderated and the sun shone outside with summer brilliance. Tom dropped his paper pellets into Herr's cell as he passed on his way to meals, or while exercising. The weather outside got hot. People congregated on the sunny side of the jail wall. Tom heard them say, "Can you believe that it is December 20?" and "Ain't it a beautiful winter—but what will the stockmen do if it don't snow?" Another voice said, "Have you seen the barometer? The hotter it gets, the lower goes the barometer."

The deputies opened the jail windows to let in the fresh breeze. Tom Horn looked at the blue sky and, in the evening, noticed the setting sun pink the creamy clouds. In the warm night he saw halos around the stars. Tom was used to the sky and sensed a storm. The next morning he woke before daylight. There was a muffled sound in the air. The deputies stamped off the snow as they came into the sheriff's office. At daylight the wind started blowing. Tom knew what that meant on the Laramie Plains, and how difficult it would make his break for freedom, but the weather was sure to moderate by the time he was ready.

To the smallest detail Tom wrote his plans. Five sticks of giant powder, purchased in Colorado where his allies could not be traced, were to be placed under the jail wall. A seamless sack, containing mittens, a warm cap, an overcoat and six-shooter, was to be left in the alley. Tom wanted extra cartridges in the coat pocket, and neither belt nor holster. An unbranded saddle horse was to be hitched to a certain rack, with two loaves of rye bread, two pounds of Bologna and two pounds of cheese in the saddlebags. He wanted a pair of number-nine shoes, already broken in for him. He cautioned his colleagues to wear socks over their shoes, so they would leave no tracks around the jail.

In another note Tom explained that when everything was ready a snowball should be placed in a window in St. John's Hall across the street. Tom said that he took his exercise every night in the corridor between six and six-thirty. He ran much of the time to keep his muscles hard and his wind sound. On the first evening after he saw the snowball, Tom explained, he would strike a match to light a cigarette as he entered the corridor. This would be a signal in the darkness that he saw the snowball; and on the second night, when he lighted the match, the wall should be blown up.

Tom ate a hearty New Year's dinner and enjoyed a cigar. His plot was well conceived. He was almost gay. He laughed at the funny papers allowed him in jail—Happy Hooligan, Foxy Grandpa and the Katzenjammer Kids. A week before the date when Tom expected Hubert Herr to be released with his message, a chinook hit Wyoming. The hot wind blew sixty-five miles an hour. Tom knew that this would temper the frozen plains for his escape.

Tom and Hubert exchanged no look of recognition when their

eyes met. In January, as Hubert's last day in jail approached, another boy was committed to jail for forging some checks. This boy was to be Tom's undoing. He sobbed, and cried aloud, and babbled about how sorry he was for himself. It disturbed everybody's composure. The prisoners could not read nor write letters nor sleep. When the jailers were around, no one dared say anything, but as soon as they closed the sheriff's office door Tom yelled at the kid to shut up and jeered at him, calling him "Big Baby," "Calf," "Bud," "Kid" and "Damned idjit." He was in one of his overbearing, taunting moods, and it disgusted Hubert Herr, who began to think about his part in the plot. He didn't like Tom Horn. Tom was a hard-boiled egg. The condition of life in a jail had opened Hubert's eyes. What assurance had he that these friends of Tom Horn would pay him when he brought out the information? They would be more likely to knock him on the head, so that he could never tell who the accomplices were. They had already killed one innocent kid, Willie Nickell. He might be the next.

Came the fourteenth of the month and Hubert Herr checked out of the "crowbar hotel," but instead of giving his small library of accumulated manuscripts to Tom's accomplices, he gave them to a newspaper reporter and fled on the first westbound train. He was thoroughly frightened, and said he did not intend to stop until he reached San Francisco. The editor smoothed out the bits of paper and assembled the details of the plot. Part of the information was on the back of a torn letter from Dixon, a small town a few miles from Baggs, Wyoming. So Tom had some friends down there! It was close to the place where he had relayed horses, after the Isam Dart murder. The old letter referred to Butch Cassidy. But there was not enough of the original paper left for the editor to decipher it. The story, as far as it went, was published in the morning paper—a great scoop. DISCOVER PLOT TO LIBERATE TOM HORN.

Sheriff Smalley read the story in the morning paper. This was his first knowledge of the plot to blow up his own jail. Smalley strode away to see the editor. Why had the paper not let him in on the story and given him warning? Why inflame the people who might now force the jail and lynch Tom Horn? There was a reward of twenty-five thousand dollars on Butch's head. The gambling houses had immediately employed extra guards as soon as the paper disclosed that the great bandit was in the country again. The people were sure to be infected with the dangerous excitement and there was no telling what they might do. Smalley was really angry—a rare thing for him. He pounded on the editor's desk, then hurried back to the jail and warned the deputies not to tell Tom that his plot was discovered or allow him to see a newspaper.

One day the snowball appeared in the window of St. John's Hall. A horse was found saddled at the designated place. Smalley told his deputies not to let Tom out of his cell alone for one moment; to give him no chance to strike the first match. Tom must have suspected that his plot had gone awry but nothing was said. A few days later a plump, hearty fellow, Charlie Irwin, came into the sheriff's office with five sticks of giant powder, saying, "Look what I found under the jail wall!" Suspicious people looked to see if Charlie was breaking in a pair of number-nine shoes. Sheriff Smalley recognized Charlie Irwin as a local rodeo man and good friend of Horn's. If Irwin knew anything about the plot he concealed his knowledge to the time of his death in 1934.

The first date—January 9, 1903—set for Tom's execution passed. The barons had made good their first promise. Lacey said that Tom was safe from the law for at least five and a half months, certainly plenty of time to work out another plot.

January passed, then February. A second blizzard came in March. On the thirtieth Judge Lacey filed another appeal and told Tom, whatever might happen, his life would be spared until 1904. Settlers in their cabins said, "I'd think that the big outfits would be afraid to pull that again. Tom will sure catch on before long."

Tom, watching from the jail window, saw the trees outside blowing in the winds of April. In May, President Theodore Roosevelt, coming from the West, stopped at Laramie, and rode horseback the thirty-five miles across the range to Cheyenne. The best horses in Wyoming were used for the relays. The President rode part way on

Ora Haley's Yellow Bird, a favorite horse of Horn's. On one side of the President rode Joe Lefors. On his other side, mounted on a single-footing racer, sat Senator Warren, the cattle baron who had run to President Harrison to save the Johnson County raiders. Tom could hear the crowd cheer the horsemen as they came into town to stop at the Inter-Ocean Hotel.

Tom still seemed to trust his wealthy friends, although the failure of his first plot taught him a lesson about the loyalty of accomplices. His next break for freedom was executed from within. Tom whispered through the jail to his fellow prisoners to be ready for a riot on the Fourth of July. He had got a piece of lead pipe from the sink where the prisoners washed in the corridor. He would hit Deputy Proctor on his bald walrus head as the prisoners marched to dinner on the Fourth. This would be the signal for a general riot.

Independence Day came. Proctor, the veteran, noticed that Tom's trouser leg did not look natural. He undressed him with the same authority Nancy had used to find out whether he had been swimming on the Lord's Day, and the weapon was discovered.

Tom tried the same game again on July 16. He persuaded another prisoner to get the pipe but the plot was foiled once more.

Ed Smalley kept these designs from the public. Laramie County's youngest sheriff felt his responsibility. He was aging markedly. He complained to the county commissioners that the "old tin can" of a jail was not adequate for a prisoner like Tom Horn. If the people knew the danger they would lynch the condemned man at once. The commissioners shook their heads. The county was still in debt from the Horn trial and could do nothing about it.

Tom became sullen. His three attempts to escape had failed. He stared morosely out the window on Ferguson Street. The sidewalks were in shadow from the cottonwoods now. He had been a prisoner for eighteen months. Twice he had seen that sidewalk shaded in July; twice he had seen it snow-white and striped with purple shadows that waved as the wind blew the bare cottonwood branches.

He knew by sight the women and men who lived in the houses

across the street and the children who ran in and out of the gates. He heard that one philosophic woman had said, on learning that the houses across from the jail rented cheaply, that *she* thought it would be a good place to live, as the example of looking at the jail every day would be good for little Asa.

The sheepmen of Wyoming suffered immense losses among their flocks in the spring blizzard of 1903. Many of them lost thirty percent of their herds. This had a strange bearing on the fate of Tom Horn. The loss in the herds was offset by a ten percent increase in the price of wool which reached the unprecedented value of seventeen cents a pound. New operators crowded into the sheep business, spreading their flocks out across the state of Wyoming. Some cattlemen in the north around Meeteetse hired a "Tom Horn" by the name of Jim Macleod to intimidate the sheepmen and keep them off their range. Being a perfect counterpart of Tom physically, but his inferior mentally, Macleod was soon arrested for killing a sheepherder. The officers, sure that he would be lynched if incarcerated at Meeteetse, sent him to Cheyenne. Smalley put him in the same cage with Tom.

Now this Macleod, or "Driftwood Jim," as he was called on the Greybull River, plotted with Tom during the hot days of July and August, while Cheyenne prepared for its annual Frontier Days, "The Daddy of Them All!" A society man named Harry K. Thaw promised Cheyenne that he would take in the festivities as he returned from the Corbett-Jeffries fight at San Francisco. A delegation of Shoshoni Indians came down from the north in a Locomobile to see the show.

Two years before, Tom had introduced his brother to the competing cowboys and also to his friend, Joe Lefors. They had sat in the grandstand together to watch the old days revived. This year Tom Horn and Driftwood Jim schemed to revive the violent days of old themselves, and Proctor was again the proposed victim.

A merry-go-round man with a calliope set up his display on a concession across from the jail. The first tune or two pleased Tom and he whistled and sang with the organ. After a day or two he loathed the thin, shrill music that started professional gaiety at nine in the morning and lasted until midnight.

Tom and Jim noticed that the giant Proctor walked around the cell room unarmed. They believed that if they could lay hold of the old walrus at a time when no one was present, they could get his keys and escape. They planned to lure him into their cell before breakfast, when Sheriff Smalley and his bride were still asleep in their house joining the jail, and when the rest of the deputies would either be busy with the prisoners' breakfasts, or would not yet have reported at the jail. With this in mind Driftwood Jim, pretending to be sick, ordered some medicine that should be taken before meals and induced Proctor to bring it to him prior to breakfast. Shortly before eight o'clock on the ninth day of August 1903, Proctor fell into this ambush. He unlocked the door to the cell room and came in alone with Jim's medicine. Macleod's and Horn's time had come! They watched Proctor's broad back as he relocked the door. He was unarmed as usual. Deputy Snow, as the plotters hoped, was sitting on the courthouse steps, enjoying the cool morning air with his great wolfhound. The possibility of Horn's escape hung always above Snow as a threat of death. Like Kels Nickell, he felt safer by reassuring himself almost constantly that the prisoner was safe.

Proctor climbed the iron steps to the cell gallery and put the key into the lock of the two convicts' cell. He opened the door wide enough to hand in the medicine and a tumbler. The two men sprang against it like caged animals. Proctor pushed with all his might against the iron door, but he could not hold it against them both. The door opened wider. Driftwood Jim slipped out and grappled with his jailer. Proctor turned from the door, picked Jim bodily from the gallery and lifted him above the iron railing, to throw him to the floor below. Instantly Tom clutched the jailer by the throat and choked the strength out of him. The three men sank in a heap on the gallery floor. From all the cells many eyes peered at them. Macleod shook himself free from the tangled arms and legs and ran down the iron steps, got a window cord and ran back with it. The two men tied Proctor's hands and feet and demanded his keys. Proctor, panting after his fight, but neither dazed nor sluggish, began to think for his life. He knew the deputies would arrive in a few minutes to serve breakfast, so he played for time. "The keys are in the safe in the office," he said.

The prisoners also knew that the breakfast hour was close, and that their only hope lay in getting away at once. They worked with feverish haste. Had they been more composed they would have remembered that Proctor had opened the doors and locked them again with the keys. That the key to the outer door was in the safe was palpably false. The two men dragged Proctor to the office and hunted frantically for weapons. Proctor was trying to kill time as much as the escaped men were trying to save it. Outside, Leslie Snow looked at his watch, got up from the courthouse steps and walked in the direction of the sheriff's office with his beautiful dog beside him.

Macleod found a Winchester on top of a wardrobe but failed to find a closet full of guns at one side. He stuck the gun at Proctor's head, racked back the hammer and ordered him to open the safe. Proctor looked at him and said, "Give me a chance. I can't work the combination with my hands tied." This sounded reasonable to the prisoners, so they untied him just enough to let him set to work. Proctor turned the brass wheel back and forth and listened to it click. Deputy Snow, playing with his dog, neared the sheriff's office. Tom Horn saw Proctor's game and said, "Open that safe and open it by-Jesusly quick or I'll blow your head off." There was something sincere in the way Tom Horn said this, and Proctor got to work in earnest. Since the keys were in his pocket he would not be able to produce them when the safe doors swung open, but Proctor knew there was a gun in the safe and, if he could get it without the prisoners seeing him, he would be a match for them, even with his hands tied. As Proctor heard the last bolt click into place, he turned to Tom, saying, "If you want to save time, look in that desk drawer and get the inside key." Macleod, with the Winchester, turned to the desk and Proctor threw open the safe and grabbed the pistol.

Tom Horn sprang like a cat on Proctor and bore him to the floor. Macleod bounded back from the desk and jumped on the two men. All three of them rolled over and over on the floor, upsetting the office furniture. In the tangle of arms and legs, Proctor fired twice, the second shot inflicting an unnoticed wound in Macleod's leg. Both men started twisting Proctor's arms and legs cruelly, and pounding his face with their fists. They realized that they had been duped. They began to search through Proctor's pockets. Macleod was the first to find the jingling bunch. He jumped up to open the iron gate to freedom.

Leslie Snow, who had not heard the shots in the brick building, sauntered casually into the room to serve breakfast. He was met by Macleod's Winchester. The worst he could imagine had happened. The dreaded Tom Horn was loose at last. The amazed wolfhound thought Les Snow wanted to romp as he ran from the building, firing his pistol in the air, shouting, "Tom Horn has escaped!" These four words were all that were necessary to turn Cheyenne into an insane asylum.

A resident of Cheyenne who claimed to have seen the subsequent antics of his fellow citizens described them as follows: A few minutes before Les Snow gave the alarm a man by the name of Durbin, who had been doing some early-morning shopping, stepped into the courthouse to call his wife on the phone and find out what else she wanted for breakfast besides a bottle of milk. When he heard Snow's cry he dropped the receiver and, clutching his milk bottle, ran from the building. Les Snow, hearing a man run down the steps behind him, supposed Tom Horn was after him, and sprinted for the nearest corner where he intended to stand and fight. Durbin, seeing the deputy sheriff running ahead of him with all his might, decided that there must be some real danger behind, and ran his best. Snow reached the corner of the armory that faced the jail. He turned at bay and shot hurriedly at his pursuer. The bullet missed Durbin but came close enough to turn him like a polo pony and, still clutching at the neck of the milk bottle that had been broken, he raced for the opposite street corner. Leslie Snow then jumped out from behind the armory and pulled back the hammer of his gun for another shot.

The old-timer of Cheyenne continued:

"Joe Cahill was county recorder in them days. Do you know Joe? The best-looking boy in town—a strong round chin like the toe of a moccasin—with a dimple in front. Joe always liked big things—big hats—runs our Frontier Days celebrations. Well, the time I'm tellin' you about: it was Sunday morning and Joe was passing the plate in church across from the jail and when he heard Les Snow shootin' he dropped the offering on the floor and started to ring the church-house bell. It made a musical accompaniment to Snow's pistol shots as Durbin was 'smoked' up the street. The people downtown ran up from Main Street. They found themselves the backstop for this bombardment and the 'leaders,' retreating to safety, knocked down and ran over the 'wheelers.' A quiet western Sunday! Laugh! I thought I'd split."

Instead of leaving the building by the door which Snow and Durbin had used, Macleod, as soon as he had repulsed Les Snow, ran back through the jail fumbling with the keys, and unmindful of Proctor and Horn as they panted and struggled on the floor, he found the key that fitted the jailyard door, swung it open and ran out.

Tom Horn, swearing in gasps, continued to wrestle with Proctor. It was a fight to get the pistol in Proctor's tied hands, and Tom clutched the deputy's wrist and twisted his hand one way and the gun the other. The trigger guard almost tore off Proctor's finger and in pain he gasped, "Well, if you want that gun, leggo my arm, and I will give it to you." He slipped the safety onto the mechanism and dropped it into Tom's hand. The gun was a German Luger that Tom had noticed Proctor carry in the jail, and he had asked about the strange mechanism, but Proctor had refused to show it. Now that Tom had the pistol, he was unable to work it although he pulled the blocked trigger a few times in Proctor's face. He turned away and ran out the door that Macleod had left open.

Both men were now armed and at liberty. Ten or fifteen city blocks either to the east or the west would put them on the ocean of grassland where they were as much at home as the wolves and antelope.

Sheriff Smalley was sitting down to breakfast in his undershirt, trousers and slippers when he heard all the bells in town start ringing. He looked out the window and saw a long-legged man leading his pet horse out of the stable. He recognized him instantly, and muttering, "Tom Horn has escaped," he ran to the door with his .44 Colt revolver in his hand. Steadying the barrel of his big pistol on the doorjamb, he fired at the moving mark. The man went over backward with a thud, as though he had walked into an invisible clothesline.

Smalley ran down the steps toward the prostrate man, who had only been creased across the back of his neck. The fugitive struggled to his feet, hid behind the horse and pointed a gun at the officer across the horse's back. Smalley ran for the shelter of the nearest telephone pole and, resting his pistol barrel on his left forearm, took a careful aim at the only part of the fugitive he could see. As he aimed he noticed that his escaped prisoner seemed to be having trouble with the mechanism of his gun. Smalley's second shot brought down the fugitive again. He fell under the horse's hoofs. The horse shied, jumped over the body and ran away. The sheriff ran forward and the man with the charmed life jumped to his feet. The second shot had been as futile as the first. The bullet had made only a flesh wound.

Smalley shot again but his pistol snapped on an empty cylinder. The fugitive ran across the street, still clutching his gun. A mail clerk named Pat Hennessey ran out of the house next to the alley with a Spanish-American War Krag in his hands and blocked the way. The quick-witted prisoner shouted, "Tom Horn has escaped! Have you seen him?" The mail clerk lowered his rifle. The fugitive ran up the alley and a moment later the astonished Pat was confronted by another desperate man running from the jail with a pistol in his hand. He raised his Krag again and ordered him to halt. The desperate man yelled, "I'm the sheriff! Give me your gun. That's Tom Horn who just went by."

"Be Ja'sus," said Pat, "you don't look like no sheriff to me in them slippers and that undershir-r-rt."

Pat proceeded to take a careful aim. The townspeople who had been repulsed from the jail by Deputy Snow's bombardment were now coming back, and Smalley, recognizing a man in the crowd whom he knew, shouted, "Don't shoot! Ask that man. He knows I'm the sheriff."

Pat turned his head toward the newcomer and the sheriff grabbed the muzzle of the rifle and thrust it up. The excited mail clerk, feeling himself being overpowered, pulled the trigger and the bullet combed the sheriff's hair. Being reassured that Smalley was indeed the sheriff, Pat relinquished his rifle and Smalley, ejecting the empty cartridge, dropped to one knee to take aim at the little figure of a man who was now running far up the alley. He pulled the trigger and the bolt snapped on an empty chamber, for there had been only one cartridge in the gun. The next moment the sheriff saw his escaped prisoner duck into a stable and disappear. With the populace at his heels, the frantic officer ran for the street where he expected the fugitive to emerge.

At this juncture, as though his troubles were not enough, a little woman ran up to the sheriff and threw both arms around him, crying, "Go to the house! Your wife is prostrated." She clutched him so desperately that he could not free himself for some minutes and the crowd took up the chase without him.

The harassed killer of the range had ducked into an old barn when he noticed men with rifles waiting for him at the next street intersection. A young man named Lamm, another mail clerk, who lived up the street, saw the fugitive run into the barn and hide. Lamm stepped into the barnyard with a Krag in his hands and yelled, "Move and I'll kill you."

The terror of the range started to plead, "Don't shoot! I'll surrender." That was not the reply Tom's friends would have expected from him.

"Drop your gun, then," Lamm said, "and come out."

The prisoner stuck out one arm to see whether Lamm would shoot and when it was not harmed he came out and surrendered to a policeman who had just run up with the crowd that had deserted the sheriff. All started back for the jail. They met Smalley who looked at the prisoner with breathless dismay and said, "That's only Jim Macleod! Where's Tom?"

Smalley left the crowd and ran panting to the jail. Could Tom by any chance be still in prison? Young and sound, with sturdy legs and lungs, Ed arrived in record time. True to his fears the cage door that had held the two killers was standing open and both birds had flown. Inside the sheriff's wrecked office Ed found Deputy Proctor helplessly tied and wedged between the back of the desk and the wall. His mouth was stopped and wedged open with rags and a stick. Perfectly helpless, he looked up at his rescuer with his melancholy eyes.

Ed unbound him, cutting ropes and rags right and left with his pocketknife. Was it possible that Butch Cassidy's men or Coble's cowboys had raided the jail and spirited Tom away? How would he ever explain to the world that he had not accepted the twenty-five thousand dollars people believed the association had offered him to let Tom Horn escape?

Outside, an excited crowd was coming toward the jail. The police were bringing Driftwood Jim Macleod. He was badly frightened and also liberally peppered with bullet scars. He had been sent to Cheyenne to prevent the Meeteetse people from lynching him. The ugly crowd at his heels unnerved him. "Get me back to the jail, quick," he said. He scurried along, almost dragging the policemen across the jailyard. "Do you think they will lynch me?" he mumbled. "Do you think they will kill me?"

Macleod was as glad as a suddenly uncaged canary to be back in the protection of the jail where Proctor, with swollen wrists and bruised face, was in charge once more. Locked up again, Macleod said, "I don't want to run for the town sports to shoot at me."

Proctor inquired solemnly, "Do you still want your medicine?"

Jim asked about Tom Horn and Proctor replied, "It's a hot time to be asking about him after the way you ran off and left him."

As a matter of fact Driftwood's separate escape gave Tom Horn the opportunity of a lifetime. When Tom ran out of the jail he found the yard surrounding the courthouse deserted, not a soul in sight. Tom went first to the sheriff's stable and found that Macleod had taken the horse. Then he went to the hitch rack in front of the courthouse where the officers had noticed with suspicion that a saddled horse had been tied every day for two weeks—but there was no horse there today. Tom looked down the street that led to the open plains to the west. He saw the backs of a big crowd, followed by the sheriff, running down the street after Jim Macleod. The distance to open country was just as short by the streets going east, so Tom ran around the courthouse and into the first alley that led away from the crowd. Had he found a horse, one burst of speed would have put him on the prairie that lay in plain sight from the courthouse steps.

The alarm bells had been ringing for some time now and the man who operated the merry-go-round in front of the courthouse was having his sleep disturbed by the madhouse antics of the population outside his tent. Further sleep was impossible, so he got up, dressed and stepped out of his tent just in time to see Tom Horn with a pistol in his hand run into the alley. The carnival man had a .38-caliber revolver that he kept to protect his cashbox in the late hours after the banks were closed. He shoved his cashbox under his cot, grabbed this weapon and started in pursuit of the disturber of his slumbers.

Tom headed for the plains, with the carnival man half a block behind him. He ran out into the first cross street. Men with rifles in their hands stood at the street intersections in both directions. He dared not turn and thus shake off his pursuer. Tom ran into the alley across the street and went straight ahead for the open country that was so close. This gave his pursuer a good chance to shoot at him as he ran between the board fences. The carnival man was already sufficiently breathless, however, to know that his aim would not be good. He did not stop to shoot. He was gaining on Tom every jump. Horn was plainly tired after his fight. Before he reached the second cross street he could hear his pursuer panting at his heels. The merry-go-round man had made up his mind not to shoot until he was so close that he would be sure of his aim no matter how breathless he might be. It looked as though Tom's charmed life had come to an end—but he still carried his buttons.

A strange rider suddenly turned into the alley ahead of Tom and swooped toward him. He was wearing a ten-gallon hat and a black-and-white-check shirt. His red silk neckerchief increased the weather-stained red in his robust cheeks. His trousers were tucked nonchalantly into high-heeled boots. His long-shanked spurs rang merrily on the hard ground as he peddled diligently on his bicycle. Tom noticed that the rider carried one of those long Krags across his handle bars. Blocked front and rear, Tom vaulted the board fence and ran across a back yard. Armed men were waiting for him at all the street intersections. If he crossed in the middle of the block he might reach the shelter of the stables on the next alley north. Tom headed straight for the public school. He had evaded the ridiculous bicycle rider but the merry-go-round man was still at his heels. In carnivals he had hopped off and on his spinning wheel too many times to be dismayed by Tom's capers. Tom Horn could run no more. Thoroughly exhausted, he turned to fight. Vainly he tried to discharge his automatic at the onrushing carnival man who ran up to him, stuck a pistol in his face and fired.

The bullet parted the hair on Tom's head but did not knock him down. Almost as soon as Tom felt the hot lead split his scalp he felt the cold steel of a pistol beating against his temples. Groggy, almost unconscious, he struck back feebly. He could not see the men running down the street from both directions. He was tottering to a fall when they surrounded him. Two blue-coated policemen wearing cowboy hats took Tom by either arm and relieved him of the gun that had done him no good. The three men walked briskly back toward the jail, followed by an armed crowd of men and boys.

Deputy Snow trotted up on horseback. He had heard that Proctor was killed. He saw Horn staggering between the policemen. Snow jerked his horse to a stop and swung to the ground. He pulled out his rifle, struck a vicious two-handed blow at the side of Tom's head. The crowd heard the sound of crunching bones and a man swearing in pain. One of the policemen had thrown up his arm to ward off the blow from Tom's head. His wrist had been broken by Snow's rifle, but Tom's life was saved.

Back in the jail, Tom revived and ate a hearty breakfast with more relish than he had shown for many months. As he ate, he congratulated Proctor on the courage he displayed in the fight against odds. For Leslie Snow, Tom showed contempt and rage. He warned Smalley never to let Snow guard him again; to let him have nothing to do with his hanging; not even to permit him in the cell room. Tom threatened to riot, sulk, hunger-strike, "cheat the law," if that man Snow was allowed in his sight. Across the street the merry-go-round started to move. The calliope screamed:

> "Meet me at St. Louie, Louie,
> Meet me at the Fair."

Everybody admired Tom Horn for his ferocity while free, and his coolness in the face of the mob when he was captured. Sheriff Smalley, the overgrown boy, boasted that his prisoner was afraid of nothing on earth. He said proudly that Tom should be kept henceforth in solitary confinement, perhaps in shackles. Tom winced with disappointment when Proctor showed him that the pistol had contained five cartridges. Had he known which lever to push he might have made his escape.

The citizens of Cheyenne turned from accounts of Tom Horn's display of bravery to read in the newspaper and on signboards that another brave man had come to town. He was named Davalo, "the stranger to fear," who advertised that he would perform acrobatic tricks at the Opera House.

The escape hurt Tom's last appeal to the Supreme Court, and fanned smoldering resentment into flames. People came down to the jail and looked at the somber walls that had not been able to hold Tom Horn. Kels Nickell stormed through the crowd, saying, "Let's hang him."

Sheriff Smalley was touchy about such talk. He walked up to Kels in front of the crowd and said, "Now you shut up and go peddle your papers or I'll throw you in the same cell as Tom Horn." Everybody laughed but Kels. The lynching threat was ended.

Inside the jail Tom sensed the fever heat of the August sky. In the afternoon he saw black clouds gather with angry silence. Then the cottonwoods on Ferguson Street waved like reeds and the swollen sky sluiced the city. Watching the storm through a four-by-eight window, Tom Horn knew that he had no chance of escape as a lone man in hostile Cheyenne. His only hope lay with the barons and their promises—promises given by uncertain men who might, or might not, want to see him hang, depending on their faith in his casual remark that nobody ever got into trouble for hiring *him*.

If Tom could only get twenty miles out of Cheyenne he was sure that his friends would cover his trail forever. Promises delaying rescue indefinitely would satisfy him no longer. If they were going to act they must act at once. He looked now to them.

25

"KEEP YOUR NERVE."

IN SPITE of the barons' promise that the execution of Tom Horn would be stayed until 1904, his jailer told him on November 15, 1903, that, whatever his friends outside might say, he would hang on Friday, November 20. Tom was put in a single cell next to Macleod's and the deathwatch was placed over him. Tom seemed less affected than the jailer who brought the fatal news. Tom knew that John Coble and his jolly cowboys had been loafing around Cheyenne, and that this ultimatum made them leave town abruptly. To the officers, their absence seemed more threatening than their presence.

The whole town worried.

Then word was received that an army of cowboys was mobilizing fifteen miles north of town. Was the association planning to put Cheyenne under private martial law as they had the town of Buffalo a decade earlier, or had Butch Cassidy and his outlaws recruited all of Tom's cowboy friends in a desperate attempt to storm the city?

The governor called out the militia and the citizens oiled their Spanish-American War rifles and antelope guns.

The wind, following a November blizzard, had quieted and the iron cold of Wyoming gripped Cheyenne. The militiamen patrolled the courthouse square, with their feet and ears wrapped against the bitterness. One young soldier complained, "We have to eat slum and walk all night while it is forty below. That's enough to take all the pleasure out of life. Now they won't let us go home in the evening. They don't even want the women to have a good time."

Deputies, with repeating shotguns, were placed in every window in the courthouse. Over a hundred armed plainsmen were housed in the building.

Governor Chatterton took the train for Denver and went to the Brown Palace Hotel for a rest. It was rumored that he had been kidnaped and was held for the ransom of Tom Horn.

A coffin was delivered at the jail. Tom heard the hollow, ghoulish sound as it struck the gravel and said, "Here comes the wooden overcoat!" Then he added cryptically, "But I guess I won't need it."

In a harness shop, a saddler with his waxed threads and hash knives was making a strange harness that must be ready on November 20. It consisted of five straps: one to hold a man's arms tightly to his sides; a second to draw the elbows back; a third to hold the wrists close to the legs; a fourth to hold the knees; and a fifth to pinion the ankles. A man hanging in this harness would be incapable of anything but slight up-and-down movements. If the noose was placed properly, the neck would break and the body hang like a sack of sand.

While the saddler made this harness, the undertaker got his paraphernalia ready, the preachers discussed their part in the drama and the militia marched the streets. Smalley hired carpenters to report at the jail on the morning of the nineteenth to build a gallows in the corridor in front of Tom's cell. Cruel as it might seem to hang a man on his own doorsill, Smalley—and most of Wyoming— was unwilling to move this man through a mob that might call either for his blood or his rescue.

Late on the night of November 18, all was quiet except the distant sound of patrolling militia. The deathwatch heard Tom lie down on the floor. Before he could be stopped Tom whispered to Jim Macleod in the next cell that he was to be released on the following night, the nineteenth. Macleod whispered this to the prisoner next him, and so it went from cell to cell, until the whole group were prepared for freedom.

Came the morning of the great day—the nineteenth. Tom looked from his cell out the window and saw written in the snow, "Keep your Nerve." Sheriff Smalley saw the writing too, and asked the guards who had written it. An arc light hung above the writing, yet not a soul admitted that he had seen the scribe. Could some of Smalley's own men be friends of Tom Horn? The sheriff worried, too, about Tom's threat to be ugly in case Leslie Snow attended the hanging.

A canvas was hung across the front of Tom's cell so that he might not see the hammers and saws working on the massive planks of the gallows. But the sounds beat through the prison. Sheriff Smalley pressed his boyish face against Tom's cage. "How does it affect you, Tom?" he asked in his friendly manner.

"Not a damn bit more than as though the boys were putting up a corral on the ranch," Tom replied as his hands worked dexterously on horsehair fancywork.

The trap on the scaffold was supported by a beam constructed in three sections and set upright in such a manner that, when sufficient water was released from a tank to overbalance an iron weight, it dropped and jerked out the middle of the beam. Without support, the trap opened on its hinges and let the hanged man drop six feet on the end of a three-quarter-inch rope. Once the trap doors had been sprung, they were restrained by weights on pulleys to prevent them from banging against the hanging body. A pipe and a valve were attached to the tank of water. When Horn was lifted on the trap, his weight would open the valve and start the water flowing.

At noon on the day before Tom Horn was scheduled to die, the gallows was tested by big Proctor, who was to conduct the hanging. With Tom only the thickness of a canvas away, the slow solemn deputy practiced adjusting the valve and springing the trap. First Proctor tied a sack of sand weighing two hundred pounds, Tom's exact weight, on the hangman's rope, then he lifted the sack on the trap while, watch in hand, he listened to the trickle of the water until he heard the fateful *chug*.

Then he readjusted the valve, letting the water out a little faster, until he was satisfied that the beam would trip in just thirty seconds. Newspaper reporters were then admitted to examine the contraption. Unconsciously they took off their hats and tiptoed around the scaffold. Proctor explained the mechanism to them in whispers. The reporters' table was on the iron balcony where they would have to move their chairs to let Tom out of his cell. The spectators were to be below and immediately in front of the scaffold.

The state wished a legal execution with all the formality and delay required by law, but John Coble had other plans. While Proctor was explaining the intricate gallows to the reporters, Coble, who seemed to be the representative of the barons, appeared in town. He was not followed by his armed riders but came instead with his ranch foreman, his attorney and Miss Kimmell—with the same red tam o'shanter pinned to her knot of hair and a new sheaf of affidavits in her gloved hand. This group marched to the domed capitol building to make a last appeal by peaceful methods to the governor, who had returned from Denver. But the governor was obdurate. He did not even read Miss Kimmell's affidavits until the next day, when it was too late. His reply to Tom's friends was, "You may state that no respite will be granted Tom Horn. He will hang tomorrow." In talking over the phone with his political chairman in one of the northern counties, the governor asked if the settlers up there were not pleased with his stand. He compromised with Coble and his supplicants, however, to the extent of giving an evasive letter permitting one of them to visit Tom Horn if the sheriff thought it advisable.

After leaving the governor's office, John Coble gave the letter to Charlie Irwin, and disappeared. Charlie went immediately to the jail that was bristling with guns. People in saloons, seeing Irwin's gay checked shirt coming down the street, wondered what John Coble, who must now be desperate, was planning to do while Charlie Irwin was in the jail. Sheriff Smalley had issued the statement that "any attempt to storm the jail will turn out to be a terrible lesson, illustrative of the fact that frontier times and methods are not to be applied in Cheyenne, as they are in other sections of the state."

Irwin, with the governor's letter, marched singlehanded upon the barricaded courthouse. A militiaman halted him. Charlie showed his letter. The sentry called out the guard, and the officer of the guard let him pass. Charlie walked up the steps and into the big door of the courthouse where the Gatling gun was mounted.

Handsome Joe Cahill, the county clerk, and his assistants sat attempting to keep their minds on their file cases and record books. They saw Irwin, a mountain of a man in high-heeled boots, knock at the sheriff's office, and hand his letter to Smalley, as he said, "Here's a letter from the governor." Smalley, noticing the executive seal, took it, closed the door in Irwin's face and pushed the bolt. In a few minutes Irwin knocked again. The door opened just a trifle and a voice said, "Can't do it, Charlie." The door slammed and the bolt clicked. Irwin thumped across to Joe Cahill's office, sat down and fidgeted for an hour. His plump hands whittled matches onto the floor.

Sheriff Smalley was obviously too busy to be interrupted on this the most important day of his life since his marriage. Smalley knew that all the prisoners were prepared for a rescue. He was personally responsible for the gallows and Proctor's experiments and the fit of the saddle maker's harness. He must keep the deputies and visiting sheriffs—many of them years older than he—all in line. The major of the militia came to him with problems of discipline and patrol. Cooks came running with complaints that the wood and supplies were not adequate to feed so many men. Ed Smalley was constantly on the go. Once when he came in from an errand he met Charlie Irwin in the courthouse hall. "Say, Ed," Charlie asked, "can't you do it now? That's a letter from the governor."

"Why do you want to see Tom?" asked the sheriff.

Irwin looked down over the globe of his stomach at his high-heeled boots. "Well, you see, it's this way." Charlie seemed embarrassed. "I'm writing a book about Tom Horn and I want to find out about Arizona."

"Can't do it, Charlie," the sheriff smiled.

"But it's an order from the governor."

"Can't help it, Charlie! Nobody sees Tom Horn until he goes to the scaffold. I'll give you a pass to be there. That's all."

Smalley hurried into his office and closed the door. Irwin leaned against the doorcasing. His high peaked hat was pushed dejectedly over his plump face, his chubby hands were thrust uselessly in the horizontal pockets under the shelf of his stomach. Clerks in Cahill's office pretended not to stare at him. Suddenly Charlie straightened up, glared fiercely at the door and then turned away. Speaking to nobody and to everybody, he said, "I've got a letter from the governor, that long—" he measured eighteen inches with his hands— "and it is not recognized. They had better look out."

Charlie clumped down the front steps, crossed the street, passed the militiamen and went downtown. The county clerk's assistant, looking out the window, saw the checked shirt disappear along the sidewalk and asked, "Why do you reckon Smalley wouldn't let him see Tom Horn?"

Handsome County Clerk Cahill knew Tom Horn by reputation. His father had known Tom well. Cahill admired Tom the same way he admired his own five-gallon hat—big and western. He replied to his clerk, "I dun' know," in a way that made his assistant think that he thought he did know. Then he said, "I wonder what he and John Coble are up to now?"

Evening came. Father John Kennedy was permitted a few words with the condemned in the darkened jail. He left, and the Reverend John Watson, assistant pastor of St. Mark's Episcopal Church of Cheyenne, entered the jail, with Lovett Rockwell, a male singer from his choir, and two women. Pompous Proctor led them up the iron stairs and along the gallery to Tom's cell. He pulled back the tarpaulin that was hung to screen the ghastly timbers from Tom Horn. Tom was sitting on his bunk braiding horsehair with dexterous fingers. He got up and said, "Howdy, Doc," to the clergyman, then bowed to the ladies, who choked with emotion and could not reply.

The Reverend Mr. Watson knelt on the iron gallery in front of Tom's cell, clasped his white hands and prayed that Tom Horn might be converted before his death and so find the life everlasting. The voice, so musical and well modulated, had its effect on the condemned man. He sat down on his bunk in the dim light and buried his shaking face in his hands. When the prayer ceased, he got up and the singers started, "Jesus, Lover of My Soul." The words fell sweetly on the ears of all the prisoners and the melody floated beyond the dismal corridors into Smalley's office where a score of deputies and sheriffs from other counties were sitting. These officers, who fancied themselves to be determined men, grew restless, and strolled into the hallway out of reach of the sound. That song held melancholy memories and solemn benedictions. Every man in the office could recall, now, the funeral of some member of his family; he could hear mourners singing that song in the little cabin around a casket lined with white cloth; he could see again the silent men and red-eyed women come out of a cool cellarlike cabin into the heat and brilliance of Wyoming.

The Reverend Mr. Watson tarried in the sheriff's office as he went out. He was glad the ordeal was over even though it had been a victory. The music, the modulated voice of prayer, the dim monastic light, these things had broken down the prisoner, and the minister told the deputies in the office that Tom Horn "within his own heart is making preparations for the end. He knows there is no help for him but in God. He is ready." A horse thundered down the street. There was a sharp cry from a sentry. Deputies grabbed their guns and crowded to the door. They saw a soldier talking to a small boy on a horse under an arc light. In disgust they returned to their posts, but the interlude shook the spell of the music from their minds and one of them forgot his manners sufficiently to question the complete triumph of the church in so short a time, even hinting that Tom Horn might have been putting on the cloak of conversion for the sake of sympathy.

The Reverend Mr. Watson looked at the heretic and shook his head. "Christian thought," he said, "has entered the calloused heart of the man who had the nerves of steel and the courage of a lion, strong, indifferent, and profane. His big frame shook like a leaf and sobs escaped his lips. When a strong man, one who has led a murderous life on the plains, facing death a thousand times and never flinching—when a man like this breaks down and cries like a brokenhearted child—when the massive frame, admired by all who ever saw him, became a limp and quivering mass on the side of the low bunk, there was no acting."

Up in his cell Tom lay silently on the bunk. Suppertime came and passed. Suddenly he jumped to his feet. "Hurry along, you sons-of-bitches," he said. "I'm hungry."

Tom did not sleep soundly that night of November 19, 1903. It was to be the night of his "rescue." Cheyenne did not sleep soundly either. The saloons kept open all night and men preferred to stay in groups. Smalley had announced that only twenty-five or thirty men would be admitted to the hanging, but the country people had packed their camp outfits in their "white tops," and had made the long pilgrimage again. It would be something to talk about for the rest of their lives. The expense was heavy but the settlers deceived themselves with the argument that a fellow might meet somebody or make a trade that would net him more than the trip would cost. Then, too, it was an education for the children, for they would see a railroad train.

The saloon men opened their betting books again, this time for wagers that Tom Horn would be released before morning. Men who had lost five dollars on Tom's conviction were sure that they could win it back on his rescue. One man said, "If Coble and Haley and them fellers wants to get Tom out, they will."

So the bets were wagered between men who knew the cattle kings were gods, and those who knew the cattle kings were brutes, and the skeptics who were nervous and wanted something to do, something to make the waiting more interesting. These were the men who took a beer chaser with their whisky—a "boilermaker and his helper," this double drink was called.

Tom Horn was allowed no newspaper on his last night. Sheriff Smalley looked at his deputies with questioning suspicion as he said, "By this time tomorrow Tom will not care about William Randolph Hearst's campaign for the Presidential nomination." Hearst's political aspirations had interested Tom. The sensational newspaperman had written an editorial which had caused much comment in the Wild West that was trying to become civilized. "If bad institutions and bad men," Hearst had said, "can be got rid of only by killing, then killing must be done." Tom had discussed this with his guard. Smalley was not sure but that some double meaning lay hidden in such argument. The fear that one of his own deputies was in league with Tom and the big outfits haunted him.

Smalley ordered the lights in the cell room turned out. Tom tossed on his bunk, listening for his rescuers. Had everybody deserted him? He got up and fumbled for his hairwork. In the dark he braided, listening, thinking. He had received a letter from Nancy in the old home in Missouri. It was dated November 16 and began, "My dear, dear Tom." Nancy, his older sister, said that she was sure of his innocence. So was his other sister, who wrote him from Elgin, British Columbia. She had named her little daughter Thomasene. Tom's skilled fingers sorted the horse hairs by touch, thrust the ends through the loops he had prepared and pulled the ends in place. He knew that both his arrest and conviction had been kept from his aged mother. He had written her two letters, one dated over a year ahead. Tom did not intend to mail them yet but in case his rescue miscarried, she would never know the fate of the little boy with the big ears, whom she had taught to kill varmints that stole her poultry, nor would she be disturbed by the mockery of "Spare the rod and spoil the child."

Tom put down the hairwork and picked up a Bible the Reverend Mr. Watson had left him. He turned the pages in the dark. He knew that his two brothers Charles and Martin were in town. Surely Coble could be depended upon! Tom heard a noise in the street. The soldiers had challenged someone. A few moments of suspense, then the soldiers began marching again. A man stamped into the building. He was only a guard come to warm himself. The long night passed with military routine. At last the window paled with dawn. Tom got up from his cot.

This was the time the Chiricahua Apaches did their traveling.

Tom put on a red and white negligee shirt, and his best trousers—
the same clothes he had worn to a dance at the Iron Mountain schoolhouse. Miss Kimmell had been there.

Tom shivered. The jail was none too warm. He put his corduroy
vest over his festive shirt. Guards brought his breakfast. They were
ill at ease. Usual things looked strange to them. They seemed pale
and acted too courteous. One started to say, "What's the idea of the
glad rags?" but stopped. Tom did not share their embarrassment.
He said quite frankly, "I wish this could be put off another day. Tomorrow is my birthday and I've had a lot of good times on that day."

After breakfast he packed his valise, then asked how much time
he had left. When told that he had two hours he said, "I can do a
lot of writing in two hours." He sat down on his bunk and wrote a
long letter to John Coble denying the murder of the boy. Tom licked
the seal with his tongue and gave the letter to his guard along with
the two letters for his mother.

At ten-thirty the reporters took their seats around the table on the
cell gallery. Directly in front of them stood the nine-foot gallows
platform. Other spectators were told to stand below. One of the reporters' hands trembled. Evidently he feared that the *Denver Post*
man next to him would notice them, for he said, "It's chilly in here
since they have taken out the stove to make room for the scaffold."

The state allowed a bonus of fifty dollars for a hanging and Smalley
decided to divide this sum with his best friends. Tom had threatened
to be violent if Les Snow were allowed to help. In his place Smalley
employed Joe Cahill, the good-looking county clerk. Joe, like
Smalley, had recently married and was getting a start in life. This
money in addition to his salary would be a help. The boys had never
hanged a man before and they knew that a bungle would be over-
powering. Both relied on Proctor's age and experience to help them.
Sheriff Smalley was particularly anxious to make the whole performance a success. In the rehearsal the day before he and Joe had decided
to add a few features that would make the hanging really remarkable. They had asked Charlie Irwin and his brother Frank to sing

Tom Horn's favorite song. Now the fatal time had come for each man to play his part. Smalley and Cahill found themselves as nervous as schoolboys on Commencement Day. They were actors with stage fright, playing calm before the newspaper men and the audience below them. Smalley glanced repeatedly at his watch. At a little before eleven o'clock he nodded to Cahill, and the two boys went to Tom's cell. One of them admitted afterward that as he walked up the corridor he kept saying over and over, "I am in control of myself."

They found Tom lying on his bed reading the Bible—the Gospel of St. John. Tom rose to his full height, towering above them both. Ed opened the cell door and Tom stepped onto the gallery. He looked sharply to see if Les Snow was among the guards. Then he glanced back wistfully at some unfinished hair embroidery on the bunk in the cell that had been his home for almost two years. He had only twelve steps to go. The reporters pressed themselves against the table to let him pass. On the platform the Reverend Dr. George C. Rafter stood at one corner.

Tom looked up nonchalantly at the crossbeam. The reporters noticed that he was thin and white from his long confinement. His strong aquiline nose appeared more prominent than it used to be. He looked down at the stretcher waiting on the floor in front of the gallows between the scaffold and the spectators; then he stepped on the platform. Below him stood the Irwin brothers flanked by armed guards and visiting sheriffs with deputies—among them Leslie Snow. Tom stiffened with anger and stared fixedly at his enemy. Proctor's clear voice called, "Charlie Irwin will sing. Mr. Horn says he would like to have him do so."

"Hello, Tom!" Charlie called, waving his hand from the little crowd.

Tom's anger melted. With a smile he answered, "Hi, Charlie." Then Charlie and Frank, his brother, who was standing with him, began to sing the Baptist hymn, "Life's Railway to Heaven," with its closing verse:

"As you roll across the trestle spanning Jordan's swelling tide
You behold the Union Depot, into which your train will glide;
There you'll meet the Superintendent, God the Father, God
the Son,
With the hearty, joyous plaudit, 'Weary pilgrim, welcome
home.'"

Suitable surely for a Pinkerton scout who had guarded the railroads and done the hobo act! This hymn, which Tom and his friends could understand, coming from the untutored throats of the cowboys brought some of the spectators to the edge of hysteria. Frank Irwin weighed a hundred and ten and was as gaunt as his two-hundred-and-thirty-pound brother was plump. Frank's chin receded until it was no larger than his Adam's apple. Charlie's chin was double. Contrary to all outward appearances, the elephantine Charlie sang a canary soprano. Frank sang a bullfrog bass. Frank had to stop several times to compose himself, wipe the tears off his chin and neck, then join Charles again at the beginning of the next stanza. When the song was finished the wet-faced boys looked up at the platform as Proctor's strong voice said, "Charles Irwin will pass around to the left and come above."

"Thank you, Dick," said Tom, and both boys came up the iron steps.

"Tom," said Charlie, "did you make a confession to the murder of Willie Nickell?"

"No," said Horn. He had learned the standards of the new civilization at last.

"Well, Tom, a man's got to die only once, and it has to be; so be game."

"You bet I will. It's as well first as last, you know. Yes, it's all right."

"Well, good-by, old man. I wish I could do something for you. Is there anything you want me to do?"

"No, I wrote to Coble this morning. Good-by, boys."

"Good-by, Tom!"

If Tom intended to betray his accomplices now was his chance!

The Irwins clambered down among the spectators below, then slipped away into the sheriff's office and closed the door. They did not want to see their friend take the plunge.

Smalley, Proctor and Joe Cahill started strapping the harness on Tom Horn. Proctor passed a strap around Tom's left leg near the thigh, and then around the right. Tom turned and twisted his body to suit the length of the straps. He helped the executioners as though he were interested in the job.

"Well, Joe," he said to Cahill, "I hear you are married and doing well; that you are county clerk. Is that so?"

"Yes, Tom, it's true," came from the man stooping over a buckle.

"Well, by God, I'm glad to hear it."

Horn's hands were then securely pinioned to his body, and he was ready for the final strap around his ankles, just above his carpet slippers. With it adjusted, he hobbled with short steps over to the edge of the trap and stared up at the beams and at the noose. The Reverend Dr. Rafter started to read a prayer from his little book, while Proctor leaned down to tighten the strap on Horn's feet and ankles.

Tom Horn, lashed and harnessed, looked at the death hood and said with a ghastly smile, "I'll have to have a hand to get on that thing." Then he noticed that Joe Cahill was rubbing his Julia Marlowe chin and looking very green.

"What's the matter, Joe?" said Tom. "Ain't losing your nerve, are you?"

"Not a bit of it," grinned Joe, as the floor rocked under his feet. All the boys avoided one another's eyes. The sixteen dollars and sixty cents was not so easily earned as they had thought.

Big Proctor picked up the noose and lifted it like a rakish halo over the side of Tom's head. Tom ducked coolly and thrust his head through the noose. Proctor pulled the hangman's knot snugly to Tom's neck, like a cowboy's muffler. The minister was now praying earnestly and audibly for the doomed man's soul. Tom leaned toward Proctor and whispered confidentially, "Look at the crowd, Dick! Did you ever see so many scared sons-of-bitches in your life?"

Proctor smiled absently. His great slow mind was intent on fixing the black cap on Tom's head. He slipped it on with the gesture Tom's mother had used when she sent him to school on a winter's day in Missouri. Tom twisted his head obediently to help as she had taught him, then unconsciously tried to lift his bound hand to help. Nobody can put on a man's hat for him so it has the right feel. When the cap was fastened Proctor stepped back. With his powerful hands on his hips, he critically surveyed the job, as far as it had gone.

Then he said, "Tom, are you ready?"

"Yes," said Horn.

Cahill and Smalley lifted him on the trap while Proctor watched. Instantly there was a little click and water began to run from the tank. It sounded like the cry of mountain water, high in the eagle crags above Leadville. The reporters held their watches and counted the seconds.

Horn's hands clenched, and he stood motionless as the beams at his side. His fists became bloodless with his own grip.

Down on the street, farmers, humped out of shape with too many clothes, wiped their noses with their mittens and wondered what was happening in the big brick building. The militiamen were all on guard.

In the cell room the watches ticked on. Horn was the coolest man there, unless it was Proctor. The little stream of water ran agonizingly slow. The watches ticked the fatal thirty seconds. The trap did not spring. The watches ticked thirty-five! Smalley put his trembling hand against the gallows tree to support himself. The watches ticked forty! Smalley buried his face in the crook of his arm. Could it be that the trigger had been set for a rescue at the last moment? A nervous reporter looked at the man next to him, who was staring at his watch. Forty-five, forty-six—and the nervous reporter looked at Proctor, who was calmly listening to the water that rasped like a file on the nerves of the onlookers. Forty-eight, forty-nine! The reporter looked at his seatmate again. Then there was a chug, and he saw that the trap was open and Tom Horn dangled six feet below. The body bounded up a few times and down again, swinging around until the hooded face was away from the crowd. Dr. Rafter stood leaning in the corner, with his head bowed in prayer.

Talking Boy had "stayed with his word." Nobody who hired *him* had ever got into trouble.

Proctor's pompous voice called, "Everybody pass out—those below first." The shuffle of feet drowned the sound of the prayer. The guests, as they passed Proctor, complimented him on the faultlessness of the execution. The old walrus beamed on the handshaking line. "Success to all of you," he repeated cordially.

The militia were laughing and joking as the newspapermen reached the crisp outdoors. The nervous reporter asked his friend as they walked to the telegraph office, "Why do you suppose the trap was nineteen seconds late?"

"Don't you reckon it was because Tom was emaciated from being in jail so long?" the veteran replied. "You know the water was set for two hundred pounds."

Many people in Cheyenne breathed a sigh of relief when they heard that the end had come. The long dangerous suspense was over. The cattle barons, some of whom, tradition says, turned white-headed during the time Tom was in jail, no longer had a case of nerves when approached by any man who looked as though he might be a United States marshal.

The body had hung for five minutes when two physicians examined it, and shook their heads. Sixteen minutes later they pronounced life extinct. The corpse was then taken down, placed on a stretcher, covered with a black rubber blanket and taken to the Nineteenth Street door. Kels Nickell was waiting there beside the "deadwagon." The horses trotted to Gleason & Company's Undertaking Parlors and Kels Nickell trotted after. The body was carried into the mortuary; Kels followed, turned the poncho back and looked at the blue face with the tongue protruding. When he recognized the corpse he ran back to the jail, hunted up Smalley and, taking him by the hand, said, "You done a good job today, young feller." Then he went home to his square frame house to rest before going on duty at the railroad yards that night.

As the militia relaxed their vigil some of the ranchmen went into the courthouse, saw the gallows and found the two-hundred-pound sack of sand. "That's what I told you," said one of them. "They wouldn't let us in to see the hanging because he didn't hang. They hung that sack of sand instead. I alwus did say the big outfits would save Tom Horn."

This rumor spread over town rapidly. A coroner's inquest was ordered in the undertaking parlors, but some of the settlers still maintained, "Yes, there's a dead man there all right but it ain't Tom Horn. Ed took the twenty-five thousand dollars and got a hobo down at the train yards and hanged him instead. The newspapermen didn't know Tom Horn, and the Irwin boys wouldn't tell. I know what I'm talking about. I'd bet a hundred dollars—if I had it—that Tom Horn is on Yellow Bird right now, headed f'r Arrowzony—he had a good name there—and the schoolmarm is with him on Pacer, and if a feller knowed where to look he'd see 'em loping over a ridge somewhere *right now.*"

John Coble procured an elaborate coffin for Tom Horn. The body a sculptor would have copied for an archangel's was hermetically sealed in a cradle of white satin trimmed with silver. Charles Horn took his brother's valise and the unfinished horsehair ornaments, and accompanied the corpse to Boulder, Colorado, where Ora Haley's son attended college. Twenty-five hundred people followed the funeral cortege. It was as big a crowd as young Haley ever saw attend a football game at his college town. The funeral resembled the demonstration accorded a political martyr in Europe. Showmen coaxed Charles Horn for the privilege of exhibiting the body. A guard was kept at the grave by the Horn family until all fear of vandals had passed.

A small red granite stone bearing the words "In loving memory of Tom Horn" was placed at the head of his grave among the white slabs in the Boulder cemetery. A large white birch tree shades his last resting place. The cemetery slopes toward the north so that the only view is to the smooth, bare foothills of the Rockies, dipping into the plains that swell to the horizon. A little railway train, as full of business as a ticking watch, goes over the horizon to the Union Depot—of Cheyenne.

After the funeral Miss Kimmell boarded the train for Denver. She was very tired and very short of money after her two hopeful years which had failed. She went to work in the Equitable Building where the railroad, mining and livestock barons had their offices. Suave salesmen and pale-faced clerks, loitering by the newsstand and cigar counter, saw a short woman wearing a red tam hurry every evening from the ornate columns in the marble corridor to her humble lodgings. Inspiration and high resolve shone in her eyes. She was writing a long manuscript about a Sir Galahad horseman who "was crushed between the grindstones of two civilizations," but she never found a publisher who thought her book would sell.

It was entitled *The True Life of Tom Horn*.

THE END

ACKNOWLEDGMENTS AND
LIST OF SOURCES

ACKNOWLEDGMENTS

THE legend of Tom Horn has been told me many times in the twenty years I spent in the range-livestock business. Each neighborhood in which Tom lived cherished the various details of his adventures in a different manner. Tom Horn's Arizona life is a chapter distinct from his northern career. Sources for this part of the story are set down in the Preface. His Pinkerton experiences have never been written before. The clue that led to their discovery was given me by W. C. ("Doc") Shores, sheriff of Gunnison County, Colorado, long an employee of Pinkerton's Denver agency. William Caywood, government trapper, E. D. Stout and George Wear, both cowboys, and all pioneers of Cotopaxi and those tortuous gulches known as Bull Hell and Fern Leaf, have told me the inside story of the McCoys' train holdup. "Pistol Frank" Hudson, of New Castle, Colorado, a descendant of the Quantrill men who settled on the Arkansas, also helped with some of the details. Buster Rector of Rangely, Colorado, lived part of the winter with McCoy before Horn overtook him. Fay Gorham, long a resident of Meeker, drove the stagecoach that carried Horn from Rifle to White River. Sam Wear was the deputy who guided Tom to Utah. Reuben Ball was a pioneer hotel man in Meeker who kept his eyes open and his memory clear. Oscar Collet happened to be at the Jensen ferry when Tom came by. Mrs. W. H. Colthorp ran the boardinghouse in Vernal, Utah, where Joe McCoy ate his meals. All of these people were long-time friends of mine. The first night Horn, Stewart and Deputy Wear spent out of Meeker they stayed at the ranch which was later the headquarters for the outfit I owned in partnership with Lloyd Lewis.

Much of the Leadville material has been told to me by John Ewing, pioneer attorney at the silver city, by Charles Porter, ore-hauler and storyteller, and by Lute Wilcox, printer and railroad-construction man who was also on the Santa Fe Trail in Tom's time.

The Brown's Hole incidents in this book are all part of the lifeblood of many old neighbors of a claim I once held at the junction of Bear and Green Rivers. I enjoyed the friendship of elderly A. H. Bassett and his cowpunching children, George, Eb, Ann and Josie. Eb lost one of the finest saddle horses I have ever seen by falling through the ice as he crossed the river at my ranch one winter. Josie was a genius at making a banquet out of the limited supplies a cow camp provides. Ann, known as "Queen Ann" and sometimes "Queen Zenobey" for a near-by mountain peak, was the wit and beauty of the family. A "live" cow hand, she would ride and swear with the best of them. In town she could grace any social assemblage. The Bassett family were as intimate as anyone could be with both Matt Rash and Isam Dart.

I also knew J. S. Hoy, who prided himself on being the historian of the area—and had a brother, Valentine, shot to death there. Wilse Rankin, another settler-historian of northwestern Colorado, was a friend, too. Charles Neiman, sheriff of Routt County at the time of the Rash and Dart murders, has told me his account of what happened. Stanley Crouse and E. V. Houghy, both reared in Brown's Hole, have helped me with the story. "Doc" Middleton, Pat Whalen and Jackie Chew have all told me some of the things that they knew. I was also acquainted with grim Hi Bernard, Haley's foreman in Routt County, who astonished the neighbors by marrying Queen Ann Bassett.

The Spanish-American War episodes in this book have been fugitive. Books about this period are plentiful but references to Tom Horn are scarce. In the testimony taken by the committee investigating the conduct of the War Department a man who resembled Tom Horn is mentioned but not named. General Leonard Wood told me a little that he remembered of Tom in Cuba. Lu Dick, whose father, Senator C. W. F. Dick of Ohio, landed at Daiquiri with Shafter, repeated the stories he had heard. So did Luther Stewart of Jensen, Utah, who was among the enlisted men. Miss Florence Spofford found for me in the General Accounting Office in Washington the data on Horn's rank and pay in the transportation service.

My friend A. G. Wallihan told me about seeing Horn ride by after the Dart murder. "Walley," the famous big-game photographer of Lay, Colorado, married a woman twice his age and then grew a beard to keep up with her, so people said. Whooping "Long Horn" Thompson was another friend. He kept a collie pup for me one winter and also told me the details about his escape from Horn's bullet. Mildred MacIntosh has confirmed the account of Tom Horn's relay of horses at her father's ranch.

The two accounts of the Baggs saloon brawl, which appeared in rival newspapers, have been checked against stories told by Tom Blevins, E. W. Leggett and Hi Burch, all pioneers of Snake River. A. H. Christensen, president of the Utah Construction Company, an outsider, happened to be in the area at the time. The accounts told by these men vary as widely as those of the different newspapers.

Tom Horn always wanted somebody to write the story of his life. He hoped that the writer would be able to depict how he "felt" at certain moments. I have attempted to do this in describing the killing of Matt Rash—my contribution to the legend of Tom Horn. Other incidents recorded in this book are based on verbal or written sources. Many of them are legendary also, but an attempt has been made to check them all for accuracy.

Much of the story of Tom Horn on the Laramie Plains was printed in the contemporary press. To these accounts I have added eyewitness testimony from my friend John Kuykendall. Tom brought the carload of bucking horses to him in Denver immediately after the Nickell murder. Kuykendall came to Tom's rescue when he lay with his jaw broken in the old Windsor Hotel on Larimer Street.

Mrs. John Coble has been good enough to tell me about her husband's connection with Horn. Al Pearce, pioneer of Plum Tree, Nebraska, remembered Coble's early livestock ventures. The registrar's office at Lafayette College, Easton, Pennsylvania, traced his scholastic record for me.

Ferdinand Lafrentz, gracious New Yorker, started life as bookkeeper for the Swan Land & Cattle Company, working for the great corporation both before and after John Clay took over its management. He has told me about the organization, its holdings and its problems. To Frank Griffin I am indebted for the story of Horn and the county commissioner at Hanna. Kels Nickell and Victor Miller each told me his side of the Horn legend. So did Charles Ohnhaus, Harry Hynds, Joe Cahill, Leslie Snow, Joe Lefors and Charles Irwin, the plump showman who used to mount his horse from a chair. Sheriff Ed Smalley, who helped on many details, always maintained that Driftwood Jim Macleod was not put in his custody for murder. Contemporary newspapers told the story as I have given it. Valuable incidents about the barons and the rustlers were given me by Charles Howell at Newcastle, Wyoming, Jim Gatchell at Buffalo, and A. K. MacDougall at Rawlins. Charles Horn led me to the grave of his brother Tom at Boulder, Colorado.

Many people have helped me check through newspapers for Horn material. I am indebted to Robert Canny in the reference department of the Denver Public Library; Dawes Markwell in the Public Library in San

Francisco; and Edith Tobitt in the Omaha Public Library. The Pueblo Public Library furnished me contemporary newspaper material on the Cotopaxi train robbery. The Reno Library gave me the press account of Tom's arrest and trial in Nevada. Floyd C. Shoemaker, secretary of the State Historical Society of Missouri, gave me some of the genealogical material about the Horns in Scotland County, Missouri. Miss Mary Marks, librarian at the University of Wyoming, generously lent me books that I could not get elsewhere. Miss Lola M. Homsher, archivist at the University of Wyoming, furnished me with pictures in her files. State Historian Mrs. Marie H. Irwin checked the spelling of many names at my request.

Don Russell, military analyst and careful student of western history, found traces of the notorious Horn in books where a less patient trailer would not deign to hunt. He has generously shared his discoveries with me and by so doing added valuable works to my bibliography. William Dean Embree, New York attorney and Laramie ranchman, prominent in the American Pioneer Trails Association, has helped me with Wyoming sources. Professor Edward Everett Dale made available to me his abundant collection of western books and pictures. Professor Frank C. Lockwood was bountiful with his knowledge gained by a lifetime of studying, teaching and writing the history of Arizona. Mrs. George F. Kitt selected pictures for me in the Arizona Pioneers' Historical Society library in Tucson.

I also want to express my gratitude to Carl B. Roden and Herbert H. Hewitt, librarian and reference librarian of the Chicago Public Library, for the use of books on interlibrary loan. In the Illinois State and Illinois State Historical libraries at Springfield, Miss Margaret Flint and Miss Florence Nichol—no relation to Kels and Willie—have been resourceful and energetic scouts for western material on midwestern shelves.

Nira C. Irwin and James N. Adams have helped me with careful typing of the manuscript. Both could always be counted on to come to my rescue when work piled up and time was short.

I wish also to acknowledge my appreciation of the help given me by Mildred Eversole Monaghan, my wife. With bright eyes and a gentle heart, she has given up many social evenings to let her husband scribble. She has read his entire copy. Her skill on the unfenced range of manuscripts has guided him past sinkholes of hidden sophisms, over mountains of misplaced commas and across chasms of dangling paragraphs. All the while she has kept the fire burning cheerily on the home ranch.

LIST OF SOURCES

Adams, Andy. *The Log of a Cowboy* (Boston: Houghton Mifflin Company, 1927). Life on the Texas trail by a participant. A classic.

Adams, Ramon F. *Western Words: A Dictionary of the Range, Cow Camp and Trail* (Norman: University of Oklahoma Press, 1945). Old and new origins of western slang.

Arizona Bill in *The American Weekly* (Sunday, Dec. 20, 1936) tells the story of Horn's capture of Geronimo and his trip to Florida. Inaccurate, but author relates incidents on Florida trip not to be found elsewhere.

Army Pay Rolls, United States General Accounting Office, Washington, D. C.

"Army Rations," *American Meat Institute* (March, 1939).

Barnes, Will C. "The Chisholm Trail—For Whom Was It Named?" *The Producer: The National Live Stock Monthly* (Jan. and Feb., 1929), X, Nos. 8, 9.

———. *Tales of the X-Bar Horse Camp* (Chicago: Breeders Gazette, 1920). Ranching in early Arizona by a musician and stockman who was decorated for bravery in the Apache wars and eventually became chief of grazing in the U. S. Forest Service.

Barrett, S. M. *Geronimo's Story of His Life* (New York: Duffield & Company, 1907).

Benton, Frank. *Cowboy Life on the Sidetrack* (Denver: Privately printed, The Western Stories Syndicate, ᶜ1903). Written by a stockman in Tom Horn's Wyoming.

Bigelow, Lieut. John, Jr. "After Geronimo," *Outing* (March, 1886, to April, 1887). Diary of officer in 10th Cavalry.

Bonsal, Stephen. *The Fight for Santiago: The Story of the Soldier in the Cuban Campaign, from Tampa to the Surrender* (New York: Doubleday & McClure Company, 1899). Especially good on Rough Riders.

Bourke, John Gregory. *An Apache Campaign in the Sierra Madre* (New York: Charles Scribner's Sons, 1886). Account of 1883 expedition.

———. *On the Border with Crook* (New York: Charles Scribner's Sons, 1891). Essential for an understanding of Geronimo and his time.

Burbank, E. A. *Burbank Among the Indians*, ed., Frank J. Taylor (Caldwell, Idaho: The Caxton Printers, Ltd., 1944). Intimate anecdotes of Geronimo's last days.

Burnham, Maj. Frederick Russell. *Scouting on Two Continents* (Garden City, N. Y.: Doubleday, Page & Company, 1926). Contains vividly dramatized experiences among Apaches and in Graham-Tewksbury feud.

Burns, Walter Noble. *The Saga of Billy the Kid* (Garden City, N. Y.: Doubleday, Page & Company, 1926). Definitive description of Lincoln County War.

Burt, Struthers. *Powder River: Let 'Er Buck* (New York: Farrar & Rinehart, Inc., ᶜ1938). A chapter on Horn with firsthand information on Joe Lefors.

Canton, Frank M. *Frontier Trails: The Autobiography of Frank M. Canton,* ed., Edward Everett Dale (Boston: Houghton Mifflin Company, 1930). The big outfit's side of the Johnson County War.

Chaffin, Mrs. Lorah B. *Sons of the West* (Caldwell, Idaho: The Caxton Printers, Ltd., 1941). Occasional nuggets about the boom cattle outfits in Wyoming.

Clay, John. *My Life on the Range* (Chicago: Privately printed, ᶜ1924). Tom Horn's Wyoming by one of the biggest cattle owners.

Clum, Woodworth. *Apache Agent: The Story of John P. Clum* (Boston: Houghton Mifflin Company, ᶜ1936). Story of the San Carlos Indian agent, focused on the 1870's with some account of Geronimo's experiences in Wild West performances. Clum was also mayor and postmaster of Tombstone and founder and editor of the *Epitaph.*

Cody, William F. "Famous Hunting Parties of the Plains," *Cosmopolitan Magazine* (June, 1894), XVII, No. 2, 131-143.

Coe, Charles H. *Juggling a Rope* (Pendleton, Ore.: Hamley & Company, 1927). Contains a defense of Horn by a friend who was also a stock detective.

"Confidentially Told" (MS containing confession of Hi Bernard, lent author by Ann Bassett, wife of Hi Bernard).

Connell, C. T. "Apache, Past and Present," *Tucson Daily Citizen* (beginning March 27, 1941).

Coolidge, Dane. *Fighting Men of the West* (New York: E. P. Dutton & Company, ᶜ1932). Historical fiction with a chapter on Horn.

Cruse, Brig. Gen. Thomas. *Apache Days and After* (Caldwell, Idaho: The Caxton Printers, Ltd., 1941). Account of a lieutenant who served in the thick of it. *See also* Smith, Col. C. C.

Cullum, George W. *Biographical Register of the Officers and Graduates of the U. S. Military Academy* (Boston: Houghton Mifflin Company, 1891).

Cunningham, Eugene. *Triggernometry, A Gallery of Gunfighters* (Caldwell, Idaho: The Caxton Printers, Ltd., 1941). A chapter on Horn.

Dale, Edward Everett. *Cow Country* (Norman: University of Oklahoma Press, 1942). Summary of British syndicates in cattle business.

――――. *The Range Cattle Industry* (Norman: University of Oklahoma Press, 1930). The opening of the Northwest and the Long Drive.

Daly, Henry W. "The Geronimo Campaign," *Journal of U. S. Cavalry Association,* XIX, No. 69, 68-103. Reminiscences of a mule packer.

――――. "Scouts Good and Bad," *American Legion Monthly* (Aug., 1928), V, No. 2, 24-25, 66-70.

Davis, Britton. *The Truth About Geronimo,* ed., Milo M. Quaife (New Haven: Yale University Press, 1929). Good account of Chevelon Canyon fight but no reference to Tom Horn.

Davis, Carlysle Channing. *Olden Times in Colorado* (Denver: Privately printed). Source material on early Leadville.

Davis, Britton. *The Truth About Geronimo,* ed., Milo M. Quaife (New York: Charles Scribner's Sons, 1898). Unusual illustrations.

――――. "Our War Correspondents in Cuba and Puerto Rico," *Harper's New Monthly Magazine* (May, 1899), XCVIII, No. DLXXXVIII, 938-948.

Dobie, J. Frank. *Guide to Life and Literature of the Southwest with a Few Observations* (Austin: University of Texas Press, 1943).

Downey, Fairfax. *Indian-Fighting Army* (New York: Charles Scribner's Sons, 1941). One chapter, "Soldier vs. Apache," begins with the Cibicu fight and ends with the capture of Geronimo.

Eaton, George O. "Stopping an Apache Battle," ed., Don Russell, *Journal of U. S. Cavalry Association* (July-Aug., 1933), XLII, No. 178.

"Experiences of an Indian Scout," *Arizona Historical Review* (April, 1936), VII, No. 2, 31-73. Personal account of scout who went into Mexico with Crook's expedition.

Forrest, Earle R. *Arizona's Dark and Bloody Ground* (Caldwell, Idaho: The Caxton Printers, Ltd., 1936). Definitive account of Graham-Tewksbury feud.

Fowler, Gene. *Timber Line: A Story of Bonfils and Tammen* (New York: Covici, Friede, Inc., 1933). One chapter on Talking Boy accepts

Horn's Arizona experiences uncritically. The account of Tom's trial is valuable source material.

Gandy, Lewis Cass. *The Tabors: a Footnote of Western History* (New York: The Press of the Pioneers, Inc., 1934). Leadville in the 1880's by a onetime printer in the city.

Gatewood, Maj. C. B., comp. "Lt. C. B. Gatewood and the Surrender of Geronimo," *Proceedings of the Annual Meeting and Dinner of the Order of Indian Wars of the U. S.* (Jan. 26, 1929).

Hagedorn, Hermann. *Leonard Wood: A Biography* (New York: Harper & Brothers, 1931). Account of Horn in pursuit of Geronimo.

———. *The Rough Riders: A Romance* (New York: Harper & Brothers, 1927). Leonard Wood in Cuba.

Hall, Thomas Winthrop. *The Fun and Fighting of the Rough Riders* (New York: Frederick A. Stokes Company, ᶜ1899). A personal approach.

Hanna, Robert. "With Crawford in Mexico," *Arizona Historical Review* (April, 1935), VI, No. 2, 56-65. In this account Americans killed the scout at Huasavas because he was a straggler.

Heard, John, Jr. "The Killing of the Captain," *Cosmopolitan* (Aug., 1894), XVII, No. 4, 440-450. Captain Crawford's death in Mexico.

Heitman, Francis B. *Historical Register and Dictionary of the United States Army* (Washington: Government Printing Office, 1903).

Henry, Robert Selph. *Portraits of the Iron Horse* (New York: Rand McNally Co., ᶜ1937). Early-day trains.

———. *Trains* (Indianapolis: The Bobbs-Merrill Company, ᶜ1934). Pioneer railway trains.

History of Lewis, Clark, Knox, and Scotland Counties (St. Louis: The Goodspeed Publishing Company, 1887). A partial genealogy of the Scotland County Horns.

Horn, Tom. *Life of Tom Horn: Government Scout and Interpreter* (Denver: Privately printed. The Louthan Book Company, ᶜ1904). Source of many Horn errors.

Hoy, J. S. "History of Brown's Park" (MS, Colorado Historical Society).

Hulbert, Archer Butler. *Southwest on the Turquoise Trail* (Denver?: Pub. Stewart Commission and Denver Public Library). Santa Fe and beyond.

Hunter, J. Marvin, ed. *The Trail Drivers of Texas* (Nashville, Cokesbury Press, pub. by Old Time Trail Drivers' Association, 1925).

Inman, Henry. *The Old Santa Fe Trail* (Topeka: Crane & Company, 1914).

Karsner, David. *Silver Dollar: The Story of the Tabors* (New York: Crown Publishers, ʿ1932). Early Leadville.

Kelly, Charles. *Outlaw Trail: A History of Butch Cassidy and His Wild Bunch, Hole-in-the-Wall, Brown's Hole, Robber's Roost* (Salt Lake City: The author, 1938).

King, Brig. Gen. Charles. "George Crook," *War Papers of Loyal Legion Commandery of Wisconsin* (Milwaukee, Wis.: Burdick, Armitage & Allen, 1891), I, 251-269.

——. "Memories of a Busy Life," *The Wisconsin Magazine of History* (March, 1922), V, No. 3, [215]-243; (June, 1922), No. 4, 360-381; (September, 1922), VI, No. 1, 3-39; (December, 1922), No. 2, 165-188.

Leslie, Shane. *American Wonderland: Memories of Four Tours in the United States of America (1911-1935)* (London: Michael Joseph, Ltd., 1936). Intimate account of Moreton Frewen and the 76 Ranch.

Lockwood, Frank C. *The Apache Indians* (New York: The Macmillan Company, 1938). Excellent account of fights at Cibicu Creek and Big Dry Wash or Chevelon Fork.

——, ed. *Apaches and Longhorns: The Reminiscences of Will C. Barnes* (Los Angeles: The Ward Ritchie Press, 1911).

——. *Arizona Characters* (Los Angeles: The Times-Mirror Press, 1928). One chapter summarizes Crook's entire experiences with the Apaches.

——. "More Arizona Characters," *University of Arizona Bulletin,* General Bulletin No. 6 (Tucson: University of Arizona, 1942). Best account of Al Sieber.

——. *Pioneer Days in Arizona* (New York: The Macmillan Company, 1932). One chapter on the story of the Apache wars.

Love, Robertus. *The Rise and Fall of Jesse James* (New York: G. P. Putnam's Sons, 1926). Definitive lives of members of James gang.

Marshall, Edward. *The Story of the Rough Riders* (New York: G. W. Dillingham Co., Publishers, 1899). Illustration opposite p. 200 shows man with nosebag asleep in shade. He looks very much like Tom Horn.

Mazzanovich, Anton. *Trailing Geronimo* (Los Angeles: Gem Publishing Company, 1926). This and Horn's account are the sources of the Tupper-Forsyth incursion into Mexico. Mazzanovich's account does not include arrest but it is probable that such a formality would occur.

Mercer, A. S. *Powder River Invasion* (Cheyenne?: A. S. Mercer & Co., 1923). Also printed as *Banditti of the Plains* (Cheyenne, 1894). The author edited a livestock paper in Cheyenne.

Miles, Gen. Nelson A. *Personal Recollections and Observations* (Chicago: The Werner Company, 1897). Source of some of the laudatory references to Tom Horn.

Miley, John D. *In Cuba with Shafter* (New York: Charles Scribner's Sons, 1899). Excellent maps of the campaign. An account that does not give the Rough Riders the center of the stage.

Mullins, Richard R. *Denver Post* (Nov. 23, 1930, to Dec. 12, 1930). Horn's own story repeated uncritically. In 1934 the copyright holder of Horn's autobiography was awarded $9,000 for the infringement of this account.

Murdock, John R. "Tom Horn—A White Man Without a Forked Tongue," *Arizona Republic* (May 8, 1933). Based uncritically on Horn's own account.

Nye, W. S. *Carbine & Lance: The Story of Old Fort Sill* (Norman: University of Oklahoma Press, 1943). The last days of Geronimo.

Outlook (Aug. 4, 1920), CXXV, 607. A picture of Leonard Wood said to have been taken in Arizona in 1885.

Owen, James. "Reminiscences of Early Pueblo," *The Colorado Magazine* (May, 1945), XXII, No. 3, [97]-107.

Paxson, Frederic L. "The Cow Country," *The American Historical Review* (Oct., 1916), XXII, 65-82.

———. *History of the American Frontier, 1763-1893* (Boston: Houghton Mifflin Company, ᶜ1924).

Pelzer, Louis. *The Cattlemen's Frontier* (Glendale, Calif.: The Arthur H. Clark Company, 1936). Contains account of boom companies in Wyoming and a reprint of the 1882 brand book.

Potter, Charles N., comp., *Cases Decided in the Supreme Court of Wyoming from August 3, 1903, to April 25, 1904*, XII, 80-167.

Quaife, Milo Milton, ed. *Vanished Arizona: Recollections of My Army Life* (Chicago: The Lakeside Press, 1939). The Apache country described by a woman in the Army wagon train.

Raine, William MacLeod. *Famous Sheriffs & Western Outlaws* (Garden

City, N. Y.: Garden City Publishing Company, Inc., ᶜ1929). Accounts of Apache Kid, Graham-Tewksbury feud, Bucky O'Neill, Harry Tracy.

Rankin, Wilse. "Outlaw Life in Northwestern Colorado" (MS, Colorado Historical Society).

Report of the Commission appointed by the President to investigate the conduct of the War Department in the War with Spain (Sen. Doc.), 56th Cong., 1st sess., No. 221. Eight vols. Testimony concerning the pack train may be found in Vol. III.

Rollinson, John K. *Hoofprints of a Cowboy and U. S. Ranger; Pony Trails in Wyoming* (Caldwell, Idaho: The Caxton Printers, Ltd., 1941). Short references to Horn by a trapper who saw him on the Swan range.

Roosevelt, Theodore. *An Autobiography* (New York: Charles Scribner's Sons, 1926).

——. *The Rough Riders and Men of Action* (New York: Charles Scribner's Sons, 1926).

——. *Selections from the Correspondence of Theodore Roosevelt and Henry Cabot Lodge, 1884-1918* (New York: Charles Scribner's Sons, 1925). Letter of Aug. 10, 1886 (Vol. I, p. 44), refers to raising a cowboy regiment in case Geronimo trouble led to war with Mexico.

——. "In Cowboy Land," *The Wilderness Hunter* (New York: G. P. Putnam's Sons, 1893). Gives Roosevelt's explanation of Tom Horn.

Russell, Don. "Capt. Crawford's Last Fight," *Chicago Daily News* (March 30, 1940).

——. "Last Surrender of Geronimo," *Chicago Daily News* (April 13, 1940. *See also* March 2, 9, 16, 23, and April 6).

——. "One Hundred and Three Fights and Scrimmages. The Story of General Reuben F. Bernard," Reprinted from *Journal of U. S. Cavalry Association* (Sept.-Oct., 1935, to March-April, 1936), XLIV, Nos. 191-192 to XLV, Nos. 193-194. Chapters on campaigns against Cochise and Geronimo.

Settle, William A., Jr. "The Development of the Jesse James Legend" (Ph.D. thesis, University of Missouri, 1945).

Shields, Alice M. "Edwin J. Smalley, One of Cheyenne's First Native Sons," *Annals of Wyoming* (Jan., 1941), XIII, No. 1, 58-72.

——. "The Life of Nannie Clay Steele," *Annals of Wyoming* (April, 1941), XIII, No. 2, 93-103. Account of nursing wounded man who turned out to be "THE Tom Horn."

282

Shipp, Lieut. William E. "Captain Crawford's Last Expedition," *Journal of U. S. Cavalry Association,* V, No. 19, 343-362. Also XIX, No. 70, 278-300.

Siringo, Charles A. *Riata and Spurs: The Story of a Lifetime Spent in the Saddle as Cowboy and Ranger* (Boston: Houghton Mifflin Company, 1931). One chapter on Horn's life based uncritically on his autobiography.

Smith, Col. C. C. "The Army and the Apache," *Arizona Historical Review* (Jan., 1932), IV, No. 4, 62-70. A defense of the Army.

——. "The Fight at the Cibicu and Nock-ay-del-klinne, Apache Medicine Man," *Tombstone Epitaph* (June 2, 16, 23, 1933).

——. "Retired Army Man takes hide off Owen P. White, author of 'Talking Boy,'" *Brewery Gulch Gazette* (May 26, 1933). Extracts from Cruse diary.

Sonnichsen, C. L. *Billy King's Tombstone: The Private Life of an Arizona Boom Town* (Caldwell, Idaho: The Caxton Printers, Ltd., 1942). Tom Horn's Tombstone without Tom.

Spring, Agnes Wright. *Seventy Years: A Panoramic History of the Wyoming Stock Growers Association* (Cheyenne?: Pub. by Wyoming Stock Growers Association, 1942). Information on Frank Canton as stock detective and the Cheyenne Club as center of cowdom's social life.

——. *William Chapin Deming of Wyoming* (Glendale, Calif.: Privately printed by The Arthur H. Clark Company, 1944). Source of anecdote about Horn's playing pranks in Inter-Ocean Hotel, Thanksgiving, 1901.

Sykes, Godfrey. *A Westerly Trend* (Tucson: Arizona Pioneers' Historical Society, 1944). Description of Chisholm Trail by an Englishman who rode it.

Thompson, John Charles. "The Hanging of Tom Horn," *The Brand Book* (mimeographed publication of the Westerners, Sept. 1, 1945), I, No. 8. Account by a Cheyenne newspaperman who was present, written forty years later.

Tittsworth, W. G. *Outskirt Episodes* (Des Moines, Iowa: Success Composing and Printing Company, no date). Only source of a great deal of Brown's Park history.

Wagon Road—Fort Smith to Colorado River (House Ex. Doc.), 36th Cong., 1st sess., No. 42. Log of government-survey party in 1858 guided by Jesse Chisholm.

Walters, Lorenzo D. *Tombstone's Yesterday* (Tucson: Acme Printing Company, 1928). Chapter on Horn from his autobiography.

Webb, Walter Prescott. *The Great Plains* (Boston: Ginn and Company, ᶜ1931). A survey: encyclopedic and entertaining.

Wellman, Paul I. *Death in the Desert* (New York: The Macmillan Company, 1935). Contains the Geronimo war, 1883-1886, with Horn's participation.

White, Owen P. "Talking Boy," *Collier's Magazine* (Feb. 18, 1933), pp. 18-40. Based on Horn's own story.

White, William Allen. *Boys—Then and Now* (New York: The Macmillan Company, 1926). Kansas in Tom's day.

Willison, George Findlay. *Here They Dug the Gold* (New York: Coward-McCann, Inc., 1931). Leadville in Horn's time.

Wister, Owen. *Red Men and White* (New York: Harper & Brothers, ᶜ1895). Apache days in color with entertaining description of General Crook.

Writers' Program of the Works Projects Administration. *Wyoming: A Guide to its History, Highways, and People* (New York: Oxford University Press, ᶜ1941). Interesting as an example of historical trend. Horn in this narrative defends cattle from sheep—not big owners from little ones.

NEWSPAPERS

The Cheyenne Leader, 1892, accounts of the Johnson County invasion. The editor got a horsewhipping for these articles.

The Cheyenne Tribune, 1892, 1901-1903, accounts of Johnson County invasion and trial of Tom Horn.

The Craig Empire, 1900-1901, the Rash and Dart assassinations.

Denver Post, 1900-1903, Horn trial; April 15, 1928, statement of W. C. Shores; May 14, 1930, history of James P. Julian water-trap gallows.

Denver Tribune, April 20, 1882, account of George Sterling's death; 1903, the trial of Horn.

Harper's Weekly, 1886, many pictures of Geronimo and the soldiers.

The Meeker Herald, Jan. 9, 1892, Horn's passage through town on the Joe McCoy chase.

Newcastle Journal, June 19, 1891, the lynching of Tom Waggoner.

The Omaha Bee, 1892, Johnson County War.

Omaha World-Herald, 1892, Johnson County War.

The Pueblo Chieftain, Sept. 1, 1891, account of D & R G train robbery.

The Reno Evening Gazette, April to Sept., 1891, Horn's Reno trial.

Rocky Mountain News, 1892, Johnson County War.

The San Francisco Bulletin, 1886, Apache wars in Arizona.

The San Francisco Examiner, 1886, the Geronimo chase.

Steamboat Pilot, 1908-1909, picturesque news about Haley and the Brown's Hole settlers.

INDEX

INDEX

OTHER TITLES BY JAY MONAGHAN
AVAILABLE IN BISON BOOKS EDITIONS

Abraham Lincoln Deals with Foreign Affairs

Civil War on the Western Border, 1854–1865

Custer: The Life of General George Armstrong Custer